TOO LATE FOR GOYA

WORKS BY FRANCESC TORRES

CURATED BY

MARILYN ZEITLIN

"But wherever there is a secret there is a rumor."
"Pero allí donde haya un secreto habrá un rumor."
Susan Griffin, *A Chorus of Stones*

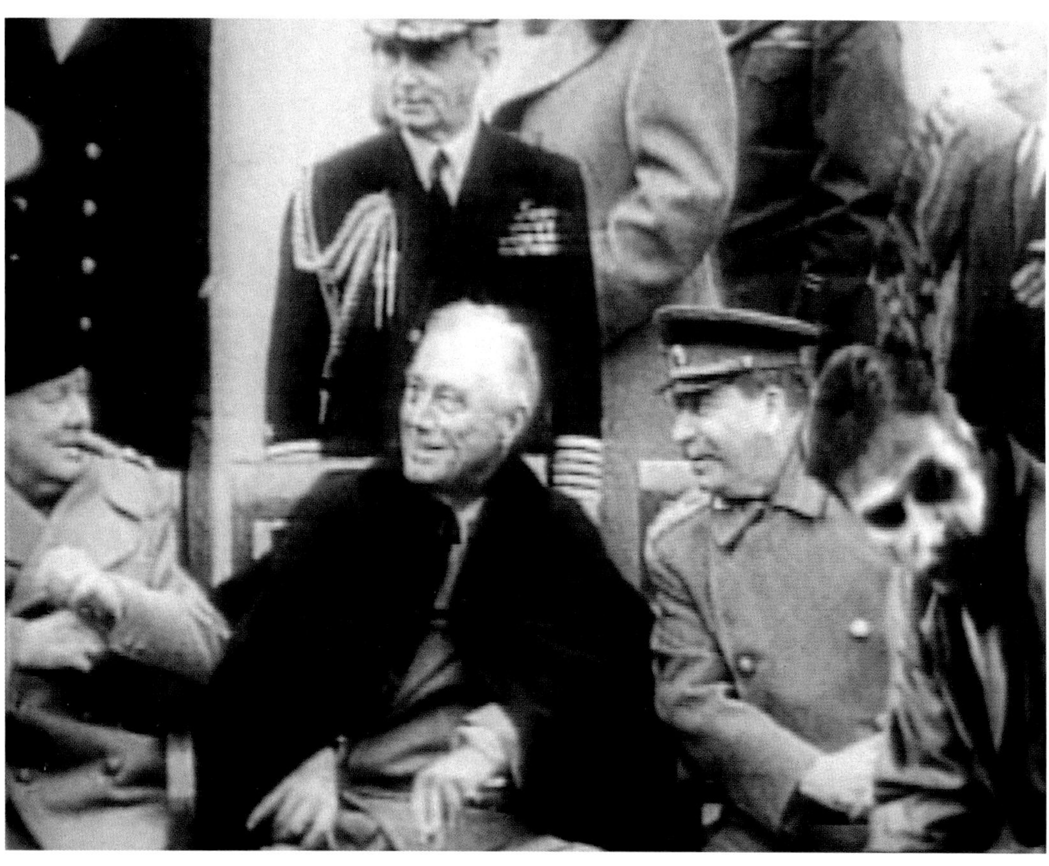

Yalta Conference, 1945
Winston Churchill, Franklin Delano Roosevelt,
Joseph Stalin, Francesc Torres
Video Still

Too Late for Goya, 1993

TOO LATE FOR GOYA

WORKS BY FRANCESC TORRES

ARIZONA STATE UNIVERSITY ART MUSEUM

Essays by

Thomas McEvilley
Juan Antonio Ramírez
Francesc Torres
Marilyn Zeitlin

Editor

Marilyn Zeitlin

Published in conjunction with the exhibition
TOO LATE FOR GOYA: WORKS BY FRANCESC TORRES
Organized by Marilyn Zeitlin, *Director and Chief Curator*
Arizona State University Art Museum

Exhibition tour (at time of publication)
Arizona State University Art Museum
5 November 1993 - 6 February 1994

Museo Nacional de Arte Moderno
Mexico City, Mexico
24 March - 13 June 1994

Center for the Fine Arts
Miami, Florida
Spring 1996

TOO LATE FOR GOYA: WORKS BY FRANCESC TORRES
is supported by the Rockefeller Foundation;
National Endowment for the Arts (a federal agency, Washington, DC);
The Bohen Foundation; California Tamarack Foundation;
Caja de Asturias, España and Friends of the Arizona State University Art Museum.

Library of Congress Cataloguing in Publication Data

Zeitlin, Marilyn A., 1941-
Too Late for Goya: Works by Francesc Torres

Published in conjunction with the exhibition,
Too Late for Goya: Works by Francesc Torres,
5 November 1993 - 6 February 1994, Arizona State University Art Museum.
Includes bibliographical references.
1. Torres, Francesc - Exhibitions. I. Torres, Francesc.
II. McEvilley, Thomas. III. Ramírez, Juan Antonio.
IV. Zeitlin, Marilyn A.
V. Arizona State University Art Museum. VI. Title.

ISBN 1-879286-07-6

Arizona State University Art Museum, Nelson Fine Arts Center, Box 872911, Tempe, Arizona 602/965-2787

Printed in the United States of America

Funders of the Exhibition

The installation **Too Late for Goya** was commissioned by *Montage 93*, Rochester, New York, and made possible, in part, by a media arts grant from the National Endowment for the Arts, a federal agency, Washington, DC.

The project at the Arizona State University Art Museum has been supported by generous contributions from

The Rockefeller Foundation, New York

The National Endowment for the Arts, a federal agency, Washington, D.C.

The Bohen Foundation, New York

California Tamarack Foundation, San Francisco

Caja de Asturias, España, Oviedo, Spain

American Heritage Fund

The Museum Store

Friends of the Museum

Lenders to the Exhibition

The Bohen Foundation, New York

Arizona State University Art Museum, Tempe, Arizona

Terry Berkowitz, New York

The artist

Acknowledgments

A project as complex as this one involves experts and supporters, problem-solvers and organizers. The origination of the multi-media installation of the title work was made possible through the sponsorship of *Montage 93*. Nathan Lyons, director of *Montage*, supported the artist in realizing the project and graciously cooperated in making it available for this exhibition. I wish to thank him and the sponsors of *Montage 93* for their generosity.

The project received support from many sources. Special thanks go to Tomas Ibarra-Frausto of the Rockefeller Foundation for his enthusiasm and understanding of Torres' work; to Fred Henry, president of the Bohen Foundation, for his strong ongoing support of the artist and of this project. The Bohen Foundation's support came through funding and generous loans of many important works. Ann Hatch of the California Tamarack Foundation, a long-time supporter of Torres' work, and Blas Eduardo Fernández Gallego of the Caja de Ahorros de Asturias, Oviedo, Spain, appreciated the concept of a major exhibition originating in the U.S., and both responded with alacrity to support the project. The support of the Museum Program of the National Endowment for the Arts is much appreciated.

Within the museum and university, support has come from the Art Heritage Fund and Museum Store for purchase of Torres' work and in support of the project. The Friends of the Museum and the Advisory Board contributed to the project, recognizing the quantum leap in scale and complexity that the exhibition represents for the museum.

The artist wishes to express his special thanks to Wayne Armour, multi-media systems integrator, for his expert help in making **Too Late for Goya** possible, and for his unshakable grace under pressure. The artist also wishes to thank Clara Casanovas, New York, for her logistical help; Fran Antmann, New York, for proofing the texts; and Elba Benítez, Madrid, and Sylvie Ferré, Lyon, for their assistance in Europe. I wish to thank Chuck Williams of State Farm claims department for assistance in locating the motorcycle carcass; and Patti Clarke of the Institute for Study in the Arts of ASU for technical video assistance.

Terry Berkowitz, designer of the catalogue, has once again found a visual language to present the complexity of Torres' work with clarity and elegance. Her work goes beyond the call, as always. The translators were Alisa Tager and Teresa Sàrries. Many thanks to them.

At Memorial Art Gallery of the University of Rochester, Candace J. Adelson, Curator of European Art, coordinated the project for *Montage*. James Smith, Manager of Facilities, supervised installation. Many thanks for their contributions and cooperation.

Everyone on the staff of the Arizona State University Art Museum participated in making this complex project possible. Special thanks go to Linda McAllister, for her work as coordinator of the publication; to Mary Jane Williams, registrar, for attending to details of shipping and loans; to Jean Makin, print collections manager, who did her normal round of trouble-shooting; to Heather Lineberry, for proofing the English text; and to Deanna Stulgaitis, Administrative Assistant, who kept us all working as a team. Stephen Johnson, Chief Preparator, and Greg Strange, Assistant Preparator, outdid themselves in creative problem-solving and precision installation.

The administration of the university and in particular Seymour L. Rosen, Dean of the College of Fine Arts, recognized the value of the project for our university and broader audiences. I wish to thank them for their comprehension of the importance of the work.

My association with Francesc Torres as both colleague and friend dates back to 1979. Francesc sets a standard for himself that radiates from him and the work to inspire everyone involved in its presentation. He establishes a force-field of creative energy that has an impact on everyone, making them aware that they are involved in something momentous. He has been an important influence on me as a curator. My conviction that Torres is one of the most intellectually provocative artists of our time is once again affirmed. It is a privilege to work with him. Many thanks, Francesc.

—*Marilyn Zeitlin, Director and Chief Curator*
Arizona State University Art Museum

Francesc Torres or The Man with Three Brains

Thomas McEvilley

Francesc Torres is among the most philosophical of artists. His work exists in a discourse of thinkers as much as in the usual critical discourse surrounding the visual arts. The material it arises from and deals with is composed not only of human experience but of theories about human experience—its sources, its meanings, and its destiny. His work derives in part from a kind of shadow-play on a cavern wall, the spectacle of the wrestling of the figures whom he calls Combat Philosophers. These figures seem in a sense the true protagonists of history or, as Percy Bysshe Shelley said of poets, the unacknowledged legislators of mankind. In Torres' work they are acknowledged, albeit with a certain irony. He focuses his artwork on that vision of the world where it seems that human destiny is at this very moment being fought out by philosophers. His own work seems to assume that today the artist is not only an observer of the Combat Philosophers but a participant in their fights.

On a purely art critical level Torres' work has been much and well discussed.[1] A critical groundwork is already in place, with which I more or less agree, and which I will not repeat at any length. But to understand the types of actions that art is engaged in here, it is necessary to enter into some of the philosophical thematics involved in the oeuvre, without pretension to completeness in this area.

Hegel and Fifty Rains

Torres has referred to some of his works as "Hegelian scenographies."[2] The phrase might be applied with special appropriateness to **Fifty Rains**, 1991, in which he dealt with three moments in Spanish history: the height of the period of political repression in 1943, when Franco—humiliatingly to all Spanish liberals or leftists —was openly an ally of Hitler; the death (by assassination) of Franco's successor Luis Carrero Blanco in 1973, marking the end of Fascism in Spain; and 1993, a year which

[1] *In essays by John Hanhardt, David Levi-Strauss, and Mar Villaespesa, as well as in Torres' own writings.*

[2] *At the beginning of an interview in* Artscribe *magazine Francesc Torres was asked why he called one of his large complex installation works a "Hegelian scenography." He replied, "Hegel's vision or concept of history was of the materialization of reason through struggle." Suddenly the interviewer became an intervener, saying, "But in that way I take your work to be anti-Hegelian." "Well, yes," Torres replied, sounding slightly defensive. "The result of reading history according to Hegel is that you set the stage for the bloodbath which is what the history of Europe has been for the past 2000 years at least. So my work is anti-Hegelian in the sense that I am showing the consequences of that approach to history and to*

Francesc Torres o el hombre con tres cerebros

Thomas McEvilley

Francesc Torres está considerado uno de los artistas más filosóficos de nuestro tiempo. Su obra está presente tanto en las reflexiones de los intelectuales como en el habitual discurso crítico que rodea las artes visuales. El material con el que trata y a partir del cual trabaja se compone no sólo de la experiencia humana sino también de teorías acerca de ella —sus fundamentos, sus significados y su destino—. La obra de Torres proviene en parte de cierto juego de sombras realizado en la pared de una cueva, del espectáculo que ofrece la lucha de las figuras a quienes él denomina Filósofos de Combate; estas figuras parecen ser, de algún modo, los auténticos protagonistas de la historia o, como Percy Bysshe Shelley dijo acerca de los poetas, los legisladores no reconocidos de la humanidad. En la obra de Torres sí son reconocidos, aunque con cierta ironía. Este artista centra sus obras en aquella visión del mundo en la que parece que son los filósofos quienes en este mismo momento soportan el peso del destino humano. Su propia obra parece asumir el hecho de que hoy en día el artista no es únicamente un observador de los Filósofos de Combate, sino que también participa en sus luchas.

A nivel puramente de crítica de arte, la obra de Torres ha sido plenamente discutida;[1] ya existe un fundamento crítico con el que estoy más o menos de acuerdo y que ahora no tengo intención de repetir. Pero para entender los tipos de acción a las que su arte se compromete, es necesario examinar algunos de los temas filosóficos presentes en el conjunto de su obra, sin pretensión alguna de abarcarlos por completo.

Hegel y Cincuenta lluvias

Torres ha calificado algunas de sus obras de "escenografías hegelianas".[2] La expresión es especialmente idónea si la aplicamos a **Cincuenta lluvias**, 1991, en la que el autor reflexionaba sobre tres

[1] *En ensayos de John Hanhardt, David Levi-Strauss y Mar Villaespesa, así como en los escritos del mismo Torres.*

[2] *Al principio de una entrevista en la revista* Artscribe*, se le preguntó a Francesc Torres por qué denominó una de sus grandes y complejas instalaciones "escenografía hegeliana". El respondió: "La visión o el concepto hegeliano de la historia consistía en la materialización de la razón a través de la lucha". Súbitamente el entrevistador intervino: "Pero de este modo asumo que su obra es antihegeliana". "Bueno, sí"— respondió*

immediately followed the Barcelona Olympics, the Quincentennial of the "discovery" of America, Expo 92 in Madrid, and the economic unification of Europe including Spain—all factors that suggested "the point at which Spain has overcome that 50 year heritage."[3] Each of the three moments is represented by an elaborate installation of furniture, some wrecked and burned, some new; cars (like the one Carrero was killed in); and pictures (a painting of the Spanish flag done in the style Jasper Johns used in his painting of the American flag, 10 Cibachrome enlargements of magazine photographs, and photos of marching boots in the trashed and burned out room of '43, abstract paintings with the impersonal new furniture of '93); and other things.

In viewing this as "a Hegelian scenography," one is faced at once with the question, Which Hegel? For in terms of the reception of his writings, there are several. On the one hand there is Hegel the evil dictator of philosophy, the Hegel on whom so much of the tragedy of modern history has been blamed for well over a century (at least since Rudolf Haym's *Lectures on Hegel and His Time*, published in Berlin in 1857).[4] This negative attitude toward Hegel recurred in the 1960s and early '70s, a period of "flight from reason" in which the hostility toward Hegel was second only to the hostility toward Aristotle (on whom Timothy Leary, in about 1967, blamed the mind's tendency to falsify experience by categorizing it).

This reception of Hegel received an influential articulation in Alexandre Kojève's *Introduction to the Reading of Hegel*. This series of lectures on the *Phenomenology of Spirit*, while not intended as antagonistic to Hegel, nevertheless emphasized the power-and-dominance aspect of the Master-Slave relationship discussed in the first six chapters of the *Phenomenology*.[5] This allegory or parable embodied a reflection on power that derives in part from reflections on the French Revolution, and that

political and social processes."

A reader cannot avoid the uneasy feeling that something has been left out. The interviewer's aggressive intervention—no matter how obviously right it was in terms of the overall thrust of Torres' work—seems to have prevented Torres from saying something more interesting about his motives in titling his work after Hegel.

[3] Artscribe *interview p. 45.*

4 Rudolf Haym, Vorlesungen über Hegel und Seine Zeit, *Berlin, 1857. The so-called Young Hegelians, with whom Karl Marx was associated in various ways, began the critique of Hegel before 1848.*

5 Alexandre Kojève, Introduction to the Reading of Hegel: Lectures on the Phenomenology of Spirit, *English translation by James H. Nichols Jr., Ithaca, NY: Cornell University Press, 1969.*

acontecimientos de la historia de España: 1)El inicio de la época álgida del fascismo en 1943, después de la Guerra Civil, cuando Franco —humillando a todos aquellos españoles liberales o de izquierdas— se declaró abiertamente aliado de Hitler, 2) La muerte en atentado del sucesor de Franco, Luis Carrero Blanco en 1973, hecho que supuso el inicio del final del fascismo en España, 3)1993, un año que ha seguido inmediatamente al de los Juegos Olímpicos de Barcelona, del quinto centenario del "descubrimiento" de América, de la Expo 92 de Sevilla y de la supuesta unificación económica de Europa, España incluida.

Todos ellos son factores que evocaban "el momento en el que España superaba la herencia de los últimos cincuenta años".[3] Cada uno de estos tres momentos está representado mediante una elaborada instalación de mobiliario, en parte destrozado y quemado, en parte nuevo; un coche (como el automóvil en el que asesinaron a Carrero Blanco), imágenes (una pintura de la bandera española realizada con el mismo estilo utilizado por Jasper Johns al pintar la bandera americana, 10 ampliaciones en Cibachrome de fotografías de revistas, y fotografías de botas en marcha en la expoliada y quemada sala del 43), y otros elementos adicionales.

Al contemplar esta obra como "una escenografía hegeliana" uno se enfrenta súbitamente con la pregunta: Cuál Hegel? Puesto que, por lo que se refiere a la interpretación de sus escritos, hay varios. Por una parte está el Hegel dictador malvado de la filosofía, el Hegel al que durante más de un siglo (al menos desde la aparición de la obra de Rudolf Hayms, *Conferencias sobre Hegel y su época*, publicada en Berlín en 1857)[4] se ha culpado tanto de la tragedia de la Historia Moderna. Esta actitud negativa hacia Hegel se repitió en los años sesenta y a principios de los setenta, en un período de "abandono de la razón" en el que la hostilidad hacia Hegel sólo se vio superada por la hostilidad hacia

Torres, algo a la defensiva—,"el resultado de haber leído la historia según Hegel se traduce en una escenificación del baño de sangre que la historia de Europa ha sido en los últimos 2000 años como mínimo. Mi obra es anti-hegeliana en el sentido de que muestro las consecuencias de dicha lectura de la historia y de los procesos políticos y sociales".

El lector no puede evitar tener la molesta sensación de que se ha omitido algo. La agresiva intervención del entrevistador -aunque naturalmente lógica por lo que respecta al impulso global de la obra de Torres- parece haber impedido a Torres decir algo más interesante sobre los motivos por los que calificó su obra de Hegeliana.

[3] *Entrevista en* Artscribe *pág.45.*

[4] *Rudolf Haym,* Vorlesungen über Hegel und Seine Zeit *Berlín, 1857. Los llamados Jóvenes hegelianos, con los que Marx estaba en diversos modos asociado, empezaron a criticar a Hegel antes de 1848.*

superseded Machiavelli's Renaissance concept of power. Hegel's parable of the Master-Slave relationship lies in the immediate background of Nietzsche's analysis of power, and hence of Michel Foucault and much more that has been recently incisive. Delivered between 1933 and 1939, Kojève's lectures seemed to forecast the war which hangs like a brooding but presiding spirit over much of Torres' work.

At the moment of high modernism's cracking open, the anti-Hegelian reaction took either the form of the Hegelian revisionism of Western Marxism or the pre-modernist revivalism of the flower-child culture: the activist intervening in history and the drop-out withdrawing from it. Torres lived in Paris in the May '68 era and was involved in the Marxist version of the Hegelian problematics for a while. This tendency still shows itself in his work's preoccupation with questions of social justice and the overall direction of history. The other option—of dropping out of Hegel's Work of culture into the surround of nature which Hegel had called Madness, and affirming this madness to be the true sanity—also shows itself in Torres' work, but not as a dominant note.

However favorably Kojève may have intended his Hegel, his vision of the philosopher of power nevertheless seems to have presaged the fascistic Hitlerian strife of the war and the Franco regime. But there is another Hegel, whose contours can be seen in a somewhat different version of the redemptive modeling of history set out in a series of essays written between 1956 and 1968 by Joachim Ritter — *Essays on the Philosophy of Right*.[6] Ritter emphasizes the revolutionary Hegel rather than the Hegel who asserted that the Prussian society of his own day was the culmination of history. For Ritter's Hegel, "the Revolution represents the principle of European history."[7] "There is no longer any possibility of turning back from the Revolution."[8] "The unity of freedom and man's being is... the principle of world

[6] *Joachim Ritter*, Hegel and the French Revolution: Essays on the "Philosophy of Right," *English translation by Richard Dien Winfield, Cambridge, MA: The MIT Press, 1982.*

[7] *Ibid., p. 57.*

[8] *Ibid,. p. 52.*

Aristóteles (a quien Timothy Leary, alrededor de 1967, culpó de la tendencia de la mente a falsificar la experiencia categorizándola).

Esta acogida de Hegel halló una influyente articulación en Alexandre Kojeve y su *Introduction to the Reading of Hegel*. Si bien esta serie de conferencias sobre *Fenomenología del espíritu* no pretendía crear un antagonismo con Hegel, dio énfasis al aspecto de poder y dominación de la relación Amo-Esclavo discutida en los primeros seis capítulos de *Fenomenología*.[5] Esta parábola o alegoría materializó una reflexión sobre el poder, derivada en parte de reflexiones sobre la Revolución Francesa y que reemplazó el concepto renacentista del poder de Maquiavelo. La parábola hegeliana de la relación amo-esclavo está basada en los orígenes inmediatos del análisis del poder de Nietzsche, y por lo tanto también de Michel Foucault, y en otras corrientes de pensamiento más recientes. Realizadas entre 1933 y 1939, las conferencias de Kojeve parecían pronosticar la guerra que, como un espíritu, preside y se cierne sobre gran parte de la obra de Torres.

En el momento culminante de la eclosión del modernismo, la reacción anti-hegeliana adquirió la forma, bien del revisionismo hegeliano del marxismo occidental, bien del renacimiento pre-modernista de la cultura hippie: el activista que interviene en la historia y el que abandona y se aparta de ella. Torres vivió en París durante el Mayo del 68 y estuvo durante algún tiempo comprometido con la versión marxista de la problemática hegeliana. Esta tendencia aún se aprecia en su obra, preocupada por cuestiones de justicia social y por la dirección global de la historia. La otra opción —la de abandonar la obra cultural de Hegel por un entorno de naturaleza al que Hegel denominó Locura, y la afirmación de que esta locura es la auténtica cordura— también se observa en la obra de Torres, aunque no como nota dominante.

[5] *Alexandre Kojeve*, Introduction to the Reading of Hegel: Lectures on the Phenomenology of Spirit, *traducción inglesa de James H. Nichols Jr., Ithaca, N.Y.: Cornell University Press, 1969.*

history."[9] For this Hegel, a person is only a person through living a self-willed life not subject to dominance, essentially a democratic idea in which, as Ritter says, freedom and human nature are synonyms, as Aristotle before him had taught in the *Metaphysics*.

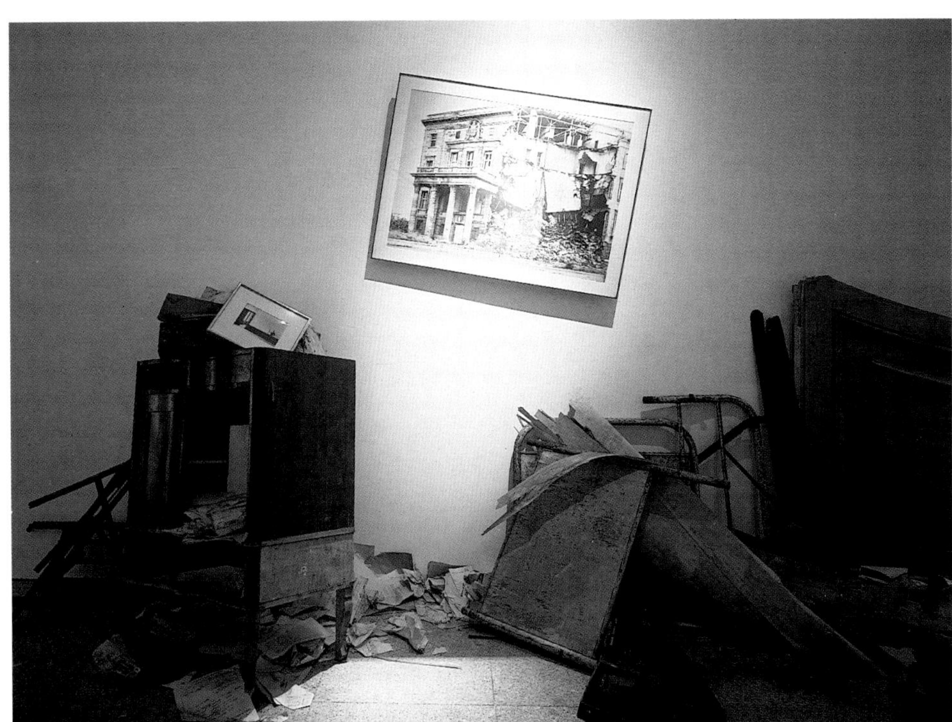

FIFTY RAINS, 1991

Which is the Hegel who presides over Torres' selection of three moments from **Fifty Rains**? Despite Torres' distanced and ironic and complexly layered attitude toward these matters, the selection of the three moments—starting in Fascism, witnessing its downfall, turning toward the future—seems to involve a redemptive sense or posited resolution. The triadic sequence suggests an Aristotelian beginning, middle and end structure, and even a Christological trinitarian view such as Joachim of Flores' and Hegel's own. At the same time, layered upon those structures of culmination, a Hegelian syllogism of thesis, antithesis and synthesis can be seen: Fascism, the negation of Fascism, and some resolution of a new future direction.

[9] *Ibid.*, p. 50.

Por más favorable que sea la definición que Kojeve realiza de Hegel, su visión del filósofo del poder parece, no obstante, presagiar el conflicto bélico fascista de Hitler y el régimen de Franco. Pero existe otro Hegel, cuyo perfil puede apreciarse en una versión algo diferente del modelado redentor de la historia expuesta en una serie de ensayos escritos entre 1956 y 1968 por Joachim Ritter, *Essays on the Philosophy of Right*.[6] Ritter da más importancia al Hegel revolucionario que al Hegel que afirmó que la sociedad Prusiana de su época era la culminación de la historia. Para el Hegel de Ritter "la Revolución representa el principio de la historia de Europa".[7] "Después de la Revolución ya no hay posibilidad alguna de volver atrás". [8] "La unión de la libertad y el ser humano es... el principio de la historia mundial"[9] Para este Hegel una persona sólo es una persona si vive una vida de constante autoafirmación, no sujeta a dominación alguna. Ésta es, esencialmente, una idea democrática en la que, según Ritter, y tal como Aristóteles explicó anteriormente en su *Metafísica*, libertad y naturaleza humana son sinónimos.

¿Cuál es el Hegel predominante en la selección realizada por Torres de los tres momentos de **Cincuenta lluvias**? A pesar de la actitud distanciada, irónica y complejamente estratificada de Torres respecto a estas cuestiones, la selección de los tres momentos —empezando con el fascismo, siendo luego testigo de su caída, y dirigiendo finalmente la mirada hacia el futuro— parece encerrar un sentido redentor o una resolución declarada. Esta tríada sugiere una estructura inicial, media y final aristotélicas, e incluso un punto de vista trinitario cristológico como el de Joachim Flores o el del mismo Hegel. Al mismo tiempo, estratificado sobre las estructuras de culminación, puede percibirse un silogismo hegeliano de tesis, antítesis y síntesis: fascismo, la negación del fascismo y cierta resolución encaminada hacia una nueva dirección futura.

[6] *Joachim Ritter*, Hegel and the french Revolution: Essays on the "Philosophy of Right", *traducción inglesa de Richard Dien Winfield, Cambridge, Massachusetts: The MIT Press, 1982.*

[7] Op.cit., *pág.*57.

[8] Op.cit., *pág.*52.

[9] Op.cit., *pág.*50.

This last is the most dynamic of the three models, for in the tripartite historical logic of Hegel which, with some revisions, is the structural main-frame of Marxism too, the synthesis, as a part of unending process, becomes the thesis of a new linked syllogism. So at the moment it is posited as a synthesis it is ambiguous, undefined, potential; subsequently, it tilts this way or that, and becomes defined at the same moment that it ceases to be a synthesis and becomes a new thesis. It is understood that this third limb, the new thesis, will emerge by the mysterious process of sublation (*Aufhebung*), whereby the thesis somehow incorporates its own negation in order to spring to a higher plane. In this way the three-staged logical argument of Torres' piece is caught at the early moment of unclearness; a redemption is implied by the first two limbs of the syllogism—yet it may be forestalled when the third limb reveals its inner nature still obscured in the creative turmoil of the sublation. It is still possible that the as-yet-undefined synthesis may tilt toward a new and more horrific disaster at the next, presently unseen, moment, as if with an ignoble cyclicity. Torres' third stage installation seems to have all this suspension and potentiality and non-commital energy in it: the flag painting exudes a slightly sinister threat of apolitical expediency; the anonymous new furniture reveals nothing yet of what will occur upon it.

In **Fifty Rains** and in some other works, Torres seems to tilt toward both the Aristotelian Hegel of the democratic self as expressed by Ritter and the Nietzschean Hegel of Terror as expressed by Kojève. Hegel's own phrase to describe the French Revolution, in the *Phenomenology*, acknowledges this linkage: "Absolute Freedom and Terror." As that phrase suggests, Torres' seemingly mixed feelings about Hegel are not uncommon. It is due to this ambivalence that the realization is spreading that so-called postmodernism might better have been called late modernism, because it increasingly seems

---

Este último es el más dinámico de los tres modelos, puesto que en la lógica histórica tripartita de Hegel que, con algunas modificaciones representa también la estructura principal del marxismo, la síntesis se convierte en la tesis de un nuevo silogismo que forma parte de un proceso infinito. De modo que cuando es declarada síntesis ésta es ambigua, indefinida y potencial; posteriormente se inclina hacia una u otra dirección y, en el momento en el que deja de ser síntesis para convertirse en una nueva tesis, adquiere definición. Se sobreentiende que este tercer componente, la nueva tesis, surgirá del misterioso proceso de sublación (*Aufhebung*), por medio del cual la tesis incorpora de algún modo su propia negación para así poder acceder a un nivel superior. De este modo el argumento lógico en tres escenas de esta pieza de Torres se halla en la etapa temprana de confusión; las dos primeras partes del silogismo implican una redención, que puede pronosticarse cuando la tercera parte revela su naturaleza interna, todavía oculta en el caos creativo de la sublación. Aún es posible que la síntesis "todavía por definir" se incline en el momento sucesivo, oculto por ahora, hacia un desastre nuevo y más siniestro, como si siguiera un infame movimiento cíclico. La tercera escena de la instalación de Torres parece encerrar en sí misma toda esta suspensión y potencialidad: la imagen de la bandera exuda cierta siniestra amenaza de conveniencia apolítica; el mobiliario nuevo, anónimo, aún no revela lo que le sucederá.

En **Cincuenta lluvias** y en otras de sus obras, Torres parece inclinarse a la vez hacia el Hegel aristotélico de naturaleza democrática de Ritter y hacia el nietzscheano Hegel del terror de Kojeve. La expresión utilizada por el mismo Hegel para describir la Revolución Francesa en su *Fenomenología* admite esta conexión: "libertad y terror absolutos". Tal como la expresión sugiere, los sentimientos contradictorios de Torres acerca de Hegel no son inusuales. Debido a esta ambivalencia se está extendiendo la opinión de que el llamado postmodernismo debería haberse llamado modernismo

more a revision of Hegel than a rejection—more a tilting toward one Hegel than another; specifically it is a revision of Hegel's idea of the end of history, seen by him as unitary (Prussian) but now seen as more pluralistic (multicultural), with an overall acceptance still of the idea of History itself.

Torres' work, with its undefined but threateningly artificial-looking third stage, is not buying into postmodern utopianism uncritically. The overall mood of the work is tough-minded in William James' sense; at any rate it presents itself as such, though perhaps with a tender-minded inside (a flower child lurking in the other room); he seems to have chosen neither to relax back into pre-modernism nor to flee from a discredited modernism into an unknown postmodernism but to balance on an interface, that is, to stay on the fence. In refusing to locate himself definitively, Torres avoids another problem with the idea of postmodernism, which is that it implies a *tabula rasa*, the dawning of a definitively new era. It is thus a somewhat wishful term, a kind of magical mantra designed to convince us that we are free of the past or have somehow gone beyond it. Torres' work does not seem to involve this hidden religious conviction.

Thus Torres' work could be called post-ideological in the ambivalence that it shows to a variety of ideological positions. Shaped for a while by May '68, when he was a student in Paris and, as he puts it, attended daily demonstrations "religiously,"[10] he now speaks of a "fall away" (compare the phrase "fallen away Catholic"): "The fall, not away from Marxism but from its practice, from the everyday political activity and what I encountered there, was certainly a disenchantment."[11]

The fall and disenchantment, and the post-ideological position that comes with them, lead to what John Hanhardt has called a "radical skepticism" in Torres' attitude.[12] The radical skepticism may be seen as a result of making Hegel ambiguous, of seeing more than one Hegel, and Hegels at war with

10 Artscribe *interview 43.*

11 *Ibid.*

12 *John Hanhardt, "Francesc Torres: The Limits of Discourse,"* Francesc Torres: Works from the Field, a Selection. *Ithaca: Herbert F. Johnson Museum of Art, Cornell University, 1982, p. 4.*

tardío, puesto que parece cada vez más una revisión que un rechazo a Hegel, es una tendencia más inclinada hacia un Hegel que hacia otro; especficamente es una revisión de la idea hegeliana del final de la historia, vista por él como unitaria (Prusiana) y ahora considerada más pluralista (multicultural), si bien el concepto general de historia es el mismo.

La obra de Torres, con una tercera escena indefinida pero amenazadoramente artificial, no acepta la idea utópica postmodernista sin criticarla. El espíritu general de la obra es enérgico, en el sentido que William James daba a este adjetivo; en cualquier caso la obra se presenta a ella misma como tal, aunque quizás con un interior algo tierno (un hippie escondido en la otra habitación). Torres no ha elegido ni descansar en el premodernismo ni huir de un modernismo desacreditado para refugiarse en un desconocido postmodernismo, sino que está en equilibrio en una superficie de contacto, es decir, nada entre dos aguas. Al rehusar ubicarse definitivamente, Torres elude otro problema relacionado con la idea de postmodernismo, el hecho de que éste implica hacer *tabula rasa*, iniciar definitivamente una nueva era. Éste es, en cierto modo un término desiderativo, una especie de mantra mágico destinado a convencernos de que nos hemos liberado del pasado o de que una forma u otra lo hemos superado. Pero la obra de Torres no parece incluir esta oculta convicción religiosa.

Así pues, la obra de Torres podría denominarse post-ideológica por la ambivalencia que muestra ante diversas posturas ideológicas. Influenciado durante algún tiempo por los sucesos ocurridos en mayo del 68, cuando él estudiaba en París y, según sus propias palabras, asistía "religiosamente" a las manifestaciones,[10] Torres habla ahora de una "apostasía" (comparable con la expresión "católico apóstata"): "La apostasía, no del marxismo sino de su práctica, de la actividad política cotidiana y lo que allí encontré representó, ciertamente, un desengaño".[11]

10 *Entrevista en* Artscribe, *pág.43.*

11 *Op.cit.*

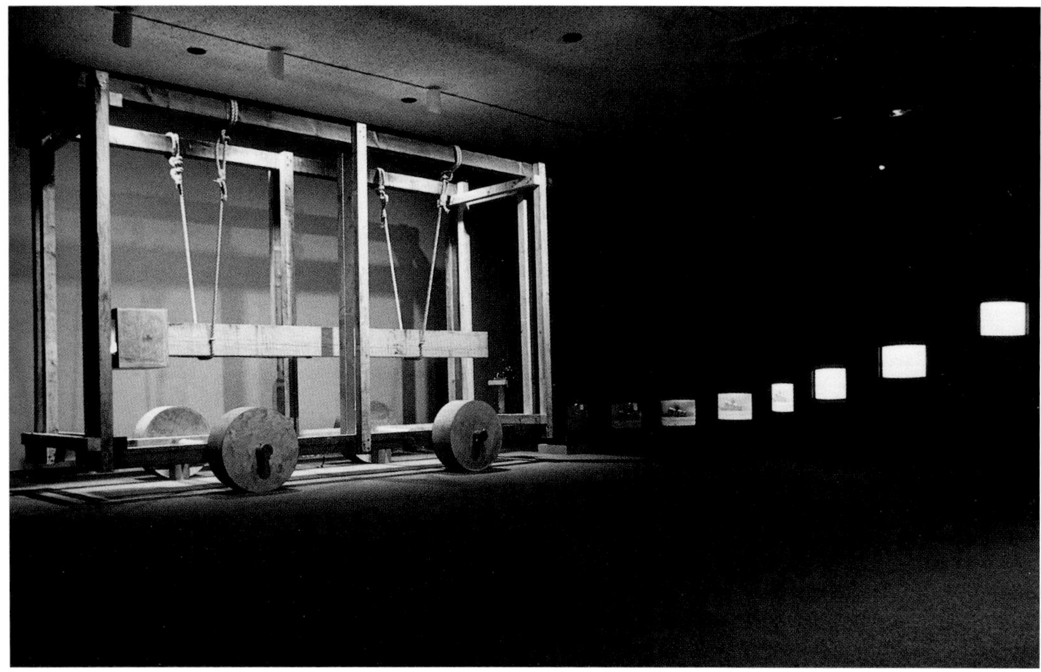

THE HEAD OF THE DRAGON, 1981

one another, annihilating one another's positions. There is then a dilemma pointed to by Torres' work—a moral-reflective dilemma which can be approached as a conflict between Kojève's and Ritter's Hegel, or in other ways.

MacLean and the Dragon

One of these other ways is seen in Torres' incorporation, alongside Hegel's free-wheeling historicism, of the biologistic determinism of neurologist Paul MacLean's theory of brain formation. MacLean argues that the different parts of the physical brain—the brain stem, the cerebral cortex, and the intermediary system—reflect and in effect preserve different stages of evolution: the brain stem, for example, is viewed as reptilian, and the other components as having developed at post-reptilian stages of evolution. Each stage is regarded as having frozen in a special formation and remained alive and active to this day, albeit overlaid by later layers that may

---

La apostasía, el desencanto, y la postura post-ideológica que ambos conllevan, condujeron a Torres a lo que John Hanhardt ha denominado un "escepticismo radical".[12] El escepticismo radical puede ser considerado como el resultado de la interpretación ambigua de Hegel, del hecho de percibir diversos Hegels que están en guerra entre ellos y se niegan entre sí. La obra de Torres apunta además un dilema de reflexión moral que puede enfocarse como un conflicto entre el Hegel de Kojeve y el de Ritter.

[12] *John Hanhardt, "Francesc Torres: The Limits of Discourse"*, Francesc Torres: Works from the Field, a Selection. *Ithaca: Herbert F. Johnson Museum of Art, Cornell University, 1982, pág. 4.*

MacLean y el dragón

Otra manera de enfocar este dilema se puede apreciar en cómo Torres incorpora, junto con el historicismo libre de Hegel, el determinismo biológico que encierra la teoría de la formación del cerebro del neurólogo Paul MacLean. MacLean afirma que las diversas partes del cerebro físico —el tronco cerebral, la corteza cerebral y el sistema intermedio— reflejan y en realidad conservan diversos estadios de la evolución. Por ejemplo, se cree que el tronco cerebral es reptil, mientras que los otros componentes parecen haberse desarrollado en fases evolutivas post-reptiles. Como si cada estadio evolutivo se hubiera congelado con una estructura especial y hubiera permanecido vivo y activo hasta nuestros días, bien que cubierto por capas posteriores que pueden amortiguar o mediar sus impulsos —"como si tuviéramos tres cerebros distintos" dice Torres—, aunque al aplicarse la teoría, el nivel medio tiene tendencia a desaparecer, convirtiendo el sistema en dualista.[13] En diferentes momentos y aspectos de la vida social, Torres percibe la ascendencia parcial o momentánea de una u otra de estas etapas evolutivas previas. La etapa reptil regula el comportamiento vinculado con la territorialidad y la agresión, "algunas de las... zonas de actividad social potencialmente más peligrosas

[13] Artscribe, *pág.51.*

muffle or mediate its impulses—"as if we had three separate brains," Torres says—though in applications of the theory the middle level tends to disappear and the system becomes dualistic.[13] In different moments and aspects of social life Torres sees the momentary or partial ascendancy of one or another of these previous evolutionary stages. The reptilian stage regulates behavior involving territoriality and aggression, "leading to the paradox," Torres comments, "of having some of the most potentially dangerous areas of social activity regulated by the oldest and most atavistic part of our brain."[14]

13 Artscribe, *p. 51.*

14 The Head of the Dragon (Anthology), *Madrid: Museo Nacional Centro de Arte Reina Sofia, 1991, p. 51.*

The Head of the Dragon, 1981, consists of a battering ram on which a small steam engine labors, facing a door behind which is a live boa constrictor whose image is transmitted to a monitor on the head of the battering ram. Behind the ram, as its "tail," a row of eight monitors shows a loop of a racing car crashing. A film projection shows a man dancing while a snake (drawn onto the film) moves about. On a wall eight prints show a snake coming into focus, followed by a diagram of the brain with MacLean's tripartite division marked out. On the floor the pieces of a jigsaw-puzzle map of the world lie scattered.

A mythical (Beowulfian) read-ing might take the boa constrictor behind the door as the "worm" (as the Anglo-Saxon calls it) guarding the treasure in the cave—or preventing the exercise of reason. The battering ram with the steam engine on its back driving it relentlessly onward is modernism rushing apace to break down the barriers of instinct and superstition; yet it bears within its own brain the very reptile that it presumes to assault—thereby rendering its assault suicidal; the suicide/homicide issue is further complicated by another (baby?) snake just taking form as the monster History's tail and about to either drive it on or attack it from behind. So the idea of

están reguladas por la parte más primitiva y atávica de nuestro cerebro —observa Torres—, lo cual es una paradoja".[14]

14 The Head of the Dragon (Antología), *Madrid: Museo Nacional Centro de Arte Reina Sofía, 1991, pág.51.*

The Head of the Dragon (La cabeza del dragón), 1981, es una instalación compuesta por un ariete sobre el que está montada una pequeña máquina de vapor en funcionamiento; este ariete está situado frente a una puerta colgante tras la cual hay una boa constrictor viva cuya imagen se transmite a un monitor colocado en la cabeza del ariete. Tras el ariete, como si fuera su "cola", una hilera de ocho monitores muestra incesantemente la colisión de un coche de carreras. Asimismo se proyecta una película que muestra un hombre bailando mientras una serpiente, dibujada sobre la película, acompaña al bailarín. Sobre una pared, ocho imágenes correlativas muestran una serpiente cada vez más definida; estas imágenes van seguidas de un diagrama del cerebro en el que está trazada la división tripartita de MacLean. En el suelo aparecen esparcidas las piezas de un rompecabezas que representa el mapamundi.

Una lectura mítica (Beowulfiana) podría identificar la serpiente tras la puerta con el "gusano" (tal como le denominan los anglosajones) que protege el tesoro de la cueva —o que impide el ejercicio de la razón—. El ariete, con la máquina de vapor en su parte dorsal que lo empuja inexorablemente hacia adelante, es el modernismo que se apresura a romper las barreras del instinto y la superstición. Sin embargo, en el interior de su cerebro anida el mismo reptil al que cree atacar, convirtiendo por lo tanto este ataque en suicida; la cuestión suicidio/homicidio viene ulteriormente complicada por otra serpiente (¿una cría?) que se convierte en la cola del monstruo de la Historia, a punto de empujarlo hacia adelante o de embestirlo por detrás. Así, para un ser con tres cerebros, la idea de progreso es una idea extremadamente conflictiva en la que una parte del dragón del yo puede traicionar y oponerse a otra.

15 Aristotle's formulation of the self-willed existence in the Metaphysics*: "That person is free who exists for him or herself rather than for another."* Met. 982b25f (anthropos ... eleutheros ho autou heneka kai me allou on). *It's interesting that Aristotle expressed it as being rather than as will, though clearly, since for Aristotle being means selfhood, the two are closely related.*

The idea of Will in Hegel comes directly from Aristotle—the only classical ethicist, East or West, who said that you had to have a certain amount of money to be happy. The idea is not that the individual human will be materially well provided for and live under favorable climatic conditions and have a good sexual relationship and own his or her own home. The idea is that even under the worst material and social circumstances this individual will somehow shape the ends of his or her life out of pure identity/will, as the whiplash on the end of the impact of desire: that Will should shape Self in a pure disinterested way except for self-expression and self-realization. The

progress, for a being with two or three brains, is a deeply conflicted idea in which one part of the dragon of the self may betray and oppose another.

A complex of ideas hovers in the air around the work: genetic coding, evolutionary stages versus historical stages, what Torres calls the "dance of biology," skeptical contemplation of the idea of progress as manifest in the industrial revolution, the speeding onward thrust of capitalist modernism and its crash, culture as a dialectic that always involves the negation of what is there in favor of a new development.

In Torres' oeuvre MacLean's tripartite brain or soul acts out the same dilemma found in the wavering attitude toward Hegel. It is implicitly Hegelian while renouncing Hegelianism. Its positive Hegelianism consists in its tendency to reflect the mid- and late-19th century equation of Darwinism with the Hegelian idea of progress—a tendency that Darwin—a Hegelian himself—was involved in. Meanwhile, the reptilian theme derived from MacLean's rereading of Darwin oozes an anti-Hegelian fog of pessimistic determinism. It implies that human life is not carried out *bei sich*, or in *Bei sich selbst sein*, "self-contained existence," as Hegel called it. It negates the idea of the democratic individual posited as the governing subject of late bourgeois capitalism. In this aspect, it not only presents human existence as carried out in bondage, but in a deeper bondage than the Master-Slave relationship could ever account for: an actual biological bondage. The result is that, in effect, it offers an excuse to humanity: that it is not altogether human. Murders, wars, holocausts—these are momentary takeovers by the reptilian brain—alienated actions in which the human actor is literally not in his right mind. For, in the Aristotelian-Hegelian view, only the democratic mind can have an identity as an individual subject—a "self-contained" or "self-willed" mode of existence.[15]

---

[15] *La formulación aristotélica de la existencia autoafirmativa en su obra* Metafísica: *"Es libre aquella persona que existe para él o ella misma más que para otro".* Met.982b25f (anthropos... eleutheros ho autou heneka kai me allou on). *Es inte-resante el hecho de que Aristóteles lo exprese como ser en vez de como voluntad, aunque es evidente, puesto que para Aristóteles ser significa individua-lidad, que ambos conceptos están estrechamente relacionados.*

La idea de Voluntad en Hegel proviene directamente de Aristóteles, el único pensador ético clásico, de oriente u occidente, que dijo que para ser feliz es necesario poseer cierta cantidad de dinero. La idea no es que el individuo humano posea recursos económicos, viva bajo condiciones climáticas favorables, tenga una buena relación sexual y posea su propia casa. La idea es que incluso en las peores circunstancias sociales y materiales dicho individuo dará forma a los objetivos de su vida mediante su identidad/voluntad, como el latigazo al final del impacto

Un complejo de ideas flota alrededor de esta obra: códigos genéticos, estadios evolutivos contra etapas históricas, lo que Torres denomina "danza de la biología", la contemplación escéptica de la idea de progreso como manifiesto en la revolución industrial, la súbita aceleración del modernismo capitalista y su caída, la cultura como una dialéctica que siempre implica la negación de aquello que está a favor de un nuevo impulso.

En la obra de Torres, el cerebro o alma tripartita de MacLean reproduce el dilema de su indecisa actitud hacia Hegel. Es implícitamente hegeliana y al mismo tiempo renuncia al hegelianismo. Su evidente hegelianismo radica en la tendencia a reflejar el paralelismo, establecido a mediados y finales del siglo XIX, entre el darwinismo y Hegel, tendencia que el mismo Darwin —también hegeliano— compartía. Simultáneamente, del tema reptil que deriva de una relectura de Darwin realizada por MacLean emana una niebla anti-hegeliana de determinismo pesimista. Ello implica que la vida humana no tiene lugar *bei sich*, o en una *Bei sich selbst sein* o "existencia autosuficiente", como la denominó Hegel, y niega la idea del individuo democrático como sujeto dominante del último capitalismo burgués. En este aspecto, no presenta la existencia humana simplemente como una existencia en estado de esclvitud, sino que esta esclavitud es más dura que la que cualquier relación Amo-Esclavo podría nunca justificar. El resultado, en realidad, ofrece una excusa a la humanidad: la de no ser completamente humana. Asesinatos, guerras y holocaustos representan momentáneas tomas de poder del cerebro reptil, acciones enajenadas en las que el agente humano ha perdido literalmente el juicio. Desde el punto de vista hegliano-aristotélico, únicamente la mente democrática puede tener identidad como sujeto individual en un tipo de existencia "autosuficiente" o de "autoafirmación".[15]

Beuys and Haacke

This type of tension in Torres' oeuvre can be seen again in the antinomy between Joseph Beuys and Hans Haacke, two artists who were formative on his oeuvre at an early stage—not on the style or shape of the work but on its internal directionality in relation to society. It has been remarked that Torres' work is in a sense situated in between theirs:[16] less oceanic than Beuys', less specific than Haacke's. One way of focusing this antinomy is by considering the distinction between time and history. Time is an oceanic flow of moments with neutral value judgment placed on them. History is a selected thin stream of moments saturated with a sense of values; it is the series of explicit moments we pluck out of the shapeless mass of time to embody a shape according to which we define ourselves.

In Torres' **Fifty Rains**, for example, the three moments selected and focused on are distinctly historical; they represent a story with a specific shape and a precise value. Yet the title, **Fifty Rains**, views the story as embedded in the value-free, shapeless or cyclical matrix of nature. The aspect of the work which deals with explicit political events is in the direction of Haacke's oeuvre, the aspect which retreats into the rainy universality of nature has more in common with Beuys running across and sinking into the peat bog, or escaping from the nightmare of history on a sled into the wilderness.

The two aspects of experience recognized by Hegel—his dichotomy of nature and culture—are again implied. This dichotomy is encountered frequently in Torres' work, but usually as revised by MacLean. Nature and culture both exist within humanity, one as the reptilian brain, the other as the cortex. There is a hidden Zoroastrian-like dualism of human nature here, which recalls the Apollonian-Dionysian dichotomy as well as the Christian dichotomy of the divine soul and animal instinct.

reasoning is somewhat circular: if the will already realizes what it wants to be then it is not disinterested. Still, there is something there, or can seem to be.

This idea of Aristotle's is at the basis of Hegel's distinction between life bei sich *and* für sich. *The idea is that the exercise of citizenship in a democratic society matures a reality principle leading to a self-willed willed self—a kind of solipsism of self-realizing will that is covertly based on the religious idea of the self-caused cause—the standard Aristotelian and Scholastic slogan-definition of God.*

[16] Artscribe, *p. 44.*

Beuys y Haacke

Este tipo de tensión en la obra de Torres puede apreciarse de nuevo en la antinomía entre Joseph Beuys y Hans Haacke, dos artistas que tuvieron influencia formativa en un primer período de su obra, no en el estilo ni en la forma de la obra, sino en su orientación interna en relación con la sociedad. Se ha comentado que la obra de Torres se halla, en cierto sentido, entre la de aquéllos:[16] es menos oceánica que la de Beuys y menos específica que la de Haacke. Un modo de enfocar esta antinomía sería considerar la distinción entre tiempo e historia. El tiempo es una corriente oceánica de momentos con un juicio de valor neutral. La historia es una corriente fina y selecta de momentos saturados con un sentido de valores; es la serie de momentos explícitos que arrancamos de la informe masa temporal para dar cuerpo a la forma según la cual nos definimos.

Por ejemplo, en **Cincuenta lluvias**, los tres momentos seleccionados y enfocados son claramente históricos; representan una historia con una forma determinada y con un valor preciso. No obstante, el título, **Cincuenta lluvias**, ve la historia como fijada en la matriz de la naturaleza, cíclica, informe o exenta de valor. La parte de su obra que trata de acontecimientos políticos explícitos está en la línea de la obra de Haacke; la parte que se refugia en la universalidad de la naturaleza tiene más en común con la escapada de Beyus y su hundimiento en la turbera o con su huida de la pesadilla de la historia en un trineo, adentrándose en lo desconocido.

Los dos aspectos de la experiencia reconocidos por Hegel, su dicotomía de naturaleza y cultura, están de nuevo implícitos. Esta dicotomía está presente con frecuencia en la obra de Torres, pero generalmente aparece con la revisión de MacLean. Naturaleza y cultura coexisten en el hombre, una como cerebro reptil, la otra como el córtex. Aquí se observa un dualismo zoroástrico oculto de la

del deseo: que la Voluntad dará forma al Yo de modo absolutamente desinteresado, excepto en la expresión de la propia personalidad y la propia realización. Este razonamiento es en cierto modo circular: si la voluntad se da cuenta de lo que quiere ser ya no es desinteresada. De todos modos, algo de ello puede haber o puede parecer que lo hay.

Esta idea de Aristóteles yace en la base de la distinción que realiza Hegel entre la vida bei sich y für sich. *La idea es que el ejercicio de la ciudadanía en una sociedad demo-crática hace madurar un principio de realidad que conduce a un yo con voluntad de autoafirmación, una especie de solipsismo de voluntad de autorealización basado secretamente en la idea religiosa del origen que se ha originado a sí mismo, la definición-lema aristotélica y escolástica de Dios.*

[16] Artscribe, *pág.44.*

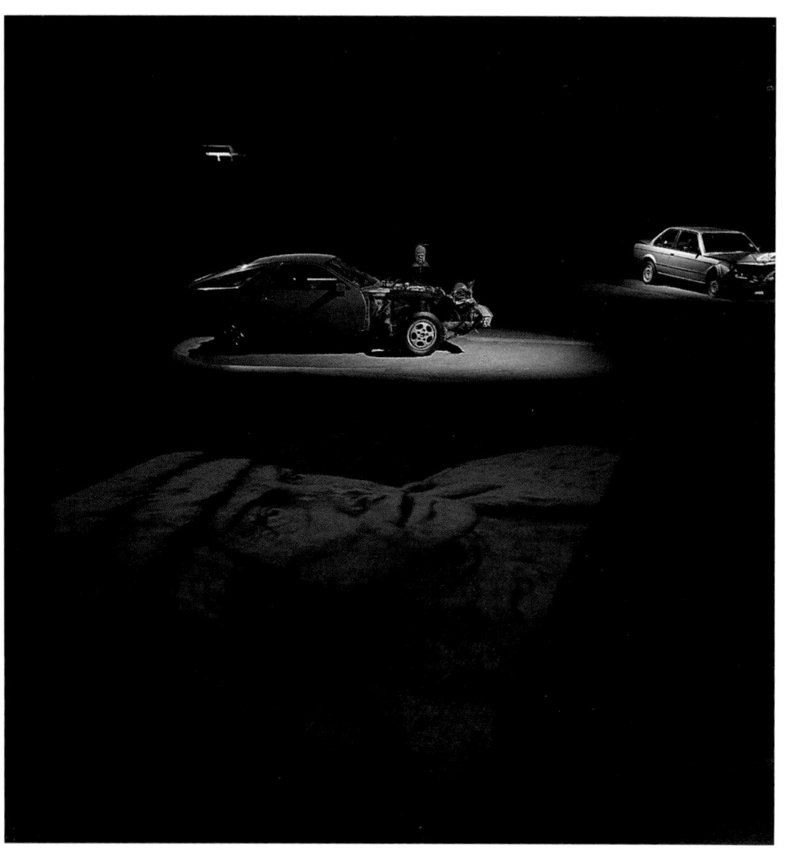

DESTINY, ENTROPY AND JUNK, 1990

Ritter notes that "every present and future legal and political order must presuppose and proceed from the Revolution's universal principle of freedom."[17] This principle underlies all of Torres' work as an inborn yearning, a final cause, almost a prayer. But equally omnipresent is the pull of the reptilian brain which, like the worm that Blake says hides inside the rose, is everywhere. It is nature sucking culture down into the abyss. It could not begin to comprehend the idea of individual action arising from individual self-conscious will.

CALLIGRAPHY

Another avenue into Torres' work is offered by Eisenstein's description of the derivation of his own imagery from Japanese calligraphy viewed as an analogue to Hegelian dialectic.[18] Eisenstein wrote of how two calligraphic signs would be combined to create a third meaning, like thesis and antithesis making synthesis. Torres' work often follows a structure of internal dichotomy or antinomy not unlike this. A semiotic ideogram emerges from the combined counterforces of this and that. One example is a kind of

---

naturaleza humana que recuerda la dicotomía apolíneo-dionisíaca y también la dicotomía cristiana del alma divina y el instinto animal.

Ritter observa que "todo orden político y legal presente y futuro debe reconocer y proceder del principio de libertad universal de la revolución".[17] Este principio es la base del conjunto de la obra de Torres, un ansia innata, una causa final, casi una oración. Pero igualmente omnipresente es la influencia del cerebro reptil que, como el gusano que según Blake se esconde en la rosa, se halla en todas partes. Es la naturaleza absorbiendo naturaleza hacia el abismo. Este cerebro no puede llegar a comprender en absoluto la idea de acción individual que surge de la voluntad del individuo.

CALIGRAFÍA

Otra manera de abordar la obra de Torres es a través de la descripción que Eisenstein hace de su propia imaginería, derivada de la caligrafía japonesa y vista como algo análogo a la dialéctica Hegeliana.[18] Eisenstein escribió acerca de cómo dos signos caligráficos combinados crean un tercer significado, del mismo modo que tesis y antítesis originan la síntesis. La obra de Torres sigue a menudo una estructura de dicotomía interna o antinomía no muy diferente. Un ideograma semiótico emerge de la combinación de fuerzas opuestas de una y otra ideas. Un ejemplo de ello es una especie de firma de Torres, la combinación de un coche y un monitor de vídeo. En **Field of Action (Campo de acción)**, 1982, un Jeep (repintado como un cuadro de goteo de Jackson Pollock) se apoya, no sobre cuatro ruedas, sino sobre cuatro monitores de vídeo; en la parte posterior, donde debería ir colocada la rueda de recambio, hay otro monitor. En **Belchite/South Bronx**, 1988, un monitor de vídeo descansa sobre el techo aplastado de un coche destrozado y abandonado mientras otros dos monitores brillan bajo el

[17] *Ritter, pág.52.*

[18] *Sergei Eisenstein, "The Cinematographic Principle and the Ideogram", en* Film Form: Essays in Film Theory, *New York:Harcourt, Brace and World, 1949, págs.28-44.*

signature image for Torres, the combination of a car and a video monitor. In **Field of Action**, 1982, a Jeep (repainted like a Jackson Pollock drip painting) stands not on four wheels but on four video monitors; on the rear end, where the spare tire would be mounted, is another monitor. In **Belchite/South Bronx**, 1988, a video monitor rests on the crumpled roof of a wrecked and abandoned car while two more glare from under its hood, from the engine compartment. In **Dromos Indiana**, 1989, a racing car stands on a field of monitors lying on their backs with their screens broadcasting upward. In **Destiny, Entropy and Junk**, 1990, wrecked cars surround a video projection on the floor. In **The Hay Wain**, 1991, a large truck is involved with a series of video projections. Related images combine the monitor with a variety of weapons ranging from the battering ram of **Head of the Dragon** to the dive bomber of **Airstrip**, 1982, and the cannon of **The Gladiator's House**, 1985. In still other cases video monitors or projections show cars in various social relations, from the crashing racing car of **Head of the Dragon** to the windshield washing activity of **Oikonomos**, 1989.

The car represents transportation through the body, the TV through the mind; the car is in effect an extension of the body, the video screen an extension of the mind. The car is an old style modernist machine, the TV a postmodernist machine in Jameson's sense, meaning an instrument not of production but of reproduction.[19] The car is about the production of new experiences, the quest for something, the need to get somewhere, to bring something home, the whole project of going out upon the earth as opposed to the postmodern project of sitting home and viewing reduced-scale images of things out there. The car is a modernist image of questing for empire, the video a postmodern image of diffusing one's consciousness into the stream of simulacra. In a sense the

[17] *Ritter, p. 52.*

[18] *Sergei Eisenstein, "The Cinematographic Principle and the Ideogram," in* Film Form: Essays in Film Theory, *New York: Harcourt, Brace and World, 1949, pp. 28-44.*

[19] *Frederic Jameson,* Post-Modernism, or, The Cultural Logic of late Capitalism, *Durham, North Carolina: Duke University Press, 1992, p.37.*

capó, en el compartimento del motor. En **Dromos Indiana**, 1989, un coche de carreras está colocado en una superficie llena de monitores que apoyan su parte posterior en el suelo y cuyas pantallas emiten hacia arriba. En **Destí, entropia i ferralla/2 (Destino, entropía y chatarra/2)**, 1991, coches destrozados rodean una proyección de vídeo en el suelo. En **The Hay Wain (El carro de heno)**, 1991, una serie de proyecciones de vídeo envuelven un camión de gran tonelaje. Imágenes afines combinan el monitor con diversas armas que abarcan desde el ariete de **Head of the Dragon** al avión de bombardeo de **Airstrip (Pista de aterrizaje)**, 1982, o al cañón de **The Gladiators House, (La casa de los gladiadores)**, 1985. Otros monitores de vídeo o proyecciones muestran coches en diversas relaciones sociales, desde el accidente del coche de carreras de **Head of the Dragon** hasta la acción de lavado del parabrisas en **Oikonomos**, 1989.

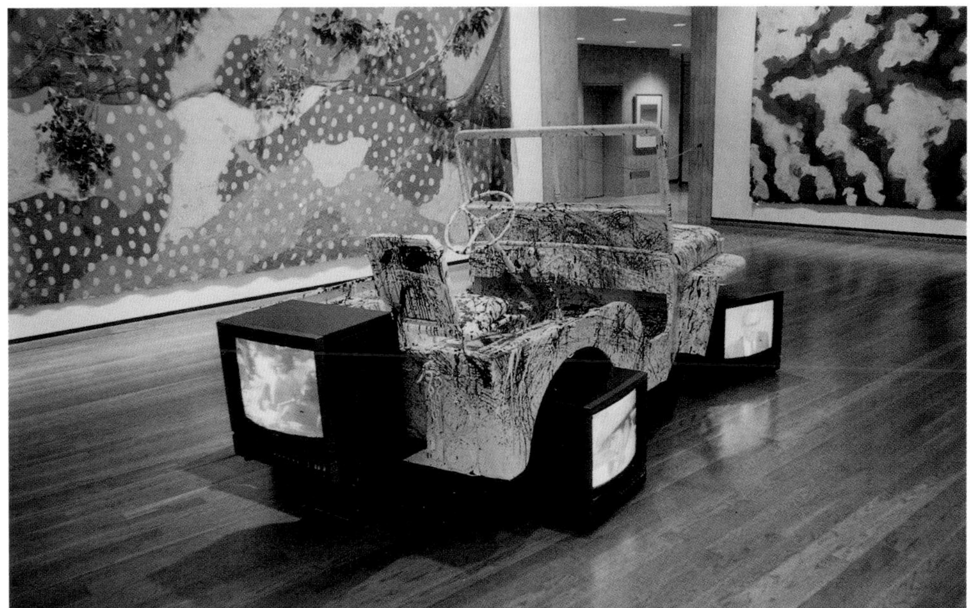

FIELD OF ACTION, 1982

El coche representa el transporte a través del cuerpo, el televisor, el transporte a través de la mente;

conjunction of car and TV is an allegorical picture of the dualistic human nature of MacLean's theory—the car representing the drive for territoriality and aggression, the video involved in contemplation of such drives and activities. Their relationship is dynamic, however, like a truncated syllogism, thesis and antithesis interacting without yet having produced a synthesis.

BELCHITE/SOUTH BRONX

Somewhat similar structures of dichotomous superimposition occur in **Belchite/South Bronx: A Trans-Cultural and Trans-Historical Landscape**, 1988, which is dedicated "to those whom Hegel doesn't mention by name." The large and complex work involves certain abstract relations between a small town in the northeast of Spain that was destroyed in the Spanish Civil War and an area of New York City that was destroyed by peacetime urban blight produced in part by changing immigration patterns. Here again Torres is working extremely closely with philosophical ideas and texts, especially those of the French sociologist Paul Virilio.[20] Virilio has stressed the parallelism between the working class in a peacetime economy and the infantry in war. In total war as defined by Karl von Clausewitz (based on the Napoleonic example), an entire population is mobilized in one way or another into a war effort. Little distinction remains between the military and the industrial proletariats. Carried further, this parallel suggests that forces like those of war exist and operate among civilian populations. Divisions within a population, when charged with sufficient hostility, amount to a state of war, and the destruction of the South Bronx is presented as a form of civil war "because it was violence perpetrated by Americans on Americans, by a nation on itself."[21] Belchite and the South Bronx, in other words, were destroyed by the same forces operating now

[20] *Especially relevant are Paul Virilio and Sylvere Lotringer,* Pure War, *New York: Semiotext(e), 1983, and Paul Virilio,* Speed and Politics, *New York: Semiotext(e), 1986.*

[21] *Francesc Torres,* Belchite/South Bronx: A Trans-Cultural and Trans-Historical Landscape, *Amherst, Mass.: University Gallery, University of Massachusetts, 1988, p. 86.*

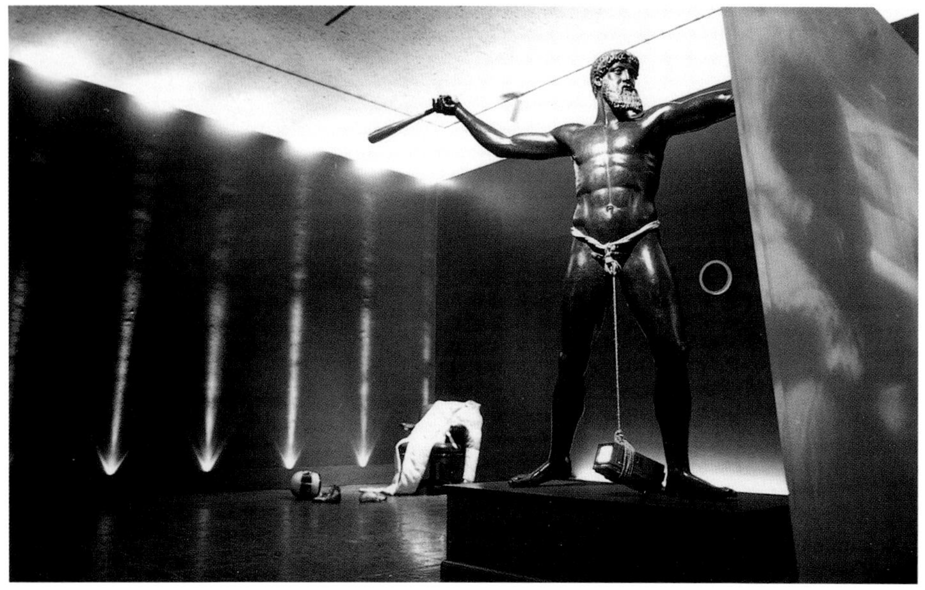

OIKONOMOS, 1989

el coche es, de hecho, una extensión del cuerpo, la pantalla de vídeo lo es de la mente. El automóvil es una máquina modernista antigua, el televisor una máquina postmodernista tal y como la concibe Jameson, como un instrumento no de producción sino de reproducción.[19] El automóvil representa la realización de nuevas experiencias, la búsqueda de algo, la necesidad de ir a alguna parte, de llevar algo a casa, la idea de cruzar la tierra que contrasta con la idea postmodernista de quedarse en casa viendo imágenes de objetos del exterior a escala reducida. El coche es una imagen modernista de la búsqueda del imperio, el vídeo una imagen postmoderna de la difusión de la propia conciencia en la corriente de los simulacros. En cierto sentido, la conjunción de automóvil y televisor es una imagen alegórica de la dualidad de la naturaleza humana que hallamos en la teoría de MacLean; el coche representa el viaje hacia la territorialidad y la agresión, mientras que el vídeo se ocupa de la contemplación de dichos viajes y actividades. Es, de todos modos, una relación dinámica, como un silogismo truncado en el que tesis y antítesis interaccionan sin haber aún producido la síntesis.

[19] *Frederic Jameson,* Post-Modernism, or, The Cultural Logic of late Capitalism, *Durham, North Carolina: Duke University Press, 1992, pág.37.*

openly, now covertly, within a society inherently in a state of total war merely because of its class divisions. "Any nation," Torres writes, "whether capitalist or socialist, that lives with the permanent stigma of unfairly distributed wealth (or the incapacity of generating wealth for the majority of its citizens) is perpetrating an act of violence on a massive scale, a definite attribute of war occurring in peacetime. The homeless, just to mention one group of victims, are the refugees of a social arena where only the strong (warlords?) can survive."[22]

[22] *Torres,* Belchite/South Bronx, *p. 87.*

The installation **Belchite/South Bronx** was extensive and complex, involving ruined buildings (smaller than life yet still large enough to suggest an urban milieu) based on both locales, wrecked cars, trashed furniture, a South Bronx style neighborhood basketball court, video monitors drawing analogies between the Spanish Civil War footsoldier and the teenage street basketball player, and more. The viewer wandered through it as through a ghost town, a civilization that had voided itself. In this case the two entities which were conflated together are less clearly thesis and antithesis. At first they seem so: Belchite as war and the South Bronx as peacetime; but the piece, as it sublates them within one another, reaches a third term that is seen as underlying both—the concept of total war, war as a force saturating all human activities. This saturation is seen not only in the destruction of both cities, but in the imbrication of team sports with military training and military-like competitions, especially in international arenas such as the long ideological competition between the US and the USSR played out on the athletic courts of the world. Thus the ghostly panorama is called trans-cultural and trans-historical because it points to forces active in human societies at many times and places—"Beirut and Dresden and the slums of Mexico City and Port-au-Prince."[23] In this sense it is the reptile's legacy again.

[23] *Torres,* Belchite/South Bronx, *p.102.*

Belchite/South Bronx

Estructuras de superimposición dicotómica similares podemos hallarlas en **Belchite/South Bronx: A Trans-Cultural and Trans-Historical Landscape (Belchite/South Bronx: Paisaje transcultural y trans-histórico)**, 1988, dedicada a "aquellos a quienes Hegel no menciona por su nombre". La obra, grande y compleja, implica ciertas relaciones abstractas entre un pequeño pueblo del nordeste de España destruido durante la Guerra Civil española y una zona de la ciudad de Nueva York destruida por la plaga urbana de los tiempos de paz, ocasionada en parte por las cambiantes pautas de inmigración. Aquí Torres trabaja de nuevo muy estrechamente con ideas y textos filosóficos, sobre todo los del sociólogo francés Paul Virilio.[20] Virilio hace hincapié en el paralelismo entre la clase obrera en tiempos de paz y la infantería en tiempos de guerra. En la guerra total, tal y como la define Karl von Clausewitz (basada en un ejemplo napoleónico), toda la población se moviliza de un modo u otro como una fuerza bélica. Poca es la distinción que se puede hacer entre los proletariados militar e industrial. Este paralelismo, llevado aún más allá sugiere que fuerzas de tipo bélico existen y actúan entre la población civil. Divisiones en la población cargadas con la suficiente hostilidad pueden alcanzar un estado de guerra; la destrucción del South Bronx se presenta como una forma de guerra civil "porque era violencia perpetrada por americanos contra americanos, por una nación contra ella misma".[21] En otras palabras, Belchite y el South Bronx, fueron destruidos por las mismas fuerzas que operan ora abiertamente, ora en secreto en una sociedad en estado de guerra total inherente a causa de las divisiones de clase. "Toda nación", escribe Torres, "capitalista o socialista, que vive con el estigma permanente de una injusta distribución de la riqueza (o con la incapacidad de generar riqueza para la mayoría de sus habitantes) está perpetrando un acto de violencia a escala masiva, un atributo de guerra

[20] *Especialmente relevantes son Paul Virilio y Sylvere Lotringer,* Pure War, *New York: Semiotext(e), 1983, and Paul Virilio,* Speed and Politics, *New York: Semiotext(e), 1986.*

[21] *Francesc Torres,* Belchite/South Bronx: A Trans-Cultural and Trans-Historical Landscape, *Amherst, Mass.: University Gallery, University of Massachusetts, 1988, pág.86.*

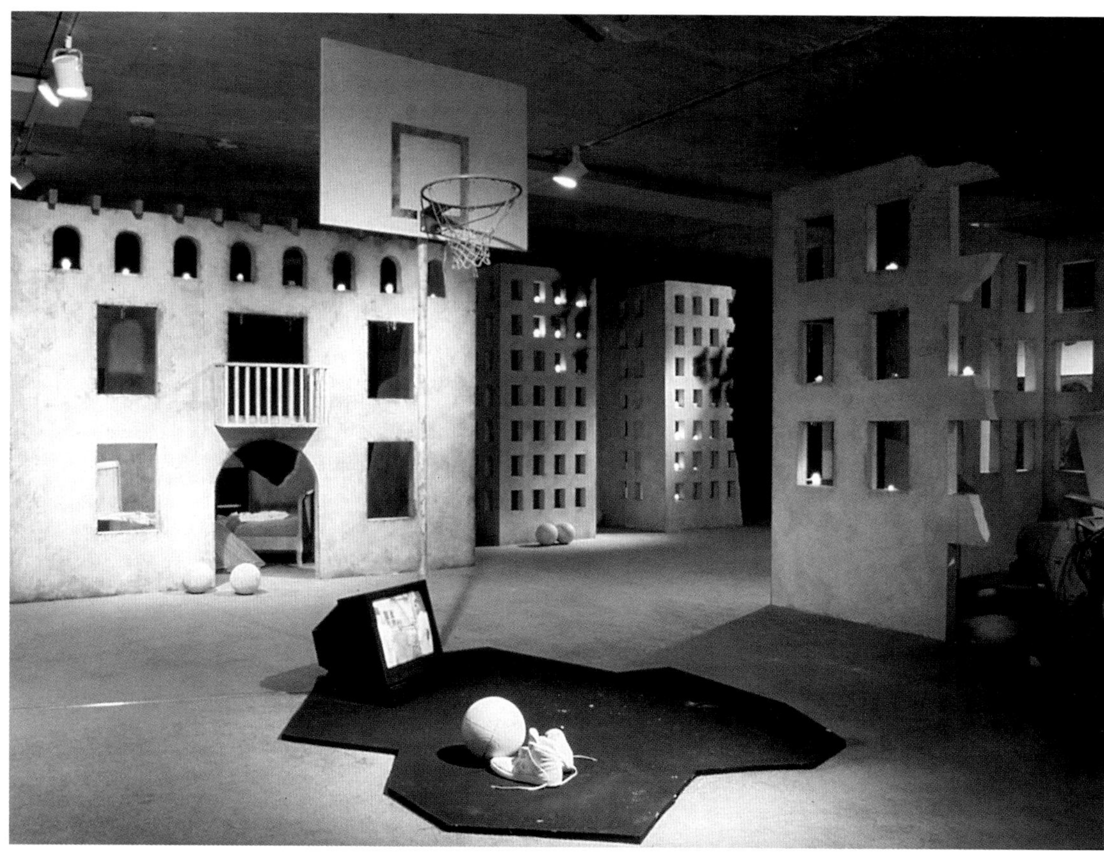

BELCHITE/SOUTH BRONX, 1988

en tiempos de paz. La gente sin hogar, por mencionar un grupo de víctimas, son los refugiados de un ruedo social en el que sólo los fuertes (¿señores de la guerra?) pueden sobrevivir".[22]

[22] *Torres,* Belchite/South Bronx, *pág.87.*

La instalación **Belchite/South Bronx** era extensa y compleja, con edificios en ruinas (menores que el tamaño natural pero lo suficientemente grandes como para sugerir un entorno urbano) basados en ambos lugares, coches destrozados, muebles rotos, una pista de baloncesto al estilo del vecindario del South Bronx, y monitores de vídeo mostrando analogías entre el soldado de infantería de la Guerra Civil española y el adolescente jugador de baloncesto callejero, entre otras. El espectador se paseaba por ella como por una ciudad fantasma, por una civilización que se había anulado a sí misma. En este caso las dos entidades combinadas representan menos claramente tesis y antítesis. A primera vista lo parecen: Belchite en tiempos de guerra y el South Bronx en tiempos de paz; pero la pieza, al sublacionar una con otra, alcanza un tercer término que yace bajo ambos: el concepto de guerra total, de guerra como fuerza que satura todas las actividades humanas. Esta saturación no se percibe únicamente en la destrucción de las dos ciudades, sino también en la superposición de deportes de equipo, entrenamiento militar y competiciones de tipo militar, sobre todo en el ámbito internacional; como la larga competición ideológica entre E.E.U.U. y U.R.S.S. llevada a cabo en estadios de todo el mundo. Así pues, este fantasmal panorama se denomina transcultural y trans-histórico porque señala las fuerzas activas en las sociedades humanas en muchas épocas y lugares: "Beirut, y Dresden, los barrios bajos de Ciudad de México y de Puerto Príncipe".[23] En este sentido es de nuevo el legado de los reptiles.

[23] *Torres,* Belchite/South Bronx, *pág.102.*

EL TEATRO DE LA GUERRA

A menudo —pero sobre todo en **Belchite/South Bronx**— las instalaciones de Torres poseen cierta

The Theater of War

Often—but above all in **Belchite/South Bronx**—there is a theatricality or staginess to Torres' installations; they seem like sets on which a dramatic action is either about to take place or has recently taken place. This haunting presence-in-absence is a quality of poetic evocativeness in the work. There is a sense that perhaps the work is more evocative (Beuysian) than provocative (Haacke-esque)—more the work of an artist evocateur than provocateur. Like Beuys, Torres is not a purely political artist, but a poetic /political artist. The crumpled car on the monitors has an evocative emotional artistry too, and a sense of high drama.

The complex and laborious installations are struck like stage sets, too, some parts being stored, some discarded; but, except for the brief periods of exhibition, they do not strictly exist as themselves. They are thus like archaeological sites, uncoverings of ancient theaters where the Combat Philosophers wrestled, archetypal arenas where the reptile and the video screen gaze uncomprehending at each other. The exhibition space of art thus acts as an arena where human destiny strives to take new form, through combats and mutual incorporations of the different visions of itself.

teatralidad o posibilidades de escenificación: son como escenarios en los que parece que la acción ha tenido lugar recientemente o está a punto de tener lugar. Esta obsesionante presencia-ausencia denota una cualidad de evocación poética en su obra. En cierto sentido la instalación quizás es más evocativa (Beuysiana) que provocativa (como Haacke), es más la obra de un artista evocador que provocador. Al igual que Beuys, Torres no es un artista puramente político, sino un artista poético-político. El coche aplastado que aparece en los monitores también posee una cualidad artística emotiva y evocativa, además de un gran sentido dramático.

Las complejas y laboriosas instalaciones también se desmontan, como escenografías teatrales, de las que se almacenan algunas partes mientras que otras se desechan; pero excepto durante los breves períodos de exhibición no existen como tales. Son como excavaciones arqueológicas, antiguos teatros desenterrados donde lucharon los Filósofos de Combate, arenas arquetípicas en las que el reptil y la pantalla de vídeo se observan sin comprender. El espacio artístico de la exhibición se convierte así en una arena en la que el destino humano lucha por adquirir una nueva forma, mediante combates y mutuas incorporaciones de las diferentes versiones de sí mismo.

FRANCESC TORRES:
EMBLEMS, ALLEGORIES,
THEATER OF MEMORY...

JUAN ANTONIO RAMIREZ

It is very tempting to consider Francesc Torres as an extreme case of formal evolutionary coherence. It is as if he had consciously passed from the austere and purified simplicity of his early works to the extreme complexity of his most recent installations. His career reads like an instruction manual for the formation of an artist: first work with volumes, exercise with materials, control the space; later go on to study yourself, your own world, verify what it is you want, where you come from and where you are going; finally, as you expand to delirious heights in your technical resources, direct your critical attention to all of society or to the natural universe from which life has emerged. We have here an educational program of fantastic dimensions—rather romantic and Wagnerian. Or is it, perhaps, a type of *Emilio* for the twentieth century? (First soak yourself in the clarity of "natural" forms and then advance to the knowledge of human beings...).

In any case, in Torres' work, one detects a journey similar to that which has appeared in certain established narrative structures. On the one hand, we discover the history of the hero who has passed through tough initiation rights (unsteady reckonings, exile, internal tearing), he conquers (and avenges) the father, and emerges in the triumphant continuation as a universal artist. It is not much different from marvelous tales nor from many mythic ancestral stories. On the other hand, adopting the historic-artistic paradigm of the "life of forms," we would have a confirmation, in the terrain of the individual, of some supposed inexorable evolution of styles beginning with an Archaic phase (simple and elemental) through a Baroque one, passing through the tranquil restraints of a Classic period.

Torres has decided that his "artistic career" began in 1968 when he conceived prototypes for his polyester and cardboard multiples. They are wonderfully clean geometrically and have a direct relationship to minimalism. But, the fact that they are meant to be models for a desirable multiple

---

FRANCESC TORRES:
EMBLEMAS, ALEGORÍAS,
TEATRO DE LA MEMORIA...

JUAN ANTONIO RAMÍREZ

Es muy tentador considerar a Francesc Torres como un caso extremo de coherencia en la evolución formal, como si hubiera pasado conscientemente desde una inicial simplicidad austera y depurada hasta la máxima complejidad de sus instalaciones ulteriores. Parece el manual de instrucciones para la formación de un artista: trabaja primero los volúmenes, ejercítate en los materiales, controla el espacio; pasa luego a estudiarte a ti mismo, a tu propio mundo, averigua qué quieres, de dónde vienes y a dónde vas; finalmente, mientras enriqueces hasta el delirio los recursos técnicos, dirige tu atención crítica a toda la sociedad o al universo natural en el que ha surgido la vida. He aquí un programa educativo de dimensiones fantásticas, romántico, algo wagneriano. ¿O es, tal vez, una especie de *Emilio* del siglo XX? (Empápate primero con la claridad de las formas "naturales" y avanza después en el conocimiento de los hombres...).

En cualquier caso, sí puede detectarse en el trabajo de Torres un recorrido semejante al que se aprecia en ciertas estructuras narrativas consagradas. Por una parte hallamos la historia del héroe que pasa por duras pruebas iniciáticas (tanteos vacilantes, exilio, desgarramiento interior), vence (y venga) al padre, y emerge a continuación triunfando como artista universal. No hay tanta diferencia con los cuentos maravillosos ni con muchos relatos míticos ancestrales. De otro lado, adoptando el paradigma argumental histórico-artístico de la "vida de las formas", tendríamos una confirmación, en el terreno individual, de la supuesta evolución inexorable de los estilos desde una fase arcaica (simple y elemental) hasta otra barroca, pasando por la serena contención de una etapa clásica.

Torres ha decidido que su "carrera artística" empieza hacia 1968, cuando concibió los prototipos para sus múltiplos de poliéster o de cartulina. Son piezas de una estupenda limpieza geométrica, emparentadas con el minimal. Pero el hecho de que se trate de modelos para una deseable fabricación

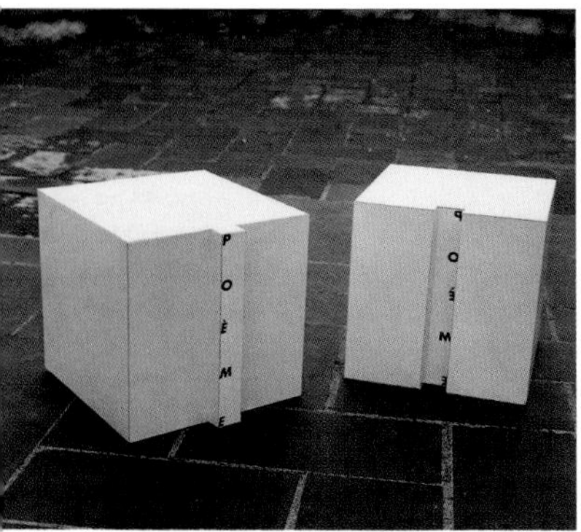

POEME, 1968

production introduces a factor that is not foreign to the universe of Pop Art. Besides, **Poeme** is clearly a literary piece which would not have been unworthy of the Spanish "visual poet" Joan Brossa. It seems to me that Torres wanted, even then, to transcend all language and to erase the disciplinary boundaries between the arts. This is a very revealing aspect of his most recent installations. It was inevitable that he would practice street or "ecological" art with hybrid experiences of notable formal interest. This is apparent in works such as **Suspension** and **Meniscus** (both of 1969), or **Information on the Existence of a Shining Triangle at Sheridan, Corner of Belmont** and **Tracing a Diagonal** (1972). I believe that these and other activities of that time tended to show the interaction between the rigid territories delineated because of human being's propensity for geometric reasoning and the random (risky?) behavior of certain natural phenomena. We will see the manner in which this problematic reemerges, transformed, in his later work.

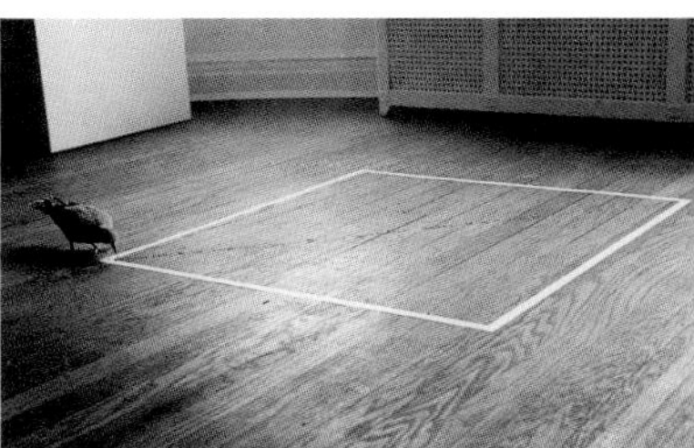

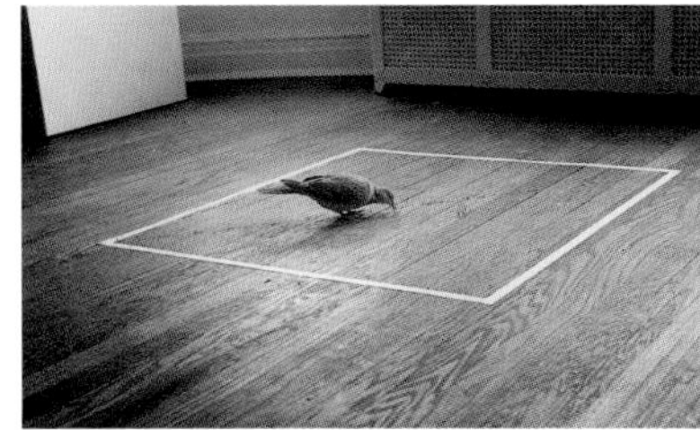

As the body of the artist is also "nature," Torres systematically began to introduce the former into his work. In **Perceptive Analysis of the Three Dimensions (Three Points of View)** (1973), he showed the exploration of a room's corner by comparing it to the identical fold in his own anatomy in three different spatial positions. It was important to show, I suppose, that the homogeneity of abstract geometric planes has nothing to do with the vision or sensation of the human being situated in various places of a determined field. Torres passed through a period in which the concrete self, subjectivity in and of itself, was converted into a reference or parameter from which all dimensions of reality were examined. This attitude appears to have culminated in the middle of the seventies with works such as **Image's Identity** (1974), **An Attempt to Decondition Myself** (1974), **Under the Dining Room Table** (1975), etc.

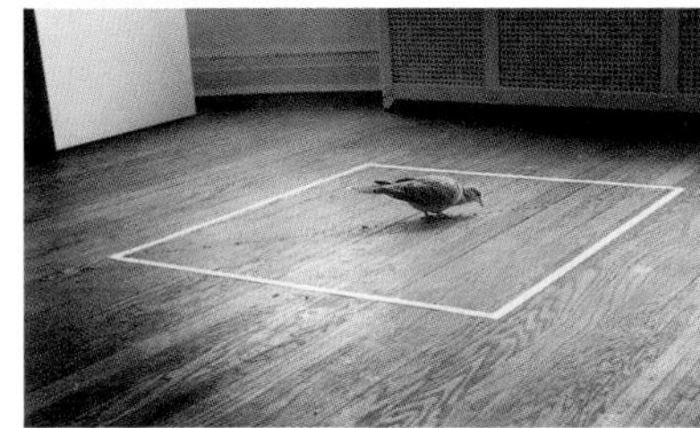

múltiple, introduce ya un factor que no es ajeno, como sabemos, al universo del pop art. **Poème** es, además, un trabajo claramente literario que no habría sido indigno de Brossa. Parece que Torres quería ya trascender todos los lenguajes, borrar las fronteras disciplinares entre las artes, lo cual es muy revelador habida cuenta del sentido de sus instalaciones ulteriores. Era inevitable que practicara el arte callejero o "ecológico" con experiencias híbridas de notable interés plástico como **Suspensión** y **Meniscos** (ambas de 1969), o **Informe sobre la existencia de un triángulo luminoso en Sheridan, esquina Belmont** y **Trazando una diagonal** (1972). Creo que con éstas y otras actividades de aquella época tendía a mostrar la interacción entre los rígidos territorios acotados por la razón geometrizadora de los humanos y el comportamiento aleatorio (¿azaroso?) de ciertos fenómenos naturales. Ya veremos de qué manera esta problemática reemerge transformada en su obra posterior.

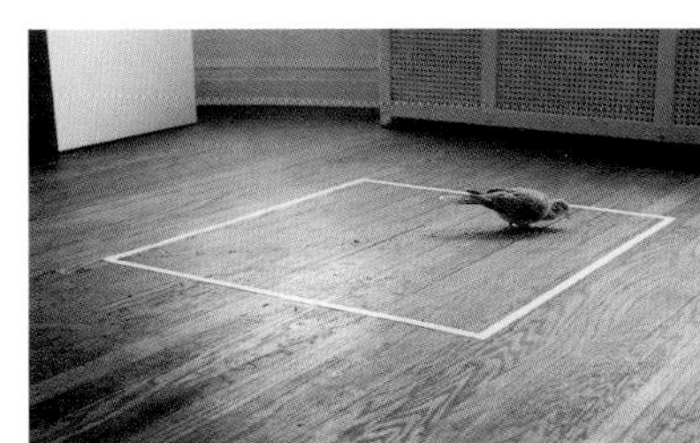

Y como el cuerpo del artista es también "naturaleza", Torres empezó a introducirlo sistemáticamente en su trabajo. En **Análisis perceptivo de las tres dimensiones (Tres puntos de vista)** (1973) mostraba la exploración de la esquina de una habitación ortogonal mediante el idéntico plegamiento de su propia anatomía, en tres posiciones espaciales diferentes. Era importante demostrar, supongo, que la homogeneidad de los planos geométricos abstractos no tiene nada que ver con la visión o sensación del ser humano, situado en varios lugares de un ámbito determinado. Torres pasó por una etapa en la que el yo concreto, la propia subjetividad, se convertía en un referente o parámetro desde el cual eran examinadas todas las dimensiones de la realldad. Esta actitud parece haber culminado a mediados de los años setenta, con trabajos como **Identidad de la imagen** (1974), **Un intento de descondicionarme** (1974), **Bajo la mesa del comedor** (1975), etc.

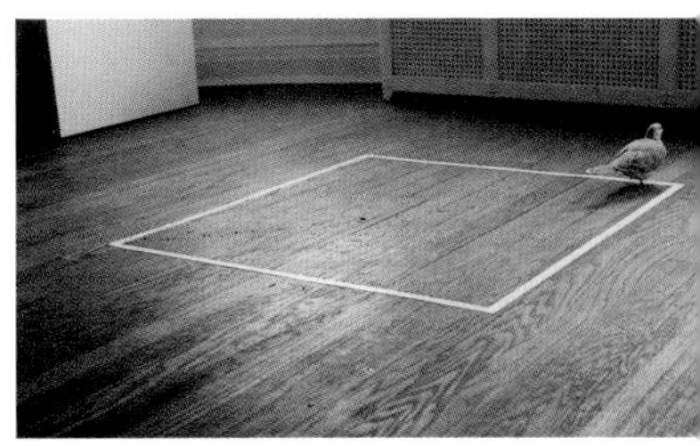

Tracing a Diagonal, 1972

El 20 de noviembre de 1975 murió, tras una larga agonía, el dictador español Francisco Franco, y

On November 20, 1975, after a long period of agony, the Spanish Dictator Francisco Franco died. I believe that this marked a watershed in Francesc Torres' work. In fact, in January of this same year he had already made an installation-performance titled **Almost Like Sleeping**. The author seemed to be sleeping in a bed next to the wall in a darkened gallery as a film loop of him biting his nails was projected behind the bed. To the right and left of this screen, one saw two large slides of Franco and Francesc's grandfather, representing opposing "cultural conditioners." The installation was completed with other projections on a lateral wall (he gathered sentences heard at random in various places) and with two speakers that each recounted the artist's life in a different manner. Here was an interesting attempt to investigate spatial exploration and appropriation; but, the formalism of his earlier exercises was giving way to a montage of grand ideological ambitions. The individual is the result of his family and socio-political circumstances (as the projected images seemed to be saying), but his life is also malleable or readily manipulated according to his own will. Or was this not the meaning of this oral autobiography, in two voices, whose meaning branched off in the middle of the story?

One would say that this was a settling of accounts which was doubly necessary. Like so many other Spaniards of that time, Torres must have felt a tremendous cathartic relief at exorcizing Franco who, during Torres' youth, represented the archetypal repressor. But, the most interesting thing is to verify how biological and artistic demands coincided with the objective historical events: the young creator frees himself at the end of the grandfather-father tutelage and commits the mythic assassination of the authority by the means of the providential death (so desired!) of the dictator. He was twenty-seven years old. Transcending the initiation rituals, he could enter the adult age "outside of himself," as an expatriate. To live in the United States and assume a new nationality is like certifying that one has

---

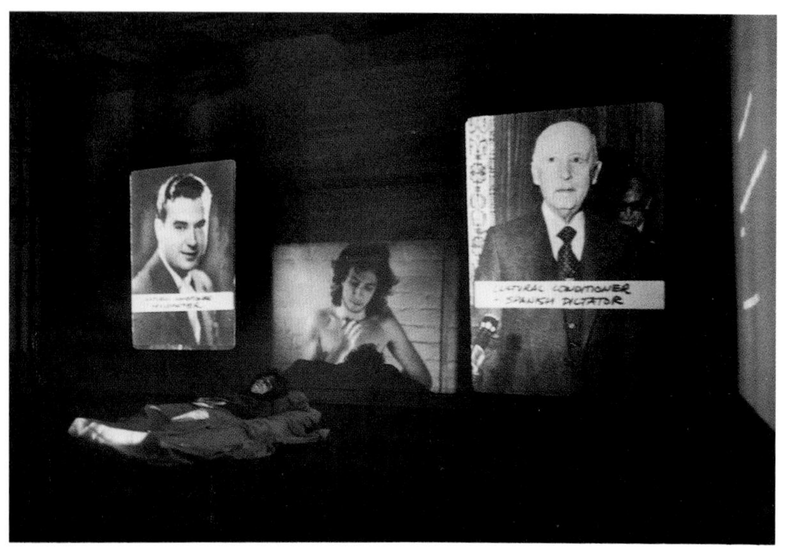

Almost Like Sleeping, 1975

creo que esto marcó una frontera en la obra de Francesc Torres. Efectivamente, en enero de ese mismo año había elaborado ya una instalación-performance titulada **Casi como durmiendo**: el autor aparecía dormido en una cama, junto a la pared de la galería oscurecida, y detrás de él se proyectaba una película sin fin que lo representaba mordiéndose las uñas; a la derecha y a la izquierda de esta pantalla, se veían dos grandes diapositivas de Franco y del abuelo de Francesc, en tanto que "condicionadores culturales"; todo ello se completaba con otras proyecciones en una pared lateral (recogían frases oídas al azar, en distintos lugares), y con dos altavoces que contaban la vida del artista de un modo diferente. Por supuesto, aquí había un intento interesante de exploración y apropiación espacial, pero el formalismo contenido de sus ejercicios anteriores cedía ante un montaje de grandes ambiciones ideológicas. El individuo es el resultado de sus circunstancias familiares y político-sociales (parecían decir las imágenes proyectadas), pero su vida es también moldeable o manipulable según su propia voluntad. ¿O no era este el sentido de esa autobiografía oral, a dos voces, cuyo sentido se bifurcaba hacia la mitad del relato?

Se diría que éste fue un ajuste de cuentas doblemente necesario. Como tantos otros españoles de aquella época, Torres debió sentir un gran alivio catártico exorcizando a Franco, que representaba al

broken the Oedipal ties and is ready to use the conquered freedom in order to explore the great matters which interest *all* of humanity.

In this manner, Francesc Torres enters a Classic period, with medium-sized installations, presumably made with a modest budget. **Construction of the Matrix**, presented in the 1976 Venice Biennial, is the first example of this new attitude. Over a mountain of earth covered with empty bullet cartridges, he projected a human figure in a fetal position. There were also two open books illuminated by reading lamps; the greatest intensity of light was directed at *The Communist Manifesto* as opposed to the weak clarity of *The Gospel According to Saint John*, thus indicating the artist's preference. I would like to call attention to the generality of this proposal. It is neither a personal nor a national matter. Torres dealt with violence as a "motor of history," the destiny of humanity, a relative measure of determinism in the choices of each individual. These matters are enunciated in a manner which is both simple and bold. Like a good theatrical function, the technical and formal problems were subservient to the clarity and efficiency of the argument.

In the following years, he maintained the same attitude, although, logically, the theme varied in each piece. **Repetition of the Novelty** critically raised the issue of artistic progress by reproducing, in the dark basements of a New York coal bin, the animals depicted in prehistoric art. **Accident** was a reflection on human's animalistic conduct, such as territorial markings (he also alludes to the "moral bankruptcy of communism"). **Scenography of Work** dealt with old matters of the political left like the annihilation of the human being by means of alienating work.

These three works of 1977 already contain the germ of the archeological preoccupations which manifested themselves in the next year with **Residual Regions**. The artist explored the remains of an

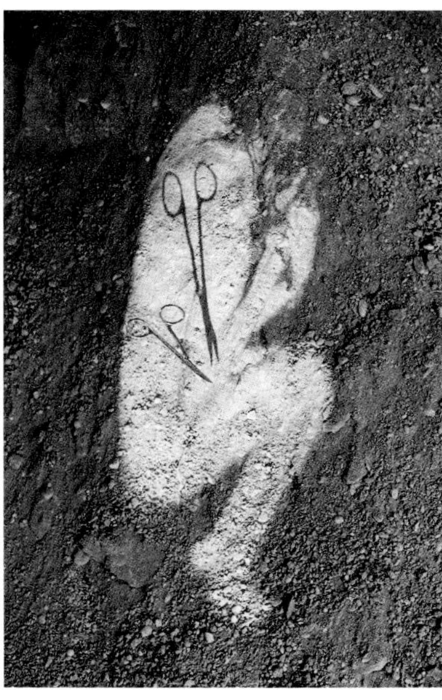

CONSTRUCTION OF THE MATRIX, 1976

arquetipo represor de su infancia. Pero lo más interesante es comprobar cómo coincidieron en el trabajo de estas fechas las exigencias biológicas y artísticas con los acontecimientos históricos objetivos: el joven creador se libera al fin de la tutela del abuelo-padre, y consuma el asesinato mítico de la autoridad mediante la muerte providencial (¡tan deseada!) del dictador. Ya tiene 27 años. Superado el ritual iniciático puede entrar en la edad adulta "fuera de sí", como un expatriado. Vivir en Estados Unidos, asumir una nueva nacionalidad, es como certificar que uno ha roto las amarras edípicas y que está dispuesto a usar la libertad conquistada para explorar los grandes asuntos que interesan a *toda* la humanidad.

Francesc Torres entra así en una etapa *clásica*, con instalaciones de mediano tamaño, realizadas presumiblemente con un presupuesto moderado. **Construcción de la matriz**, presentada en la Bienal de Venecia de 1976 es el primer ejemplo de esta nueva actitud: sobre un montón de tierra con casquillos de bala vacíos, se proyectaba una figura humana en posición fetal, y había también dos libros abiertos, iluminados por sendas lámparas; la mayor intensidad de luz se dirigía a *El manifiesto comunista*, indicando así la preferencia del autor frente a la débil claridad de *El Evangelio según San Juan*. Quisiera llamar la atención sobre la generalidad de esta propuesta. No es un asunto personal, ni nacional: Torres trataba sobre la violencia como "motor de la historia", el destino de la humanidad, el mayor o menor grado de determinismo en las elecciones de cada individuo... Estos asuntos aparecían enunciados de un modo sencillo y contundente. Los problemas técnicos y formales se supeditaban a la claridad y a la eficacia del argumento, como en una buena función teatral.

La misma actitud se mantuvo en los años inmediatamente ulteriores, aunque el tema, lógicamente, variaba en cada pieza: **Repetición de la novedad** planteaba críticamente el progreso artístico al

abandoned old country home which had served as a barracks for the Republican troops during the Spanish Civil War. Some testimonial material, photographs of the place and some film clips served as base materials for an emotional installation which was, simultaneously, a parody of archeological museums and a resonant slap in the face to the arbitrariness of the supposed "objective science" which we call history.

He moved forward with **This is an installation which has as a title...** (1979), which affected with more daring than ever the basic continuity of the creative attitudes and qualities of the human species from the remote times of the *Australopithecus Africanus* up until our time. There was here, I believe, a bitter reflection concerning (maybe non-existent) human progress. Although Torres principally dealt with the History of Art (and what *history* could there have been when one combines the creative potentials with the intervention of fate?), he could not hide his indirect reference to the *disenchantment* as a generational attitude vis-à-vis the great social and political models. This is the path taken in the following works such as **John Doesn't Know what Paul Does** (1979) and **Rock-Solid-Thin-Air** (1980).

At the beginning of the eighties, Francesc Torres already seems to have completed his repertory of fundamental obsessions. Coinciding with the conservative tidal wave of the Thatcher-Reagan-Bush era, many of these works are among Torres' most virulent, developing in their complexity and spectacularity. Although he combines techniques, means and variable sizes, there is an indelible personal stamp in everything he made from 1980 until the present. His enormous production and tremendous rhetorical ambition (in the old sense of the term), permit us to include these works in a *baroque* period (and it is a mere coincidence if this word appears to be supported by a recent international trend). With this Torres does not betray his trajectory, since one characteristic of his

---

reproducir animales del arte prehistórico en los oscuros sótanos de una carbonera neoyorquina; **Accidente** era una reflexión sobre la pervivencia en el hombre contemporáneo de comportamientos animales como el marcaje de la territorialidad (también aludía al "descalabro moral del comunismo", en palabras del propio Torres); **Escenografía del trabajo** incidía en un viejo asunto de la izquierda política como es el de la aniquilación del hombre mediante el trabajo alienado, etc.

Estos tres trabajos son del año 1977 y contienen ya el germen de las preocupaciones arqueológicas que se manifestarán al año siguiente con **Regiones residuales**. El artista exploró los restos de una vieja casa de campo abandonada que había servido como cuartel de las tropas republicanas durante la guerra civil española. Algunos testimonios materiales, ciertas fotografías del lugar, y unas filmaciones, sirvieron como materiales de base para una emocionante instalación que era, a la vez, parodia de los museos arqueológicos, y sonora bofetada a la arbitrariedad de esa supuesta "ciencia objetiva" a la que llamamos historia.

Un importante paso adelante lo dio con **Esta es una instalación que lleva por título...** (1979), pues incidía con mayor osadía que nunca en la continuidad básica de las actitudes y cualidades creativas de la especie humana, desde los remotos tiempos del *Australopithecus Africanus* hasta nuestros días. Había aquí, creo, una reflexión amarga acerca del (tal vez inexistente) progreso humano. Aunque Torres se centró principalmente en la Historia del Arte (¿y qué *historia* puede haber cuando se combinan las mismas potencialidades creativas con la intervención del azar?) no pudo ocultar su referencia indirecta al desencanto, en tanto que actitud generacional frente a las grandes soluciones políticas y sociales. Por ahí van a ir otros trabajos inmediatamente ulteriores como **Juan**

work is his capacity to reformulate and recombine the previously tried major themes in new and surprising ways. It is precisely this which allows him to create his own language, to articulate signs, to systematize and decodify them.

As such, he has revealed himself to be a great creator of enjambed metaphors, a true master of the synecdoche and the metonymy. It is not that Torres is a conscientious scholar of the old books of rhetoric; indeed, many of his linguistic tricks are in the contemporary world's iconosphere. How could advertising subsist otherwise, or on what would one base the cinematographic language itself? The new, then, is not the rhetorical tool as such, but the means used in each circumstance and the plotting intention which governs invention.

Let us look at an example. **Soldier's Complaint** (1991) is a simple assemblage which consists of a few cast iron eggs placed in the interior of a "nest" constructed inside an old metal helmet, like those used by North American soldiers during World War II. The work comes with an explanatory text in which Torres speaks of how the head "is like an egg in which the mystery of life unfolds." Looking at this work, it is impossible not to remember an emblem of Alciato which represents the abandoned helmet of a soldier which is filled with a swarm of bees. The clear message: the sweetness of peace (the honey) is preferable to the bitterness of war. Torres has done almost the same thing and, although he has oriented the reading of his visual metaphor towards apparently less "moralistic" considerations, it is obvious that he follows a more incisively pacifist political program than that of the Renaissance author. In any case, it deals with a three-dimensional modern emblem. It is the Duchampian ready-made (readjusted in this case), although devoid of thematic ambiguity and anchored by means of an explicitly literary message.

ignora lo que hace Pablo (1979) o **Sólido como la roca, ligero como el aire** (1980).

Al empezar la década de los años ochenta Francesc Torres parece haber completado ya el repertorio de sus obsesiones fundamentales. Coincidiendo con el maremoto conservador de la era de Thatcher-Reagan-Bush, muchas de las obras del artista alcanzan su máxima virulencia, ganando en complejidad y espectacularidad. Aunque combine técnicas, recursos y tamaños muy variados, hay un sello personal indeleble en todo lo realizado desde 1980 hasta nuestros días. Su ingente producción y la gran ambición retórica (en el sentido antiguo del término) de la misma, nos permiten incluir a estos trabajos en una etapa *barroca* (y es mera coincidencia si esta palabra parece apoyarse en una reciente moda internacional). No reniega Torres con esto de su trayectoria, pues una de las características de su producción va a ser la capacidad que demuestra para reformular y recombinar de un modo novedoso y sorprendente los grandes temas ensayados con anterioridad. Es esto, precisamente, lo que le permite crearse un lenguaje propio, articular signos, sistematizarlos y des-codificarlos.

Así se ha podido revelar como un gran creador de metáforas encabalgadas, un verdadero maestro de la sinécdoque y la metonimia. No es que Torres sea un estudioso aplicado de los antiguos libros de retórica, pues muchos de sus trucos linguísticos están en la iconosfera del mundo contemporáneo. ¿Cómo podría subsistir si no la publicidad o en que se basa el mismísimo lenguaje cinematográfico? Lo nuevo, pues, no es el recurso retórico en cuanto tal, sino los medios utilizados en cada caso y la intención argumental que rige la invención.

Veamos algún ejemplo. **Queja de soldado** (1991) es un sencillo ensamblaje que consiste en unos huevos de acero fundido colocados en el interior de un "nido" construido dentro de un viejo casco metálico, como los empleados por los soldados norteamericanos durante la Segunda Guerra Mundial.

Another perfect example is **Eagles' Nest** (1991). A hand grenade rests on an "executive's chair." The author's explanation eliminates any doubt about its interpretation: "The powerful lovingly incubate their own power... The infant born of so much care... has its own dynamic and can become allied with the enemy. Any king, banker or prime minister who has been blown to pieces has understood, for one one-hundredth of a second, the parricidal characteristics of pure power." Other more recent emblems are **Utopia** (a "paper" airplane made with a sheet of lead lying on a white cloth) and **History and Farce**. This last word appears written over an ordinary hammer which has a small relief of Lenin pasted onto the iron that strikes. The other inscription ("farce") appears over a small sheet of lead on which there are various images of the Soviet leader cast onto the metal by the adjacent hammer.

There are a lot of similar cases in Francesc Torres' work and I believe that it is not one of his lesser merits to have rejuvenated a literary-visual genre that was believed to have been definitively set aside with the arrival of modernity. The old books of Renaissance and Baroque emblems were true manuals of ethics and good customs; the text anchored the image and this resumed, in a concise and effective fashion, their complex literary meanings. But, in Torres' emblems, moralism becomes criticism and the visual is generally constituted by assemblages of "ready-made" objects. Political art and the subversion of the ready-mades have seduced and fertilized this traditional genre. It is no longer the candid, virginal amusement which charmed the princes' teachers, sophisticated ladies and ingenious Jesuits [see Graphic Number 1].

But many of these emblems function when inserted into more ambitious installations: the enjambed or consecutive metaphors generate waterfalls of new meaning, giving place to true allegorical

---

La obra viene con un texto explicativo en el que Torres habla de cómo la cabeza "es como un huevo dentro del cual se desarrolla el misterio de la vida". Es imposible no recordar ante esta obra un emblema de Alciato que representa a un yelmo de guerrero abandonado, dentro del cual se ha instalado un enjambre de abejas. Claro mensaje: la dulzura de la paz (la miel) es preferible a la amargura de la guerra. Torres ha hecho casi lo mismo, y aunque ha orientado la lectura de su metáfora visual hacia consideraciones aparentemente menos "moralistas", es obvio que forma parte de un programa político más incisivamente pacifista que el del autor renacentista. Se trata, en culquier caso, de un emblema moderno, tridimensional. Es el *ready-made* duchampiano (rectificado, en este caso), aunque desprovisto de ambigüedad temática, y anclado mediante un explícito mensaje literario.

Otro ejemplo perfecto es **Nido de águilas** (1991): sobre un "sillón de ejecutivo" reposa una granada de mano; la explicación del autor elimina cualquier duda respecto a su interpretación: "El poderoso incuba amorosamente su propio poder (...) La criatura nacida de tanto cuidado (...) tiene una dinámica propia y que puede aliarse con el enemigo. Todo rey, banquero o primer ministro que ha volado por los aires ha comprendido, por una centésima de segundo, las características parricidas del poder puro". Otros emblemas más recientes son **Utopía** (un avioncito "de papel", hecho con una lámina de plomo, yace sobre un paño blanco) y **Historia y Farsa**. Esta última palabra aparece escrita sobre un martillo ordinario que tiene un pequeño relieve de Lenin pegado en el hierro que golpea; la otra inscripción ("farsa") figura sobre una laminilla de plomo en la que hay ya varias improntas del líder soviético producidas con el instrumento adyacente.

Hay bastantes casos parecidos a éstos en la obra de Francesc Torres, y no creo que sea uno de sus menores méritos el haber remozado un género literariovisual que se creyó definitivamente arrumbado

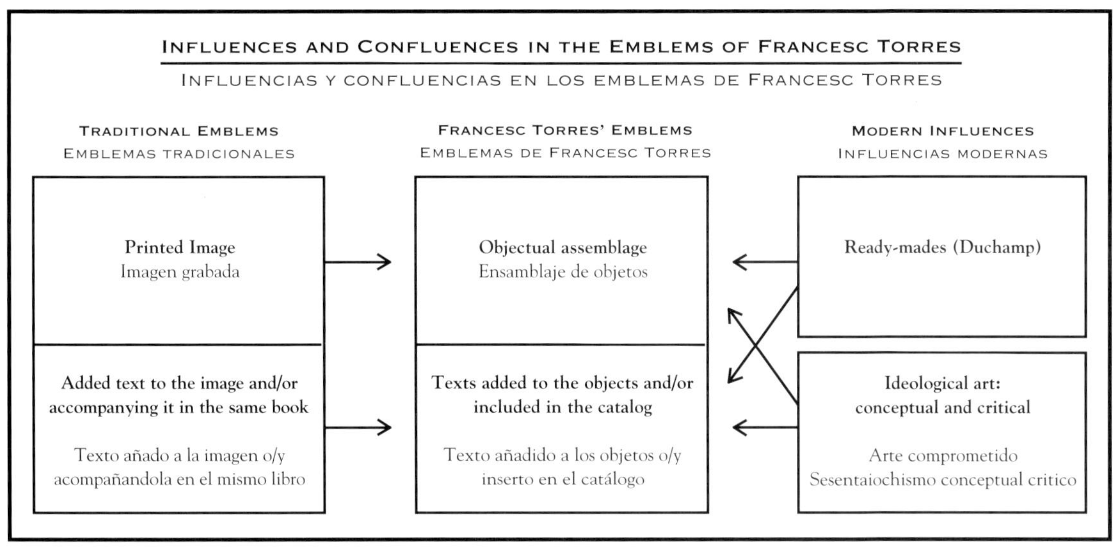

GRAPHIC NUMBER 1/GRÁFICO NÚMERO 1

cornucopias. This also pertains to my discussion on Torres' Baroque period. Perhaps he has been affected by some hidden influence of the Iberian art of the counter-reformation, with its rhetorical vehemence and its vast array of visual and conceptual tricks. Let us not forget the *fallas* from the region of Valencia—a festival of popular art wherein hundreds of elaborate papier-mâché effigies adorn the city's streets for a celebratory week and are then burned. More often than not, these incredible statues are satirical, if not outwardly bawdy, in both their content and fabrication. This festival has carried the grandiloquent use of explicit allegories and of three-dimensional jokes into present times. There is

con la llegada de la modernidad. Los viejos libros de emblemas del renacimiento y el barroco eran verdaderos manuales de moral y buenas costumbres; el texto anclaba a la imagen y ésta, a su vez, resumía de un modo sumario y eficaz los complejos significados literarios. Pero en los emblemas de Torres el moralismo se hace crítico, y lo visual está constituido generalmente por ensamblajes de objetos "ya hechos". Digamos que el género tradicional ha sido seducido y fecundado por el arte político y por la subversión de los *ready-mades*; ya no es el cándido entretenimiento virginal que encantaba a educadores de príncipes, damas sofisticadas y jesuitas ingeniosos [véase el gráfico número 1].

Pero muchos de estos emblemas funcionan insertos en instalaciones más ambiciosas: las metáforas encabalgadas o consecutivas generan entonces cataratas de nuevos significados, dando lugar a verdaderos túmulos alegóricos. A esto me refería también cuando hablaba de la etapa barroca de Francesc Torres. Quizá haya ejercido en él alguna influencia subterránea el arte ibérico postridentino, vehementemente retórico, plagado de trucos visuales y conceptuales. No olvidemos tampoco a "Las Fallas" del País Valenciano, manifestaciones del arte popular muy conocidas en toda España que han mantenido hasta hoy el uso grandilocuente de las alegorías explícitas y de los chistes tridimensionales. Hay algo más: Torres coincide con los artistas falleros en su pasión por comentar críticamente las costumbres sociales o los grandes acontecimientos de la actualidad. (Tal vez sea una casualidad, pero a mí me parece significativo que la instalación **Demasiado tarde para Goya** (1992-93) contenga un primate hiperrealista encargado a un artesano valenciano especializado en fallas).

Una de las primeras alegorías complejas de esta última etapa fue **El paradigma asirio** (Presentada por primera vez en la Rotonda del Williams College Museum of Art, Williamstown, 1980) . Torres construyó con naipes ocho sectores de una "ciudad radial"; en el centro había una especie de pilar-

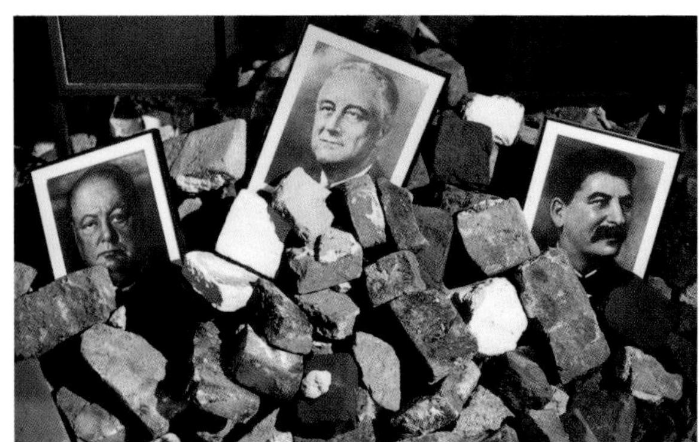

CLAUSEWITZ'S CLASSROOM AND/OR YALTA BEGINS AT SCHOOL, 1984

something more: Torres coincides with the artists of the *fallas* in his passion for critically commenting on social conventions and the great events of the present. (Maybe it is a coincidence, but it seems significant to me that the installation **Too Late for Goya** (1992-93) contains a hyper-realist primate made by a Valencian artist who specializes in *fallas*).

One of the first complex allegories of this last period was **The Assyrian Paradigm** (presented for the first time in the rotunda of the Williams College Museum of Art, Williamstown, 1980). Torres used playing cards to construct eight sectors of a "radial city"; in the center was a kind of pillar-obelisk crowned with a transparent box that held two dice and were shaken every fifteen seconds by an automatic device. Other elements of the installation were a Goya print mounted on plexiglass laminate which moved with the air generated by passing people, a burned mock-up of the Hindenburg, matches, a television, magazines, a mirror and an alarm clock. A sound track repeated a text which helped one to understand the meaning of the visual presentation: "Chance," one heard among other things, "...motivates and feeds the exercise of uncomprising curiousity which has maintained our species alive. Chance, as an intrinsic component of a social and political arrangement on a world-wide scale based in the absolute dominion of power, is a guarantee of disaster."

Other works had similar ambitions (and dimensions): **The Head of the Dragon** (1981), **Airstrip** (1982), **Steel Balls** (1983), **Clausewitz's Classroom and/or Yalta Begins at School** (1984), **Paths of Glory** (1985), **The Gladiator's House** (1985), **Oikonomos** (1989). In these and other examples, we found ourselves facing a profuse use of objects and icons combined in such a way that the storyline

obelisco coronado por un recipiente transparente en cuyo interior un par de dados eran agitados cada quince segundos mediante un dispositivo automático; otros elementos de la instalación eran un grabado de Goya montado sobre una lámina de plástico que se movía con el aire generado por los espectadores al pasar, una maqueta quemada del Hindemburg, cerillas, un televisor, periódicos, un espejo y un despertador. Una banda sonora repetía un texto que ayudaba a entender el sentido de lo que allí se veía: "El azar —se oía entre otras cosas— ...motiva y alimenta el ejercicio sin compromisos de la curiosidad que ha mantenido en vida a nuestra especie. El azar, como componente intrínseco de un arreglo social y político a escala mundial basado en el dominio absoluto del poder, es una garantía de desastre".

Ambiciones (y dimensiones) similares tuvieron otros trabajos como **La cabeza del dragón** (1981), **Pista de aterrizaje** (1982), **Bolas de acero** (1983), **La clase de Clausewitz y/o Yalta empieza en la escuela** (1984), **Senderos de gloria** (1985), **La casa del gladiador** (1985), **Oikonomos** (1989), etc. En estos y en otros ejemplos nos encontramos ante un uso profuso de objetos e iconos combinados de tal modo que el significado argumental no es difícil de descifrar para el visitante medio de las galerías de arte. Se trata de un arte de tesis, con implicaciones literarias, como si planteara la posibilidad de un nuevo género filosófico que podría definirse como "ensayo multimediático tridimensional". En efecto, aunque a tales montajes les viene bien por regla general algún texto complementario, éste (cuando existe) no lo dice todo por sí mismo. No es la obra una mera ilustración visual de un escrito precedente, sino algo distinto. Torres suele hacer una descripción o proyecto por escrito, antes de cada instalación, pero ese es un material interno (dirigido a los responsables de los museos y a los de las instituciones de apoyo a las artes) cuya finalidad es describir y presupuestar lo que el artista desea hacer. El resultado, desde este punto de vista, se parece más a la ópera que al teatro, pues mientras éste último

significance is not difficult to decode for the average art gallery visitor. They deal with an art of thesis with literary implications as if to raise the possibility of a new philosophical genre that could be defined as "three-dimensional multi-media essay." Although in some montages a complementary text is a convenient means of elucidation, this (when it exists) does not say everything in and of itself. The work is not merely the visual illustration of a written precedent, but something distinct. Torres always does a description or written text for each project prior to each installation. But this is internal material (written for the directors of museums and other institutions which support the arts) whose intent is to describe and budget that which the artist wants to do. The result, from this point of view, seems more like the opera than the theater, since the latter has been secularly supported in the primacy of the text (and from there, the viability of read theater). The opera gives more import to the musical element. Torres' montages display objects in an environment with controlled lighting and it is necessary to contemplate them (perhaps to touch them) in order to enjoy them in an adequate manner. It is a new class of opera, then, with visual primacy. Another unconscious renovation built upon new bases is the romantic idea of the *Gesamtkunstwerk* [see Graphic Number 2].

From this point of view one sees that Torres makes use of all resources, traditional or not, which can be useful in order to obtain the desired result. There is no fetishism of the "new technologies" nor unconditional adoration of the mass media industry's idols. If he frequently uses televisions, holograms or computers, it is because these things are an inexorable part of our world. The most important element is the "atmosphere," the psychological climate of the installations. Normally they are presented with a calculated semi-darkness. Torres must know the fascination of the fictitious closed paradises, like the circus, the casinos of Las Vegas, or the grand department stores: there are no

Primacy of the Elements in Opera, Theater and in the Installations of Francesc Torres
Primacia de los elementos en la opera, el teatro y en las instalaciones de Francesc Torres

	Opera/Ópera	Theater/Teatro	F. Torres/F. Torres
1	**Music — Sound** Música — sonido	**Text** Texto	**Image — Objects** Imagen — objetos
2	**Text** Texto	**Set Design** Imagen decorado	**Text** Texto
3	**Set Design** Imagen decorado	**Music — Sound** Música — sonido	**Music — Sound** Música — sonido

Gráfico número 2/Graphic Number 2

se ha apoyado secularmente en la primacía del texto (y de ahí la viabilidad del teatro leído), la ópera da más valor al elemento musical. Los montajes de Torres poseen objetos, con una iluminación controlada, y hay que contemplarlos (tal vez tocarlos) para disfrutar de ellos de manera adecuada. Nueva clase de ópera, pues, de primacía visual. Otra renovación inconsciente, sobre bases nuevas, de la idea romántica de la *Gesamtkunstwerk* [véase el gráfico número 2].

Desde este punto de vista se explica que Torres haga uso de todos los recursos, tradicionales o no, que pueden ser útiles para lograr el resultado apetecido. No hay fetichismo de las "nuevas tecnologías", adoración incondicional de los ídolos de la industria masmediática, y si usa con frecuencia televisores, hologramas, o computadoras, ello se debe a que tales cosas son una parte inexorable de nuestro mundo. Lo más importante es el "ambiente", el clima anímico de las instalaciones. Normalmente se presentan en una calculada semioscuridad. Torres debe conocer la

windows to the exterior and the things are presented like Ali Baba's magic grotto. The spectator is left hypnotized. The darkness and isolation of the reality drags them towards their unconscious. That which is seen, then, is perceived as the facsimile of a dream, an unexpected materialization of longings and fears of which one has had remote premonitions. Although the political message is always rational and can be enunciated in a linear fashion, it is framed by a heap of emotional signs and poetic circumstances.

The ideal museum for such works would not be along the lines of the painting and sculpture galleries which have been inherited from bourgeois enlightenment with the sunlight revealing the ("eternal") beauty of static objects. Instead, this museum would link other aristocratic and popular traditions. I am referring to those of the *Wunderkammeren*, with their irrational display of exotic and fascinating objects. Also, the wax museums, which are not only more or less horrifying "gothic" places, but which also contain true paintings of history constructed in three-dimensions. They are an illusory challenge to the limitations of space and time, as if those far away and famous immobile characters live together in a plane of equality (they are life size), in the shadows of each "hall," alongside anonymous live visitors.

Also, Francesc Torres' installations aspire to be new *theaters of memory*. Giulio Camillo's very famous one in Renaissance Italy was inspired by the architectonic disposition of the Roman tiers; an ideal spectator, situated in the center of the scene, could see how the concepts and information of all universal knowledge radially opened before him or her. The visual panopticon coincided with the conceptual: one sees what one knows, one knows what one sees and it is all remembered because the eye recognizes that knowledge occupies a place in space. The television is now the always evident eye: to look at the blinking lights of the screen is to commune with god himself. It is a constant presence.

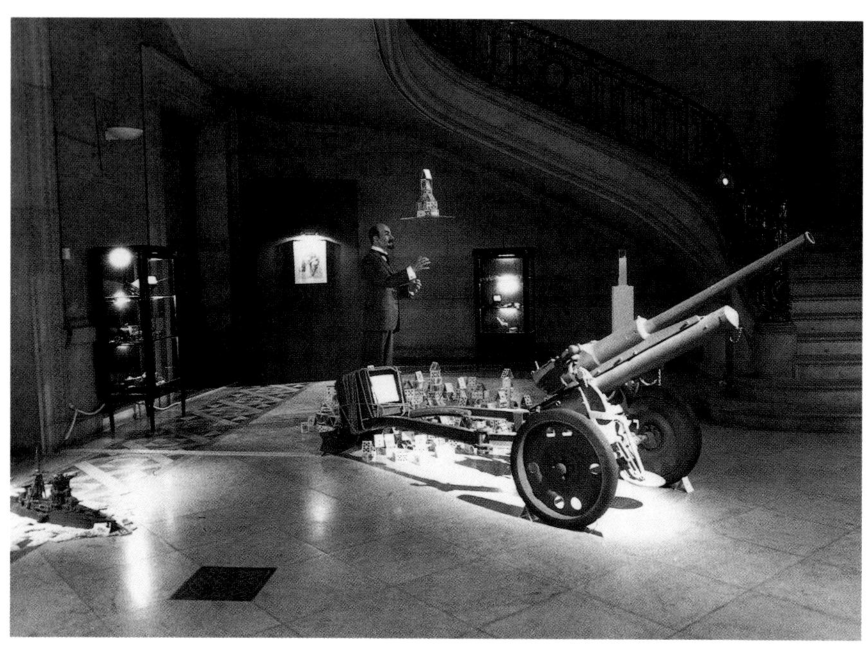

THE GLADIATOR'S HOUSE (HAS AN ATTIC), 1985

fascinación de los paraísos ficticios cerrados, al estilo de los circos, los casinos de Las Vegas, o los grandes almacenes modernos: no hay ventanas hacia el exterior, y las cosas se presentan como en la gruta mágica de Alí Babá. El espectador queda hipnotizado. La oscuridad y el aislamiento de la realidad le arrastran hacia su propio inconsciente. Lo visto, entonces, se percibe como un facsímil del sueño, una materialización inesperada de anhelos y temores oscuramente presentidos. Aunque el mensaje político suele ser racional y se puede enunciar linealmente, está aureolado por un cúmulo de signos y de circunstancias poéticas de naturaleza emocional.

El museo ideal para tales trabajos no estaría en la línea de las galerías de pintura y escultura heredadas del iluminismo burgués, con la luz solar revelando la belleza ("eterna") de objetos estáticos, sino que enlazaría con otras tradiciones aristocráticas y populares. Me refiero a la de las *Wunderkammeren*, con su despliegue irracional de objetos exóticos y fascinantes. Y también a los museos de cera, que no sólo son lugares "góticos" más o menos espeluznantes, sino que contienen verdaderos cuadros de historia construidos en tres dimensiones. Hay en ellos un desafío ilusorio a las limitaciones

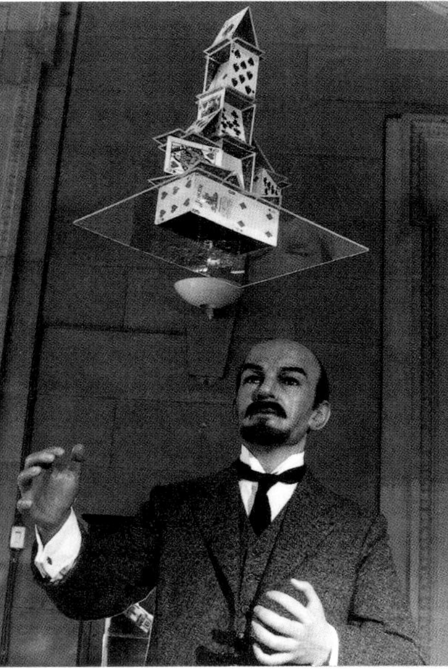

THE GLADIATOR'S HOUSE (HAS AN ATTIC), 1985

Torres registers the diverse levels of reality and translates a state of consciousness into space (or stages). The visitor to the installation is, naturally, the one who looks at this mnemonic display, the addressee of the artistic articulation. But, there are some works which possess their own spectator-watchman incorporated as part of the piece.

In **The Gladiator's House (has an attic)** (1985) a hyper-realistic, life-size Lenin controls the city of playing cards at his feet and the cannon in front of it. **Oikonomos** (1989) showed the Zeus of Cape Artemision looking at a large Plexiglas screen as he stands menacingly with a baseball bat. The screen shows images of the street people who wash windshields at the intersection of Broadway and Houston in New York (a television monitor with scenes from Wall Street dangled from the statue's genitals). **Too Late for Goya**, his most recent installation, is a monkey with a fictitious gaze who contemplates six screens that show the great historical events of our century.

Now then, given that these controllers of the media and object-driven panoptic are object-actors for the gaze of the real spectator, are we not also passive (manipulated) ingredients of another "installation"? Isn't Torres trying to make us conscious that all of our lives and that which surrounds us forms a part of an intricate machination which generates inequality and justifies oppression? This is how the universal panoptic of the media-infused society is inverted and turned over (as it is said Marx and Hegel did): to look at the spectator-controller who watches what he/she watches, is to be conscious that someone looks at me and someone controls me. Entering the work in an illusory fashion, I know better how they are playing with me and I intend to get myself out of the montage in which I am stuck. Francesc Torres' theater of memory does not stretch to encompass an ecstatic and universal knowledge,

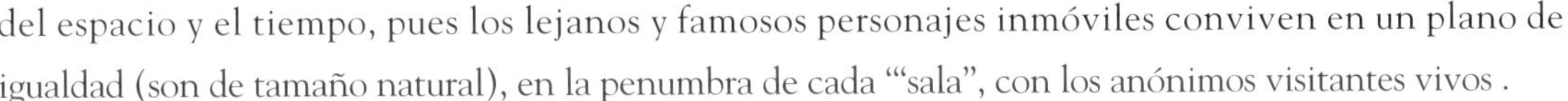

del espacio y el tiempo, pues los lejanos y famosos personajes inmóviles conviven en un plano de igualdad (son de tamaño natural), en la penumbra de cada '"sala", con los anónimos visitantes vivos .

También las instalaciones de Francesc Torres aspiran a ser nuevos *teatros de la memoria*. El muy famoso de Giulio Camillo, en la Italia renacentista, se inspiraba en la disposición arquitectónica de los graderíos romanos; un espectador ideal, situado en el centro de la escena, podía ver cómo se abrían radialmente ante él los conceptos e informaciones de todo el saber universal. El panóptico visual coincidía con el conceptual: se ve lo que se sabe, se sabe lo que se ve, y todo ello se recuerda porque el ojo reconoce que el saber ocupa un lugar en el espacio. El televisor es ahora el ojo omnividente: mirar las luces parpadeantes de la pantalla es comulgar con el mismo Dios. De ahí su presencia constante. Torres registra los diversos niveles de la realidad, espacializa (o escenifica) un estado de conciencia. El visitante de la instalación es, naturalmente, el que mira ese despliegue mnemotécnico, el destinatario de la articulación artística. Pero hay algunas obras que poseen su propio espectador-vigía incorporado como parte del trabajo: en **La casa del gladiador (tiene trastero)** (1985) un Lenin hiperrealista de tamaño natural controlaba la ciudad de naipes a sus pies y el cañón de la parte delantera; **Oikonomos** (1989) mostraba al Poseidón del cabo Artemisio mirando y amenazando con un bate de béisbol a una gran pantalla de plexiglás con imágenes de los limpiaparabrisas callejeros de la intersección entre Broadway y Houston, en Nueva York (de los genitales de la estatua colgaba un monitor de televisión con escenas de Wall Street); en **Demasiado tarde para Goya**, su última instalación, es un mono el que contempla con su mirada ficticia a las seis pantallas donde se muestran los grandes acontecimientos históricos de nuestro siglo.

Ahora bien, puesto que estos controladores del panóptico objetual y mediático son objetos-actores

but to unveil the hidden meanings of individual and symbolic materials that reality provides us with.

To state it clearly: it is an archaeological endeavor. Behind the semantic veneer of the emission in the "privileged hour" is *another* truth, the eternal presence of the media and the germ-free cleanliness of the spaces which surround big capital that lied to us. There exists detritus, the remains of degraded materials, spaces in the shadows of public attention. It is not necessary to dig very deep in order to bring them out to light so that they compose for themselves a tableau completely different from our social trajectory, from our situation in the world, from the power relations, etc. Torres has been doing some of this in almost all of his works, but he has carried it to its maximum formal and conceptual virtuosity with two of his installations from 1988: **Belchite/South Bronx: a Trans-cultural and Trans-historical Landscape** and **Plus Ultra**.

The former installation articulated a corrosive thesis—that wartime destruction is equivalent to the social and economic marginalization generated by a society in "peacetime". It was sufficient to situate the ruins of a village destroyed during the Spanish Civil War alongside those of the poorest neighborhood of New York in order to make us reflect upon the suspiciously close similarities. The other installation had a more nostalgic and poetic character which, perhaps, is not as easy to perceive for those who did not experience at close range the slow internal decomposition of Franco's regime. The ruins of the Spanish Embassy in Berlin during the Third Reich held documents and objects of 1943 Fascist Spain. As if it were a mammoth frozen between the polar ices, this emphatic "imperial" building had served as a historical refrigerator, preserving the vestiges of an infamous period thanks to the low (moral) temperatures of the Cold War. With **Plus Ultra**, Torres was "beyond" academic history and the orthodox archeological techniques. He removed memory's garbage and discovered its stench in the very

---

para la mirada del espectador real, ¿no seremos también nosotros ingredientes pasivos (manipulados) de otra "instalación"? ¿No pretende Torres hacernos tomar conciencia de que toda nuestra vida y lo que nos rodea forma parte de una alambicada maquinación que genera desigualdad y justifica la opresión? Así es como invierte, pone patas arriba (como dicen que hizo Marx con Hegel), al panóptico universal de la sociedad mediática: al mirar al espectador-controlador que mira lo que mira, tomo conciencia de que alguien me mira y me controla. Entrando ilusoriamente en la obra sé mejor cómo están jugando conmigo e intento salirme del montaje en el que ando metido. Este teatro de la memoria de Francesc Torres no tiende, pues, a escenificar un saber estático y universal, sino a desvelar los sentidos ocultos en el material visual y simbólico que nos proporciona la realidad.

Digámoslo claro: es un trabajo arqueológico. Bajo el barniz semántico de la emisión en la "hora privilegiada" late otra verdad. El eterno presente de los medios y la limpieza aséptica de los espacios que ama el gran capital son mentirosos. Existen detritus, restos materiales degradados, espacios en la penumbra de la atención pública. No hace falta excavar mucho para sacarlos a la luz y para que compongan por sí mismos un cuadro completamente diferente de nuestra trayectoria social, de nuestra situación en el mundo, de las relaciones de poder, etc. Torres ha venido haciendo algo de esto en casi todas sus obras pero lo ha llevado al máximo virtuosimo formal y conceptual con dos instalaciones de 1988: **Belchite/South Bronx: un paisaje trans-cultural y trans-histórico** y **Plus Ultra**. La primera de ellas articulaba una tesis corrosiva como es que la destrucción bélica equivale a la de la marginación económica y social generada por una sociedad "en paz": bastaba con situar en paralelo las ruinas de una población destruida durante la guerra civil española con las del barrio más degradado de Nueva York para hacernos reflexionar acerca de tan sospechosa similitud. La otra instalación tenía un carácter más

heart of the old-new capital (*Das Kapital*) of the Nazi Reich and, maybe, also of the world which is about to land on us.

It is now time to speak of the passage of time. Torres wrote about **Plus Ultra**: "In the installation, the merry-go-round plays the role of a metaphor for history as it hurls its passengers towards nothingness." One could think that because of this and other indicators the notion of human progress is not clear. One could say that all actions and desires, individual and collective, end with failure. This notion (dust to dust)is also the unconscious heir to the Catholic Baroque, wherein, perhaps, there is not much difference between Don Miguel de Manara and any other disillusioned forty-something year old. This explains the constant presence of biological permanence as an element that contrasts with the ephemerality of human events. Does Torres believe in the utility of individual force? If the response is negative, why do political art? And if it is positive, how does one articulate individual actions in the march of global history and in which manner does this combine with the biological determinations of the species? One has the impression that the artist has been torn by these interrogations for more than a decade. While sometimes he seems to indicate the primacy of individual and subjective action, in other cases he is charmed by historic morals. There were several works in which he presented great human actions as mere actualizations of primal biological impulses, as if warlike destruction and the exploitation of humans by humans were the "natural thing".

It is not that extreme coherence is something essential. At the story's end, an artist is neither a biologist nor a historian. Perhaps, the artist's highest mission is to plant questions without providing solutions or to suggest uncomfortable answers. But, something has changed in his last installation. **Too Late for Goya** shows a very precise articulation of great didactic clarity, between distinct degrees

nostálgico y poético que quizá no sea tan fácil de percibir para quienes no hayan vivido desde dentro la lenta descomposición interna del franquismo: las ruinas de la embajada española ante el III Reich, en Berlín, conservaban documentos y objetos de la España fascista de 1943. Como si fuera un mamut congelado entre los hielos polares, ese enfático edificio "imperial" había servido como una nevera histórica manteniendo los vestigios de un tiempo infame gracias a las bajísimas temperaturas (morales) de la guerra fría. Con **Plus Ultra** Torres fue "más allá" de la historia académica o de las técnicas arqueológicas ortodoxas. Removió la basura de la memoria y descubrió intacto su hedor en el corazón mismo de la vieja-nueva capital (*Das Kapital*) del Reich nazi, y tal vez también del mundo que se nos viene encima.

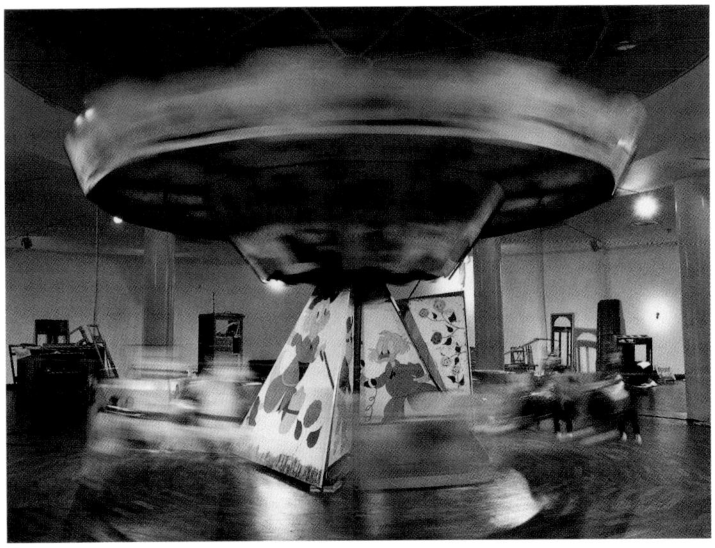

PLUS ULTRA, 1988

Y ya es hora de hablar del paso del tiempo. "El tiovivo —escribió Torres sobre **Plus Ultra**— juega en la instalación el papel de una metáfora de la historia, que precipita a sus pasajeros hacia la nada". Podría pensarse por éste y por otros indicios que no está nada clara la noción del progreso humano. Se diría que todas la acciones y anhelos, individuales o colectivos, acaban en el fracaso. También este "polvo eres" es heredero inconsciente del catolicismo barroco, pues quizá no haya tanta diferencia entre Don Miguel de Mañara y cualquier sesentaiochista desengañado. Eso explica la presencia constante de lo biológico-permanente como un elemento que contrasta con lo efímero de los

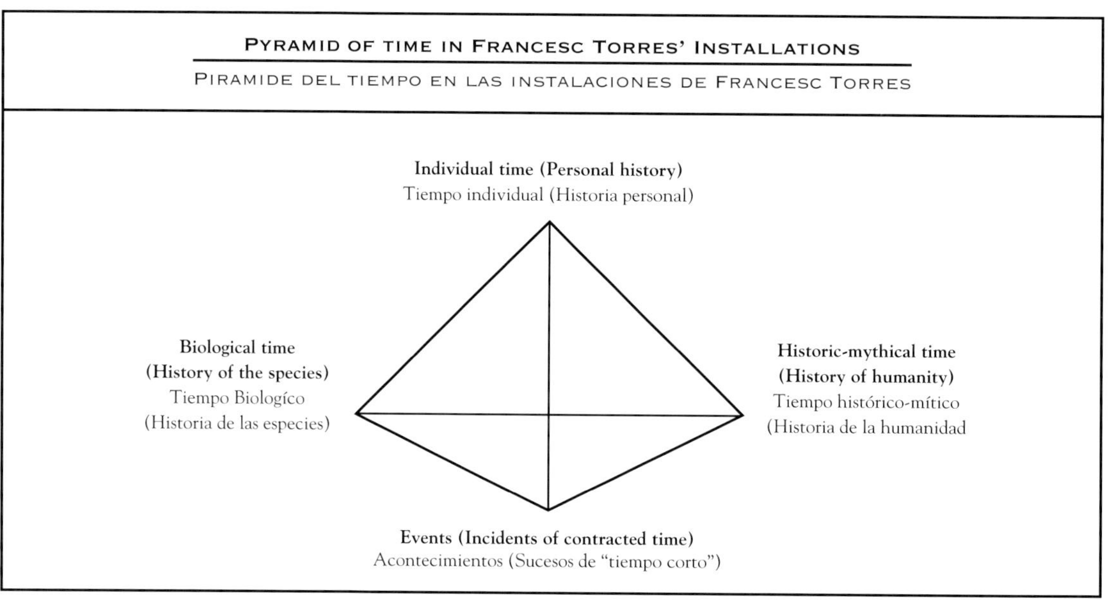

GRAPHIC NUMBER 3/GRÁFICO NÚMERO 3

of temporality. The monkey seated in a chair observes six screens which show outstanding moments of twentieth century history. The selected film fragments are spread out over time and change slowly. The adjacent television monitor (turned to the station CNN), emits non-stop news reports of the day, reflecting the great speed of events. This makes me think of F. Braudel's distinction between *événementiel* history (that which registers events) and other of *long duration* that highlights the phenomena which change slowly (eating habits, technical traditions...). In this installation, there was

---

acontecimientos humanos. ¿Cree o no cree Torres en la utilidad del esfuerzo individual? Si la respuesta es negativa, ¿por qué hace arte político? Y si es positiva, ¿cómo se articulan las acciones individuales en la marcha de la historia global, y de qué modo se conjuga todo ello con las determinaciones biológicas de la especie? Uno tiene la impresión de que el artista ha estado desgarrado durante más de una década por estos interrogantes, y mientras unas veces parecía indicarnos la primacía de la acción individual y subjetiva, en otros casos se deleitaba con la moraleja histórica. Y no eran pocos los trabajos en los que presentaba las grandes acciones humanas como meras actualizaciones de impulsos biológicos primigenios, como si lo "natural" fuese la destrucción bélica y la explotación del hombre por el hombre...

No es que la coherencia a ultranza sea algo esencial. A fin de cuentas un artista no es un biólogo ni un historiador. Tal vez su más alta misión sea plantear preguntas sin aportar soluciones, o sugerir respuestas incómodas. Pero algo ha cambiado en su última instalación: **Demasiado tarde para Goya** muestra una articulación muy precisa, de gran claridad didáctica, entre los distintos grados de la temporalidad. El mono sentado sobre el taburete observa a seis pantallas que representan a otros tantos momentos culminantes de la historia del siglo XX. Los fragmentos de las filmaciones elegidas se distienden en el tiempo, cambian lentamente. El adyacente monitor de televisión (conectado a la cadena CNN), emitiendo sin parar las noticias de la actualidad, refleja la gran velocidad de los acontecimientos. Esto me hace pensar en la distinción de F. Braudel entre una historia *événementiel* (la que registra los acontecimientos) y otra de *larga duración* que da cuenta de los fenómenos que cambian con lentitud (hábitos alimenticios, técnicas tradicionales...). Habría, pues, en esta instalación de Torres un tiempo casi eterno, identificable con las constantes biológicas (el del mono que mira a toda

a sort of eternal time, identifiable with the biological constants (that of the monkey that looks at all of history), another of slow flow (that of the culminating moments of History with a capitol "H") and another of accelerated flow (that of the daily news shown on television). Personal time, that of the artist and of the viewer, is at the crossroads of the three, like the summit of an imaginary pyramid of temporalities [see Graphic Number 3].

Each of Torres' works is situated inside of this polyhedron at a greater or lesser distance from the respective apexes, indicating, thus, the greater or lesser emphasis conferred either to the individual temporality, or to that of the "event," to that of the socio-political history (the territory of the semi-sedimented myth), or to the very slow biological evolution. These temporal levels can be inserted, by the denunciated order, like a game of Russian dolls. This is how the complicated art of multi-media installations can synthetically resolve the tensions between disciplines as diverse as psychology, history, anthropology and biology. Torres has arranged communicating vessels between the watertight compartments of knowledge. But, by connecting such different disciplines, he has extracted their blood, sucking out the juiciest part of their essence. The dracula-artist annihilates academic knowledge, he carries it to the realm of the night (again, the Gothic and the Baroque) and this is how he assures that the fragile epistemological models can live eternally.

The ephemeral art of the installation surpasses any linear discourse because it is always (literally, not metaphorically) a true palimpsest. Images and objects, static and mobile elements, texts and words, sounds, lights and colors can all go in connected harmony or disassociate themselves in alternative and contradictory discourses—like life itself. Emblems, allegories, garbage. They invite the spectator to be like the artist: a poet, a *bricoleur*, an enthusiast of riddles and an irascible archaeologist.

la historia), otro lento (el de los momentos culminantes de la Historia con mayúscula) y otro veloz, el de las noticias cotidianas que transmite la televisión. El tiempo personal, el del artista que crea o el del espectador que visita el montaje, está en la encrucijada de los otros tres, como la cúspide de una pirámide imaginaria de temporalidades. [Véase el gráfico número 3].

Cada trabajo de Torres podría situarse en el interior de ese poliedro, a mayor o menor distancia de los vértices respectivos, indicando así el énfasis mayor o menor que se otorga a la temporalidad individual, a la del "acontecimiento", a la de la historia político-social (asimilable a la semicongelación del mito), o a la de la lentísima evolución biológica. Estos niveles temporales son encajables, por el orden enunciado, como en un juego de muñecas rusas. Así es como el arte complejo de la instalación multimedia puede resolver sintéticamente las tensiones entre disciplinas tan dispares como la psicología, la historia, la antropología y la biología. Torres ha colocado vasos comunicantes entre los compartimentos estancos del saber. Pero al conectar entre sí esas disciplinas tan variadas las ha vampirizado, chupando lo más jugoso de su contenido. El artista-drácula aniquila el saber académico, se lo lleva al reinado de la noche (otra vez lo gótico y lo barroco), y así es como consigue que los frágiles modelos epistemológicos puedan vivir eternamente....

El arte efímero de la instalación supera cualquier discurso lineal porque siempre es (de un modo literal, no metafórico) un verdadero palimpsesto. Imágenes y objetos, elementos estáticos y móviles, textos y palabras, sonidos, luces y colores: todo puede ir en conjuntada armonía o disociarse en discursos alternativos y contradictorios. Como la vida misma. Emblemas, alegorías, basuras. Se invita a que el espectador sea como el artista: un poeta, un *bricoleur*, un aficionado a los acertijos y un atrabilario arqueólogo .

Too Late for Utopia

Marilyn Zeitlin

In an early passage in *Foucault's Pendulum*, Umberto Eco's protagonist Casaubon hides in the Conservatoire des Arts et Metiers after hours, concealing himself in a periscope. He is surrounded by a polyglot assortment of objects: old vehicles, obsolete machines, strange birds preserved by taxidermy, all made more mysterious by the dim light of the empty museum. At the same time that he is surrounded by the motionless paraphernalia of the past, he can look through the periscope to the street outside to observe the ambient present. Casaubon is part of a coterie of hack writers and vanity publishers who accidentally come upon clues to a Universal Plot. Their analyses employ the cabala, computers, and principles of physics. They draw on a variety of forms of knowledge and quackery in attempting to trace the perpetrators of a grand conspiracy. They have a plethora of data, yet it is impossible to see the complete pattern. The limitations of vision reflect the boundaries of intellectual mastery and the futility in seeking totalizing explanations. Casaubon, who has concealed himself to observe, attempts to link the information gleaned from arcana to present-day events and players in the scheme and acts on the basis that the elements in a conspiracy add up. But like the array of objects in the museum that, together, are purported to encompass knowledge, it is impossible to conceive the whole.

Eco's chosen setting, with its multiple levels of perceived reality, is not unlike one of Francesc Torres' media installations. The viewer, temporarily captive in a darkened area of a museum, with seemingly disparate objects and information, is challenged to draw conclusions about historiography and the manipulation of power. In the installation, video monitors or projections parallel the periscope, introducing the moving image and another layer of information imported from a distant source, one that is perpetual, constantly adding to the historic record, constantly revising the past in the present.

In the case of Torres' recent work—and really throughout his oeuvre—history is his source and his

---

Demasiado tarde para utopías

Marilyn Zeitlin

En los primeros capítulos de *El Péndulo de Foucault* de Umberto Eco, Casaubon, el protagonista, se esconde en el Conservatoire de Arts et Métiers una vez que éste ha cerrado, ocultándose en un periscopio. Allí se encuentra rodeado de un surtido políglota de objetos: vehículos viejos, máquinas obsoletas, extraños pájaros conservados mediante taxidermia. Objetos a los que la tenue luz del vacío museo da un aspecto aún más misterioso. Además de estar rodeado de la inmóvil parafernalia del pasado, a través del periscopio puede ver la calle y observar el ambiente que en ella reina. Casaubon forma parte de un grupo de escritores y editores por encargo que casualmente hallan la clave de un Complot Universal. En sus análisis utilizan la cábala, computadores y los principios de la física. Recurren a múltiples formas de conocimiento y charlatanería con el propósito de localizar a los maquinadores de una importante conspiración; pero aunque poseen multitud de datos les resulta imposible obtener una visión global de ésta. Lo limitado de su visión es un reflejo de los límites de la supremacía intelectual y de la futilidad de la búsqueda de explicaciones totalizadoras. Casaubon, oculto para poder observar, y en su intento por unir la información recogida en los arcanos con los acontecimientos y los ejecutantes actuales del plan, actúa siguiendo la teoría de que los elementos de una conspiración encajan perfectamente; pero al igual que la colección de objetos del museo, reunidos con la intención de acumular sabiduría, es imposible concebirla en su totalidad.

El escenario elegido por Eco, con sus múltiples niveles de percepción de la realidad, no es muy distinto de una de las instalaciones multimedia realizada por Francesc Torres. Al espectador, temporalmente prisionero en una zona oscurecida del museo y rodeado de objetos e información aparentemente dispares, se le provoca para que saque conclusiones sobre historiografía y sobre la manipulación del poder. En la instalación, monitores de vídeo o proyecciones son el equivalente del

nagging concern. How the events that become history are chosen and represented to encapsulate whole eras is the issue Torres examines in the works in the exhibition.

In the media installation **Too Late for Goya**, Torres places the stream of current events as they spew forth from CNN against the backdrop of sifted key moments of the past. The contemporary reportage, with its persistent banality, fast clips, and predictable repetition every twenty minutes or so contrasts with the sense of weightiness of the selected moments presented in the large-scale projections, with the dignity and authority that the elapsing of time has bestowed on the recording of turning points in the political history of the twentieth century. The moments are heroicized by scale, pace, and the presence of figures now made larger than life in the history-making process. The work simultaneously presents historical events and figures who are credited with having changed the world, and by reference to twentieth-century events, it summarizes the century and ideological struggles among socialism, fascism, capitalism, reflects the impact of more narrowly defined ideologies such as Zionism. The work raises questions about the manufacture of history, and of the validity of ideology—any ideology—in the contemporary setting, a time in which the crisis of history reflects the ubiquity and instantaneity of media manipulation. The CNN broadcast with its sound track manipulated on delivery reminds us that even the present is removed from some putative reality or objective world of facts.

In all his work, Torres selects images meticulously, to make installations, sculptural objects, prints, and large-scale Cibachrome photographs that induce an intellectual response as well as a visceral one. Often the works are brimming with visual material and reference. In his most spare installation work to date, Torres goes against the grain of much video or media installation by his forbearance in not bombarding the viewer with a firestorm of images and sound. The work is not about media overload, so

periscopio, los cuales introducen imágenes en movimiento y otra capa de información vinculada a un origen distante, perpetuo, y que constantemente añade material a los anales de la historia y revisa el pasado en el presente.

En la obra reciente de Torres —y en realidad a través de toda su obra— la historia representa un punto de partida y una constante preocupación. En las obras de la exposición Torres analiza principalmente una cuestión: cómo los acontecimientos que se convertirán en históricos son elegidos y representados para condensar épocas enteras.

En la instalación multimedia **Too Late for Goya (Demasiado tarde para Goya)**, Torres sitúa la corriente de acontecimientos actuales, tal y como los arroja la CNN, contra el telón de fondo de algunos momentos clave del pasado. El reportaje actual, con su persistente banalidad, sus rápidos cortes y las predecibles repeticiones aproximadamente cada veinte minutos, contrastan con la sensación de gravedad de los momentos seleccionados presentados en las proyecciones a gran escala, con la autoridad que el paso del tiempo ha conferido a las imágenes registradas de los momentos cumbre de la historia política del siglo veinte. Dichos momentos adquieren heroísmo gracias a la escala y al ritmo de la imagen, y también por la presencia de figuras engrandecidas en el proceso de creación de la historia. La obra presenta simultáneamente acontecimientos históricos, figuras a las que se atribuye el mérito de haber cambiado el mundo, y, en alusión a los acontecimientos del siglo veinte, resume las luchas ideológicas de este siglo entre socialismo, fascismo y capitalismo, asimismo refleja el impacto de ideologías más estrictamente definidas, como el sionismo. La obra plantea cuestiones sobre la fabricación de la historia y sobre la validez de la ideología —cualquier ideología— en el marco actual, en una época en la que la crisis de la historia refleja la ubicuidad e instantaneidad de la manipulación

it need not impersonate it. On the contrary, it requires patience and active participation through analysis from the viewer. Like Casaubon holed up in the periscope, the viewer must wait as the six image screens slowly—excruciatingly slowly—change. The slowness and sparse sound component are integral to the meaning of the piece. The work permits—even demands—slow perception, an approach to information-gathering in defiance of the disintegration of attentiveness that is a symptom of the "postmodern condition." Torres places video and film in the place held for so long by historical painting. The projections are given the dignity of the masterpieces of historical painting.

In the photographic works, Torres captures the media imagery of history from *Newsweek*, placing photographs of current events and advertising icons on an equal footing, each giving information about the nature of our time in equal measure. Torres creates a tension among the images in the three panels of the triptychs, indicating a critical option through juxtaposition. Often he will manipulate the printed page of the magazine, dissolving the inks to make marks that mimic the romantic gestures of abstract expressionism. The obliterations and blurrings obfuscate narrative context, isolating the images to iconic levels. **Triptych #26 (Newsweek Series)**[1] contrasts the mechanically reproduced image of the cover of the magazine with the individuation that Torres' manipulation imparts. The same face, of a soft-faced soldier-boy, peers from each panel. His face is slightly wounded; he looks stunned and is close to pouting. He is one of an anonymous category, "young soldier," and a particular person, somebody's son. He earned his moment by virtue of having been one of the Gulf War prisoners of war. The accident of history and *Newsweek* chose one face from the many, but the mass-production of the image reverses the process of individuation. Torres repeats the process, in reverse, repeated but then differentiating. The scale heroicizes the figure but also reveals its very ordinariness.

[1] **Triptych #26 (Newsweek Series)**, *1992, Cibachrome, 65 3/4 x 150", collection of the Bohen Foundation, New York.*

---

de los medios de comunicación. La retransmisión de la CNN, emitida con la banda de sonido manipulada nos recuerda que incluso el presente se ve despojado de cierta supuesta realidad o de un mundo fáctico objetivo.

En toda su obra, Torres selecciona las imágenes meticulosamente para crear instalaciones, objetos escultóricos, grabados y Cibachromes en gran escala, que inducen a dar dos tipos de respuesta: una intelectual y otra visceral. Material tanto visual como de referencia abunda a menudo en sus obras. En **Too Late for Goya**, hasta ahora su instalación más austera, Torres va contra la tendencia general a abusar del vídeo y de los medios de comunicación y se abstiene de acosar al espectador con un bombardeo de imágenes y sonido. La obra no trata de la sobrecarga de los medios de comunicación, así pues, no necesita representarla. Por el contrario, ésta exige al espectador paciencia y su participación activa a través del análisis. Al igual que Casaubon, oculto en el periscopio, el espectador debe esperar a que las seis imágenes cambien con lentitud —con extrema lentitud-. La lentitud de la pieza y la exigüedad de su componente sonoro forman parte integrante de su significado. La obra permite —e incluso exige— una percepción lenta, un acercamiento a la recopilación de información que menosprecia la desintegración de la atención, síntoma de un "estado postmoderno". Torres sitúa vídeo y película en el lugar ocupado durante tanto tiempo por la pintura histórica. A las proyecciones se les confiere la dignidad de obras maestras de la pintura de temas históricos.

En sus obras fotográficas, Torres capta la imaginería histórica de los medios de comunicación en la revista *Newsweek* , colocando fotografías de acontecimientos actuales e iconos publicitarios en un plano de igualdad, cada uno de los cuales proporciona en igual medida información sobre la naturaleza

The shift in visual historiography from painting to the mechanically-initiated media of photography, film, and video challenged the image-maker (in both the sense of a picture maker and one empowered to make-or-break what we now refer to as media figures) in the process of idealizing or editorializing. Goya as history painter envisioned an event he had probably not witnessed. He then conceived the visual image to convey the moment with a viewpoint that he held or was commissioned to present. Photography moved one notch closer to "truth," to the extent that the event was simultaneous with its recording. Photo journalism could bias, but it had to happen in the presence of the action. Movies and later video also had to be there when it happened, adding narrative, and gradually penetrating further into the realm of ordinariness, however historically momentous. The video camera, in particular, can intrude to record the most unheroic behavior. Athletes cannot make a "uniform adjustment" in private any longer. Political gaffs and bad angles are played and replayed. The media holds the power to condemn a candidate or leader through the means of portrayal, through the magnification of unflattering detail.

Photography, in the popular imagination, is thought to be more objective and more realistic than painting or sculpture, media that are controlled more directly by the hand. Photography, film, and video, because their use involves a mechanical process, having a seeming transparency, and in fact do incorporate fragments of the observable world not necessarily fabricated by the artist. But while the camera may be objective, its user is not. In *Evidence*,[2] Luc Sante has selected photographs taken by the police of New York City between 1914 and 1918, each made to document the scene of a murder. There was no artistic intent. They are taken from the angle, often from high above, to capture the most information. For all this indifference to esthetic value, they are filled with what Sante calls

[2] *Luc Sante,* Evidence, *New York, 1992.*

de nuestro tiempo. Torres crea cierta tensión entre las imágenes de los tres paneles de los trípticos, indicando una opción crítica mediante la yuxtaposición. A menudo manipula la página impresa de la revista, disolviendo las tintas para dejar en ella marcas que imitan el aire romántico del expresionismo abstracto. Los borrones y las manchas ofuscan el contexto narrativo, aislando las imágenes a nivel de icono. En **Triptych #26 (Newsweek Series) (Tríptico nº 26 [Serie Newsweek])**[1] la imagen de la revista, reproducida mecánicamente, contrasta con la individuación que la manipulación de Torres proporciona. La misma cara, la de un joven piloto de rasgos suaves, aparece en todos los paneles. Tiene ligeras heridas en la cara; parece aturdido y está a punto de echarse a llorar. Forma parte de una categoría anónima, "joven soldado", y es a la vez una persona concreta, el hijo de alguien. Se hizo merecedor de este momento gracias al hecho de haber sido uno de los prisioneros de guerra de la Guerra del Golfo. Una circunstancia histórica durante la cual *Newsweek* eligió una cara de tantas, pero la producción en masa de la imagen invierte el proceso de individuación. Torres repite el proceso en orden inverso, lo repite, pero también lo diferencia. La escala confiere un carácter heroico a la imagen, al mismo tiempo que revela su trivialidad.

[1] **Triptych #26 (Newsweek Series)**, *1992, Cibachrome, 65 3/4 x 150", colección de la Bohen Foundation, Nueva York.*

En historiografía visual el cambio de la pintura a los medios mecánicos como la fotografía, el cine y el vídeo representó un reto para el creador de imágenes (como pintor y como individuo que tiene el poder de crear o hundir a quienes ahora nos referimos como figuras de los medios de comunicación) en el proceso de idealizar o editorializar. Goya, como pintor de la historia, imaginaba un acontecimiento del que probablemente no había sido testigo, y después concebía la imagen visual para transmitir el momento con su punto de vista o con el que le encargaran presentar. La fotografía representó un acercamiento a la "verdad", puesto que el acontecimiento era simultáneo a su plasmación. El

[3] *Ibid., p. xii.*

"terrible eloquence and nagging silence."[3] These pictures should come as close to unvarnished truth as we can get. Instead, they suggest the lost works of an unknown genius.

Selection plays a potent role in the making of history. Completeness is impossible, so the choice of what is important is the choice of what is history. It is a choice that is never free of bias, and is always partial. Video installation gives a sense of provisional completeness. It surrounds the viewer, incorporating sound, sculpture, video, and text. It is a total, self-contained environment. The installation becomes an arena for experience, analysis, and interaction with the content of the work.

The museum of Eco's novel implies control through completeness. In the mode of the Victorian passion for taxonomy, it also introduces vicariousness as a convenience, a substitute for or even improvement over direct experience. No need to research the object in its messy context. No need to visit the colonies when we can bring the wonders of conquered worlds here to the botanical garden or the museum. Just as the museum constructs a selective reality with an underlying, biased text, the media version of history is not only a more convenient way to experience events without involvement, but is obviously a construct created to manipulate the viewer to the benefit of whoever controls the media. Taken to its logical endpoint, perhaps the event can be manipulated to the point that it can be discarded as supernumerary. The substitute for the event, the simulacrum, no longer depends upon an antecedent, leaving the media free to create history as well as to record or reflect upon it.

In contemporary Western culture, the acceptance of the copy of the copy of the model is characteristic rather than aberrant, and occurs with decreasing skepticism. I recall watching the moon landing on a television set in a store window in Zurich with my children, five and seven at the time.

---

periodismo fotográfico podía ser parcial, pero debía tener lugar en presencia de la acción. Las películas, y más tarde el vídeo, también deben estar presentes cuando ocurre la acción, le añaden narrativa y gradualmente penetran en el reino de lo habitual, por muy trascendental que sea el momento histórico. La cámara de vídeo, especialmente, puede entrometerse y grabar hasta la conducta menos heroica. Los atletas ya no pueden "ajustarse el uniforme" en privado. Los desaciertos y malos ángulos de los políticos se ven reproducidos una y otra vez. Los medios de comunicación tienen el poder de condenar a un líder o candidato al hacer un retrato de él/ella, exagerando los detalles menos favorecedores.

Normalmente se considera que la fotografía es más objetiva y más realista que la pintura o la escultura, ambas formas de arte controladas más directamente por la mano humana. El cine, el vídeo y la fotografía requieren un proceso mecánico, lo cual les hace parecer transparentes; de hecho, incorporan fragmentos del mundo observable no necesariamente inventados por el artista. Pero mientras es posible que la cámara sea objetiva, la persona que la utiliza no lo es. En *Evidence*,[2] Luc Sante seleccionó fotografías tomadas por la policía de Nueva York entre 1914 y 1918, todas ellas realizadas para documentar escenas donde se produjeron asesinatos. No tienen ningún propósito artístico; están tomadas desde un ángulo, a menudo desde cierta altura, para poder captar así la mayor cantidad de información posible. Puesto que los valores estéticos les eran indiferentes, las fotografías están repletas de lo que Sante denomina "terrible elocuencia y silencio punzante".[3] Estas fotografías deberían ser lo más cercano posible a la pura verdad. Sin embargo sugieren la obra perdida de un genio.

La selección juega un papel importante en la creación de la historia. La información total es imposible, así pues la elección de lo que es importante es la elección de lo que es la historia. Esta elección nunca está exenta de subjetividad y siempre es parcial. La instalación de vídeo aporta un

[2] *Luc Sante*, Evidence, *Nueva York, 1992.*

[3] *Op.cit. pág. xii.*

The older one assumed we were watching a simulation, and thought I was a fool to believe it was actually happening. He internalized the assumptions of Guy Debord's *Society of the Spectacle* six years before it was published.[4]

[4] *Guy Debord,* La société du spectacle*, first published in Paris, 1967.*

Debord articulates that the world presented to us is a seamless impersonation of itself, "a long striptease,"[5] a perception that can be read at every level of society and its cultural manifestations, from political machinations to the presentation of the arts, with a leveling effect that makes it possible to regard the most disposable pop icon as profound, and the reverse. Only a few metro stops from Casaubon's musty Conservatoire is one of the greatest museums and tourist attractions in the world, the Louvre. It is to Napoleon that we owe thanks for gathering these spoils of war in such a convenient place and in such plenitude. But it is Jack Lang, France's former Minister of Culture, whom we must thank for the marketing of the museum and the creation of visitor amenities. In order to accommodate the vast crowds that penetrate the museum each day, and to meet the shift in the function of museums, the Louvre's entrance was updated. The crystal pyramid entry by I. M. Pei signals the transformation of what was a dark and confusing behemoth into an art mall. It is a very pleasant place to stroll past masterpieces. Here is housed *The Coronation of Napoleon*,[6] a painting that commemorates a spectacle of power to create power. It draws one of the largest crowds, so that it is nearly obscured by people milling before it. As history painting, it prefigures the media recording of such events: its motivation is not only to reflect, but to create and magnify the event as a means of manipulating and conferring the power; it is replete with detail, ambitious to be total in its scope.

[5] *Quoted in Elizabeth Sussman, editor,* On the Passage of a few people through a rather brief moment in time: the Situationist International 1957-1972, *Cambridge, Mass. and London, 1991, p. 98.*

[6] *Jacques-Louis David,* The Coronation of Napoleón, 1805-07, *oil on canvas, 240 x 367".*

History tends to forgive the powerful. Louis XIV is exonerated in the Expiatory Chapel of

sensación de totalidad provisional; rodea al espectador incorporando sonido, escultura, vídeo y texto. Es un entorno total e independiente. La instalación se convierte en campo de experimentación, análisis e interacción con el contenido de la obra.

El museo de la novela de Eco implica control a través de la totalidad. Siguiendo la pasión victoriana por la taxonomía introduce también la experiencia indirecta como algo conveniente, como un sustituto o incluso como algo preferible a la experiencia directa. No es necesario investigar el objeto en su caótico contexto; no es necesario visitar las colonias cuando podemos traer las maravillas de los mundos conquistados aquí, al museo o al jardín botánico. Del mismo modo que el museo construye una realidad selectiva con un texto parcial subyacente, la versión de la historia que ofrecen los medios de comunicación es un modo más cómodo de experimentar los acontecimientos sin necesidad de estar implicado en ellos, incluso cuando sabemos que es una elaboración realizada para manipular al espectador en beneficio de quienes controlan los medios de comunicación. Llevado hasta su límite lógico, es posible que el acontecimiento pueda manipularse de tal modo que incluso se pueda desechar por superfluo. El sustituto del evento, el simulacro, ya no depende de un antecedente y deja libres a los medios de comunicación para que creen historia, la plasmen o reflexionen sobre ella.

En la cultura occidental contemporánea, la aceptación de la copia de la copia del modelo es algo característico más que aberrante, y se produce con un escepticismo siempre menor. Recuerdo haber visto la llegada a la luna en un televisor situado en el escaparate de una tienda de Zurich con mis hijos, que tenían entonces cinco y siete años. El mayor supuso que lo que veíamos era un simulacro y pensó que yo era tonta por creer que aquello estaba sucediendo realmente; había interiorizado las teorías de *La société du spectacle (La sociedad del espectáculo)* de Guy Debord seis años antes de que el libro se publicara.[4]

[4] *Guy Debord,* La société du spectacle*, primera edición París, 1967.*

Conciergerie, adjacent to the cells that warehoused the commoners condemned to die in the purges of the Revolution that had earlier beheaded the king. In the same building, the heroes of the Revolution are equally commemorated: the king in the chapel, Danton in a chamber above it. Memories of the bloodshed are subordinated to adulations of power and celebrity.

Torres' emphasis is clearly on the power of events rather than the personalities of history. The construction of history is built from blocks of events, selected and packaged to create a narrative that serves to support or create a political and cultural mythology. As a secondary by-product, these events are often reduced to a parade of celebrities. The media did not give birth to Adolf Hitler or cause World War II, but Leni Riefenstahl's films were a powerful force in apotheosizing the Führer, lifting him above ordinary mortals, and beyond the range of moral law.

The selling of personalities as embodiments of an ideology is not very different from the hero-centered theory of history of Thomas Carlyle.[7] The degraded, commodity-centered version of the hero-as-history is typified and at the same time parodied by sports heroes. The stars of sport like the celebrities of ideological struggles embody ideologies, ethnic identities, and national pride, a pattern baldly presented in "all-star wrestling," where racial and class caricatures struggle in parodic spectacles of exaggeration and feigned pain.[8]

Torres has made several works that use sports as analogies to other forms of institutionalized competition. Torres uses a racing vehicle in **Dromos Indiana** and fast vehicles in both versions of **Destiny, Entropy, and Junk** to explore theories of effective economic and political power. In sculptural objects, Torres uses the racing wheel to make concise analysis of a different kind of

[7] *Thomas Carlyle*, On Heroes, Hero-Worship, and the Heroic in History, *first published in 1841*.

[8] *Bruce Lincoln*, Discourse and the Construction of Society, comparative studies of myth, ritual, and classification, *New York, 1989, pp. 148-159.*

Debord manifiesta que el mundo que presentan ante nosotros es una representación uniforme de sí mismo, "un largo striptease";[5] esta idea puede percibirse en todos los niveles de la sociedad y de sus manifestaciones culturales, desde las maquinaciones políticas hasta la presentación de las artes, con un efecto de nivelación que hace posible contemplar el icono pop más fútil como si fuera algo profundo y viceversa. A pocas paradas de metro del mustio Conservatoire se halla uno de los mayores museos del mundo, que es a la vez una gran atracción turística: el Louvre. Allí se encuentra *La coronación de Napoleón*, una pintura que conmemora un espectáculo de poder, hecho para crear poder. Es a Napoleón a quien debemos la acumulación de estos botines de guerra en un lugar tan adecuado y en tal abundancia. Pero es al ex-ministro de cultura francés, Jack Lang, a quien debemos agradecer la publicidad que se ha realizado del museo y la creación de atracciones para los visitantes. Para poder acomodar a las grandes multitudes que invaden el museo cada día y para adaptarse al cambio de función de los museos, la entrada ha sido modernizada. La nueva entrada, una pirámide de cristal de I.M. Pei, marca la transformación de lo que fue una mole oscura y confusa en una avenida del arte. Es un lugar muy agradable por el que pasear entre obras maestras. Una de las pinturas que atrae más público, la monumental *Coronación de Napoleón*, de Jacques-Louis David[6] está prácticamente oscurecida por la cantidad de gente que se detiene frente a ella. Como pintura histórica prefigura la plasmación de eventos de parecidas características: pretende no sólo reflejar, sino también crear y magnificar el acontecimiento como medio de manipulación y de adquisición de poder, está repleta de detalles y ambiciona ser total en su cometido.

La historia tiende a perdonar a los poderosos. Luis XIV es exonerado en la Capilla Expiatoria de la Conciergerie, próxima a las celdas que guardaron a los plebeyos condenados a morir en las purgas de la

5 *Cit. en* On the Passage of a few people through a rather brief moment in time: the Situationist International 1957-1972, *Elizabeth Sussman, editora, Cambridge, Mass. y Londres, 1991, p.98.*

[6] *Jacques-Louis David*, La coronación de Napoleón, 1805-07, *óleo sobre tela, 240 x 367".*

competition in two objects that each embellish a sleek new racing car wheel and tire. At the hub of **European (Oneiric) Competition Wheel** is an enamel miniature portrait of Sigmund Freud. At the center of the other, **European (Historic) Competition Wheel**, Karl Marx. The two ideologues, portrayed in an old-fashioned decorative medium associated with sentimental idealized portraiture, are at the end of the axle holding the wheels that propelled the motion of modern history. Both ideologies involve the notion of struggle: Marxism, among classes; Freudianism, between the mother and the child, and by extension, between the sexes, with Freud describing the healthy female psyche as one of quiescence. The axioms that these thinkers codified have increasingly come under fire, particularly but not exclusively from feminist perspectives. By making the two objects a matched pair, Torres suggests that they may power the vehicle in tandem.

Torres' signature images are quintessentially male: racing vehicles, tanks, guns. His portrait of Freud places the founder of psychoanalysis in the same tight spot as other ideologues of theories now considered to have failed. In **Emergency Drinking Water**, Torres offers a simple work that is open to multiple interpretations, and invites either Freudian or a variety of feminist interpretations, or all of these. He places a small replica of the *Venus of Willendorf* on top of a can of Coast-Guard issue emergency drinking water. The organization of elements, with the woman on top, can be read as the dominance of a primal female, defining her as a source for survival. It is also clearly phallic. Or the pendulous breasts, usually associated with milk, maternal nurturing, and the sign for mammalian identity, are here transformed into a figurehead on a military provision, jettisoning all the baggage of motherhood and the guilt that Freud foregrounds for it. Or is the goddess, like Freud or Marx at the center of the wheel, the driving force of conflict? The woman behind the men? Feminists may be quick

revolución que poco antes había decapitado a su rey. En el mismo edificio, los héroes de la revolución que habían enviado a la guillotina a Luis, y más tarde al propio Danton, son igualmente recordados como héroes. Las memorias de la matanza están subordinadas a la adulación del poder y la celebridad.

Torres pone claramente más énfasis en el poder de los acontecimientos que en las personalidades de la historia. La historia se construye a partir de bloques de acontecimientos, seleccionados y empaquetados para crear un relato que sirva para sostener o para crear una mitología política y cultural. Como consecuencia indirecta, estos acontecimientos se reducen a menudo a un desfile de celebridades. Los medios de comunicación no dieron a luz a Adolf Hitler, ni causaron la segunda guerra mundial, pero las películas de Leni Riefenstahl dieron gran fuerza a la glorificación del Führer, elevándolo por encima de los simples mortales y más allá de toda ley moral.

La venta de personalidades como encarnaciones de una ideología no difiere demasiado de la teoría de la historia centrada en el héroe de Thomas Carlyle.[7] La versión degradada y centrada en el producto del héroe como historia viene tipificada y al mismo tiempo parodiada por los héroes del deporte. Las estrellas del deporte, al igual que las celebridades de las luchas ideológicas, encarnan ideologías, identidades étnicas y orgullo nacional. Esta fórmula viene presentada en su versión más escueta en "all-star wrestling", los espectáculos de las estrellas de lucha libre, donde caricaturas raciales y de clase combaten en espectáculos de parodia en los que el dolor es fingido y exagerado.[8]

Torres ha realizado varios trabajos en los que utiliza los deportes como analogías de otras formas de competición institucionalizadas. En **Dromos Indiana** Torres utiliza un automóvil de carreras, y en ambas versiones de **Destí, Entropia i Ferralla (Destino, entropía y chatarra)** utiliza bólidos para examinar teorías de poder efectivo tanto político como económico. En sus objetos escultóricos, Torres

7 *Thomas Carlyle*, On heroes, Hero-Worship, and the Heroic in History , *primera edición, 1841*.

8 *Bruce Lincoln*, Discourse and the Construction of Society, comparative studies of myth, ritual, and classification, *Nueva York, 1989, págs.148-159*.

to groan at the resurrected image of the goddess, but the work suggests that the female persona need not be defined as either/or the essentialist goddess of feminism of the 1960's, the equal-pay-for-equal-work feminist of the 1980's, or cyborg or fighter pilot of the 1990's.

The value of a constructed personality to embody a movement is traceable in the Bolshevik insistence upon the necessity of a vanguard at the head of the proletarian file. In fact, the Bolsheviks may have done all they could to slow the actions of the masses, and were several steps behind the people they claimed to lead.[9] It is in the interest of the leaders that everyone appear to live by the ideas articulated by the leader and to charge the barricades fueled by the charismatic leader's words and image. Yet the "mandate of Heaven" is, ultimately, revealed in the will of the people. "Hegemony is established to the extent that the world view of the rulers is also the world view of the ruled."[10]

Torres expresses the futility of historic imperatives by expressing the vanity of utopian theories. In **History and Farce**[11] Torres caps the business end of a hammer with a relief of Lenin. The lead sheet shows the random repeat of the profile of the leader embossed on the metal. Lead is replete with associations, including reference to Plato's class structure designating those who are innately destined to be of gold, silver, or lead. The *Lumpenproletariat* (those of lead) may have been hammered with Lenin's image and Leninism, but the artifact (history) records nothing but repeated effort that goes no further than image. The subtitle of Friedrich Nietzsche's *The Twilight of the Idols; how to philosophize with a hammer*[12] comes to mind. The twilight of history and the ideologies of the twentieth century make it too late not only for Goya but for Leninism as well.

Logic and the Termites[13] reduces armed conflict to the action of toy tanks swarming over a gold bar labeled with the lost elementary notation of logic: A⟶B. The tanks look earnest and silly, but

[9] *Daniel and Gabriel Cohn-Bendit, translated by Arnold Pomerans,* Obsolete Communism; the Left-wing Alternative, *New York, 1968, pp. 210-219.*

[10] *Trinh T. Minh-Ha,* When the Moon Waxes Red, *New York, 1991, p. 148.*

[11] **History and Farce**, *1992, lead panel, hammer, and brass, 13 3/8 x 16 3/4", collection of Terry Berkowitz, New York.*

[12] *Quoted in Arthur C. Danto, "John Heartfield,"* The Nation, *June 28, 1993, p. 918.*

[13] **Logic and the Termites**, *1992, brass, zinc, glass, wood, 47 9/16 x 13 3/8 x 17 7/16", collection of the artist.*

emplea la rueda del automóvil de carreras para realizar un análisis conciso de un tipo diferente de rivalidad entre dos objetos que adornan la rueda y el neumático de un flamante bólido. En el eje de **European (Oneiric) Competition Wheel [Rueda europea de competición (onírica)]** hay un esmalte con el retrato en miniatura de Sigmund Freud. En el centro de la otra rueda, **European (Historic) Competition Wheel [Rueda europea de competición (histórica)]**, está Karl Marx. Los dos ideólogos, representados en un medio decorativo asociado con un tipo de retrato sentimental e idealizado, rematan el eje de las ruedas que empujaron hacia adelante el mecanismo de la historia moderna. Ambas ideologías contienen implícita la noción de lucha: la marxista, entre clases, y la freudiana entre madre e hijo y, por extensión, entre sexos, con Freud describiendo la psique femenina sana como algo latente. Los axiomas que dichos pensadores codificaron se han visto cada vez más atacados, sobre todo, pero no exclusivamente, desde perspectivas feministas. Al combinar los dos objetos emparejándolos, Torres sugiere que ambos pueden impulsar el vehículo al unísono.

Las imágenes de firma de Torres son esencialmente masculinas: coches de carreras, tanques, pistolas. Su retrato de Freud sitúa al fundador del psicoanálisis en el mismo aprieto que otros ideólogos de teorías consideradas ahora como un fracaso. En **Emergency Drinking Water (Agua potable de emergencia)**, Torres ofrece una obra simple, abierta a múltiples interpretaciones, incitando al público a dar una interpretación freudiana, diversas interpretaciones feministas, o ambas. Sobre una lata de agua potable utilizada por los guardacostas en casos de emergencia coloca una pequeña réplica de la *Venus de Willendorf*. La organización de los elementos, con la mujer en la parte superior, puede interpretarse como el dominio de una mujer primitiva, definiéndola como una fuente de supervivencia. Es también una imagen claramente fálica. Los pechos que cuelgan de ella, normalmente asociados con la leche, la

the analogy to termites warns that while they might seem mindless and without direction, they can undermine, even gut the innards of the support system. Logic, then, is the infrastructure vulnerable to the termite action that destroys from within, leaving only the fragile shell of appearance. This analogy seems to describe the devolution of ideologically-inspired social movements that have been reduced to platitudes with promises left unfulfilled.

In **Table for Hegelian Heroes at a Business Lunch: Dining Room Storm Also Applicable to the Domestic Front**, a battle plan is set out on a long steel table. A built-in anachronism, tanks about to attack a medieval castle, associates the event with no time and all time, and undercuts the weightiness of strategy with absurdity. The arrows of the plan are red and yellow on one side; white and orange on the other—a schoolbook oversimplification of the Hegelian dialectic. The tanks, like ants, are inadequate to the challenge, but earnest. The sides appear to be evenly matched, predicting a blood bath for both sides. Remote from the action, at either end of the table, are elegant place settings for those in control of these forces. Invisible generals or presidents or kings, they will dine while the game is played out. "Domestic" brings

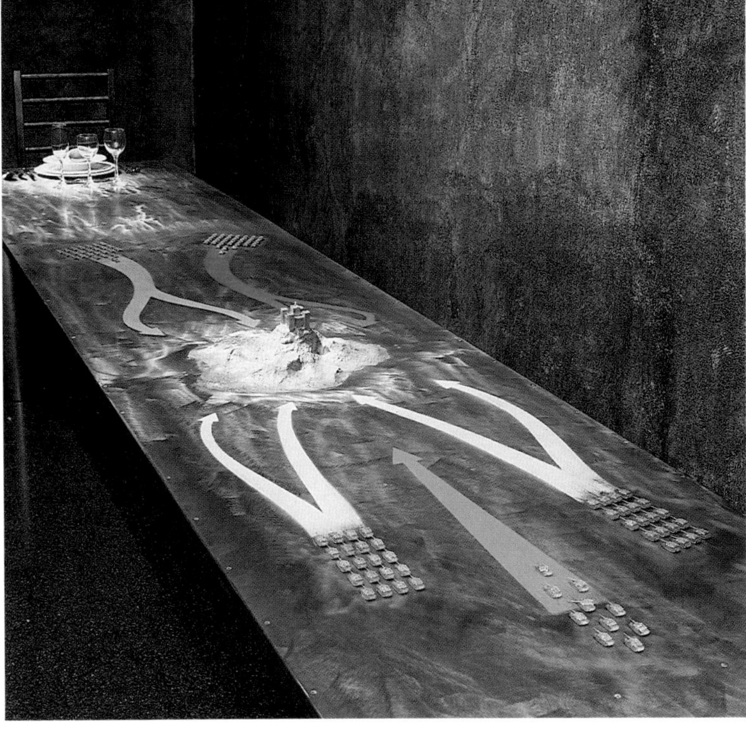

TABLE FOR HEGELIAN HEROES AT A BUSINESS LUNCH: DINING ROOM STORM ALSO APPLICABLE TO THE DOMESTIC FRONT, 1991

alimentación materna, y como signo de identidad de los mamíferos, se ven aquí transformados en el mascarón de un suministro militar que echa por la borda todo su bagaje maternal y la culpabilidad que Freud les impone. ¿O quizás es la diosa, como Freud y Marx en el centro de la rueda, la fuerza motriz del conflicto? ¿La mujer que hay detrás de cada hombre? Es posible que las feministas se quejen de inmediato a la vista de la imagen resucitada de la diosa, pero la obra sugiere que la mujer no tiene porque definirse como la diosa existencial del feminismo de los años sesenta, ni como la feminista de los ochenta a favor de la igualdad en el ámbito laboral, ni tampoco como el cyborg o el piloto de combate de la década de los noventa.

El valor de una personalidad construida para encarnar un movimiento se hace patente en la ideología bolchevique y su insistencia en la necesidad de que hubiera una vanguardia a la cabeza del proletariado. De hecho, es muy posible que los bolcheviques hicieran todo lo posible por retrasar las acciones de las masas, a las que, en vez de dirigir tal y como afirmaban, seguían a varios pasos de distancia.[9] A los líderes les interesa que todos parezcan vivir según las ideas articuladas por el líder y que ataquen las barricadas alimentados por las palabras y la imagen de los líderes carismáticos. Sin embargo, es el "mandato del cielo" el que finalmente se revela en la voluntad del pueblo. "La hegemonía se establece hasta el punto de que la visión del mundo que tienen los gobernantes es también la visión del mundo de los gobernados".[10]

Torres expresa la futilidad de los imperativos históricos declarando la vanidad de las teorías utópicas. En **History and Farce (Historia y farsa),**[11] Torres corona la cabeza de un martillo con un relieve de Lenin. La hoja de plomo muestra la copia aproximada del líder repujado en el metal. El plomo está repleto de asociaciones, incluida la definición de estructura de clases de Platón, que designaba a

[9] *Daniel y Gabriel Cohn-Bendit, traducción inglesa de Arnold Pomerans,* Obsolete Communism: the left-wing alternative, *Nueva York 1968, págs. 210-219.*

[10] *Trinh T. Minh-Ha,* When the Moon Waxes Red, *Nueva York, 1991, p.148.*

[11] **History and Farce**, *1992, panel de plomo, martillo y cobre, 13 3/8 x 16 3/4", colección de Terry Berkowitz, Nueva York.*

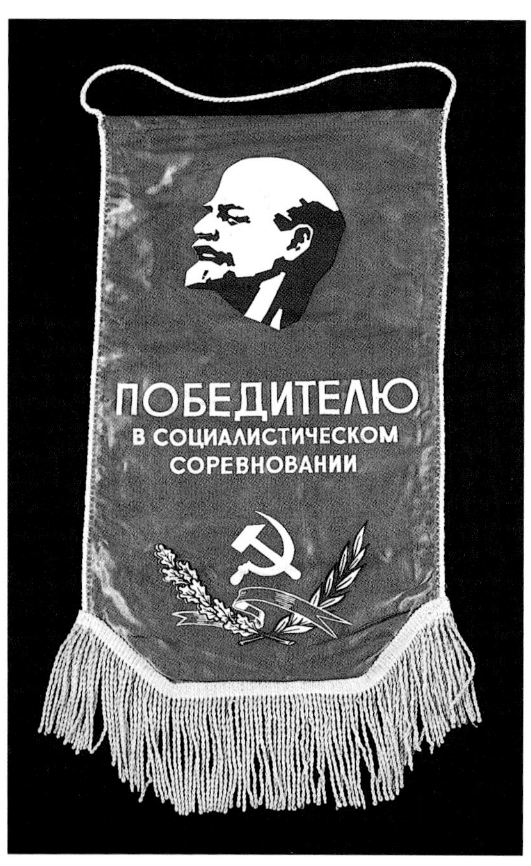

SOVIET INCENTIVE BANNER, 1930'S

the war home, to problems on the home front and to the center of the family. The prize, the castle as centerpiece, suggests a multi-layered wedding cake.

Torres' historic footage records events. Only after events, after history is written, are the personae built to embody these events and to create a means of identification of the people with the "causes" (in both senses) of these events. History is portrayed as ineluctable, the two sets of tanks converging senselessly on the castle. Leaders need to be celebrities in order to maintain the fiction of the sustained revolution or loyalty to the precepts of a constitution, a process deeply dependent upon the media. John F. Kennedy was the not the first president to exploit that observation, but he was the first to win an election through television. The craving for charismatic or at least photogenic leaders recalls the impact of the images of the saints that turned the facades of cathedrals into explicit texts. The image of the leader is equivalent to currency, where his (less often, her) profile fills a coin. Evidence of the power of the image of the leader—or the creation of the power of the leader—is reflected in the banners used in the Soviet Union to reward outstanding workers. In a society in which competitiveness was not rewarded with money, the familiar profile of Lenin on a red satin banner was awarded in lieu of a raise. It worked, for a while.

The figures that were canonized by socialism—Lenin, Stalin, Tito—all are self-created personae. Like movie stars, they made up their names, eradicating their localized ethnic identity to become universal. Stalin, for example, expunged

---

aquellos destinados de manera innata a ser de oro, plata, o plomo. El *Lumpenproletariat* (de plomo) podía haber sido martilleado con la imagen de Lenin y el leninismo, pero el artefacto (historia) hace constar repetidamente una acción inútil que no va más allá de la imagen. El subtítulo de la obra de Friedrich Nietzsche *El ocaso de los ídolos; como filosofar con un martillo*[12] nos viene a la mente. El ocaso de la historia y de las ideologías del siglo veinte hacen que sea demasiado tarde no sólo para Goya, sino también para el leninismo.

Logic and the Termites (La lógica y las termitas)[13] reduce el conflicto de la acción a un grupo de tanques de juguete que hormiguean por una barra dorada en la que figura una notación lógica básica A——>B. Los tanques parecen laboriososos y estúpidos, pero la analogía con las termitas nos advierte que, si bien parecen necios y sin dirección fija, pueden socavar e incluso vaciar las entrañas del sistema de soporte. Lógica es, pues, la infraestructura vulnerable a la acción de las termitas, que destruyen desde el interior, dejando sólo una frágil cáscara de apariencia. La analogía parece describir la degeneración de los movimientos sociales de inspiración ideológica, los cuales se han visto reducidos a tópicos llenos de promesas sin cumplir.

En **Table for Hegelian Heros at a Business Lunch: Dining Room Storm Also Applicable to the Domestic Front (Mesa para héroes hegelianos en una comida de negocios: tormenta de comedor también aplicable al frente doméstico)**, se expone un plan de batalla sobre una larga mesa de acero. Un anacronismo incorporado, tanques a punto de atacar un castillo medieval, asocia este acontecimiento con todas las épocas al mismo tiempo que con ninguna, y debilita mediante la absurdidad la importancia de la estrategia. En el plan, las flechas de un bando son rojas y amarillas, y las

[12] *Cit. en Arthur C. Danto, "John Heartfield"*, The Nation, *28 de junio de 1993, pág.918.*

[13] **Logic and the Termites**, *1992, cobre, cinc, cristal y madera, 47 9/16 x 13 3/8 x 17 7/16", colección del artista.*

his Georgian name to become a figure that rises above his regional identity.

Too Late for Goya raises the question of why some political figures are deified to become emblems of a movement—whether villains or heroes is not the issue here—while others fade into the backdrop. Images of celebrity, from fanzines to revolutionary banners, sort into those destined for longevity in recognition value and those headed for the graveyard of amnesia or the dim corridors of a museum of history.

For what is Goya too late? There is a mild scold and a sad note in the title. It is too late to commemorate heroes in painting. That is probably unarguable. Is it too late for heroes? Too late for the kinds of events that Goya recorded, the nationalistic and popular uprisings quelled by a firing line of ten to push aside disillusionment with political and cultural models and reorganize to press for social justice?

Those of us who grew up thinking revolution was not only possible but imminent find ourselves in an awkward position. With the passing of the Soviet Union and Yugoslavia, we inadvertently find ourselves mourning dictators, a few of which may have been somewhat benevolent. The revolutions of the late 1960's and early 70's took many forms, but all reached for the betterment of the dispossessed or disenfranchised: the civil rights movement that gave impetus to the black power movement; struggles for women's equal place in society. All united against the war in Vietnam, applying what they learned about colonialism to domestic as well as imperialist context. The disparate and sometimes warring parties found inspiration in varying degrees from Marxism. That the idealism of Marxism became in practice repression in Soviet and Chinese communisms did not prove the error of the theory but the flaws in application. The atrocities of the purges, the gulags, are not intrinsic to the ideology but were Stalin's crude means of repression to build and sustain his own power. But now, with the demise of

del otro bando de colores blanco y naranja; una simplificación excesivamente didáctica de la dialéctica hegeliana. Los tanques, como hormigas, son laboriosos, pero inadecuados. Las fuerzas parecen ser equilibradas, lo cual hace predecir un baño de sangre por ambas partes. La mesa está elegantemente dispuesta a ambos extremos, lista para los que ostentan el mando de los dos ejércitos, los cuales se hallan apartados de la acción. Los generales, reyes o presidentes invisibles comerán mientras se desarrolla el juego. La palabra "doméstico" acerca la guerra a los problemas del frente nacional y del entorno familiar. La recompensa, el castillo como pieza central, evoca un pastel de boda de varios pisos.

El material histórico de Torres registra acontecimientos. Sólo después de que éstos hayan sucedido, una vez escrita la historia, se construyen los personajes que encarnarán dichos acontecimientos y que crearán un medio de identificación de la gente con las "causas" (en ambos sentidos) de éstos. La historia viene representada como algo ineludible, con los dos grupos de tanques que convergen inconscientemente en el castillo. Los líderes necesitan ser celebridades para así poder mantener la ficción de la revolución continua o de la lealtad a los preceptos de una constitución, un proceso que depende en gran parte de los medios de comunicación. John F. Kennedy no fue el primer presidente en sacar partido de esta observación, pero sí fue el primero en ganar unas elecciones gracias a la televisión. El ansia por tener líderes carismáticos, o al menos fotogénicos, recuerda el impacto que producían las imágenes de los santos que convertían las fachadas de las catedrales en textos explícitos. La imagen del líder también se ve reflejada en el dinero; es el perfil masculino (o menos frecuentemente, femenino) que ilustra una de las dos caras de la moneda. Otra muestra del poder de la imagen del líder —o de la creación del poder del líder— aparece en las banderas que se utilizaban en la Unión Soviética para premiar a los mejores trabajadores. En una sociedad en la que la competitividad no se recompensaba

the Soviet Union, Marxism reviled and abandoned by much of the "intelligentsia," one of the great utopian theories of modern times has been discredited. Communist paraphernalia is now collectible. The utopian vision that served to inspire multitudes in the Third World devolved into unworkable political realities. Nostalgia for Marxism is misplaced sentiment, perhaps; but another vision for a New Society is not even conceivable in the context of the present. In political terms, with the exception of Germany, no democratic structure has arisen to replace the repressive communist regimes, and even in Germany, with racial hatred and xenophobia renewed, chaos has been loosed.

Gorbachev's attempt to liberalize the Soviet Union was his, and its, undoing. Now Boris Yeltsin, unable to deliver even the most basic goods of capitalism, faces grim crowds, gray faces below placards calling for the restoration of the bad old days of Stalin. Gorbachev is one of the figures in the historic footage in **Too Late for Goya**. In retrospect, he wears the expression of doom. In **Triptych #28 (Newsweek Series)**,[14] Torres shows the price riots in Moscow under Yeltsin. The views of civil unrest flank an image of a plunging diver. The diver is effortlessly elegant. In contrast, the trajectory of events in the side panels leads to anything but a soft landing.

The notion of a utopian ideology seems embarrassingly romantic, something that requires too much imagination and purposefulness in a world permeated by postmodern malaise. How Torres regards the future potentiality for a society emanating from an ideological base is suggested in a group of monotypes in which the image is the hull of a cargo ship sharply angled and about half way submerged into the sea.[15] Torres' ship is poised so that it can be read as sinking or emerging. The ship is the *UTOPIA*. The sinking ship view is the first to occur to most observers; yet if the emerging view

[14] **Triptych #28 (Newsweek Series)**, *1992, Cibachrome, 65 3/4 x 150", collection of the Bohen Foundation, New York.*

[15] **UTOPIA (Sinking or Refloating?)**, *1993, ink on paper, 60 x 42". From a series of four monotypes made at Segura Publishing Co., Tempe, Arizona, in April 1993.*

---

con dinero, en lugar de otorgar al trabajador un aumento de sueldo se le premiaba con una bandera de satén rojo en la que destacaba el conocido perfil de Lenin. La idea funcionó, durante algún tiempo.

Las figuras que el socialismo canonizó —Lenin, Stalin, Tito— son todas ellas personajes que se han creado a sí mismos. Modificaron sus nombres, tal como hacen las estrellas de cine, desarraigando su identidad étnica para convertirse en universales. Por ejemplo, Stalin suprimió su nombre georgiano para convertirse en una figura que se eleva por encima de su identidad regional.

Too Late for Goya plantea la cuestión de por qué algunas figuras políticas son divinizadas y se convierten en emblemas de un movimiento —el que sean héroes o canallas ya es otra cuestión— mientras que otras se desvanecen en un telón de fondo. Las imágenes de los famosos, desde los fanzines a los estandartes revolucionarios, separan aquellas cuyo valor será reconocido durante largo tiempo de aquellas destinadas al cementerio de la amnesia o a los oscuros pasillos de un museo de historia.

¿A qué ha llegado Goya demasiado tarde? El título encierra cierta reprensión y una nota triste. Es demasiado tarde para conmemorar héroes en pintura; esto probablemente es indiscutible. ¿Es demasiado tarde para los héroes? ¿Demasiado tarde para el tipo de acontecimientos que Goya plasmó, los levantamientos nacionalistas y populares reprimidos por una línea de fuego el 3 de mayo de 1808? ¿Es demasiado tarde para dejar de lado la desilusión que han producido los modelos políticos y culturales, y reorganizarse para conseguir justicia social?

Los que crecimos pensando que la revolución no sólo era posible sino inminente nos hallamos ahora en una incómoda posición. Con el paso a mejor vida de la Unión Soviética y Yugoslavia nos encontramos, sin darnos cuenta, llorando la muerte de dictadores, algunos de los cuales es posible que fueran hasta cierto punto benevolentes. Las revoluciones de finales de los años sesenta y principios de

prevails, then utopia will spring, like Aphrodite, reborn from the sea. The image is a terse statement of Torres' play on a multiple level of tensions. It is grim and funny. With the balance of interpretation in so precarious a balance, the work leaves responsibility for envisioning the future in the eyes of the beholder, as if to say, "It's up to you whether we sink or float."

Torres was one of the young ones in Paris in 1968. The experience of engagement in participatory politics, to put it mildly, and in the debate that examines Marxism anew underlies Torres' entire body of work. While his work always carries a look of precision and minute attention to detail, it is also elusive. He offers ideas, he suggests interpretation; but, at its best, his work offers no crisp answers. The installations, too, leave the viewer to decide whether the ship is sinking or rising to the surface.

Torres' work is not for the pedestrian traversing the museum. **Too Late for Goya** demands that the viewer fit together visual elements and associations they evoke to read a hypothesis. Historical events that conditioned the present slowly unfold in the six projections while the issues of the moment speed by on CNN. A monkey seated like a dunce on a tall chair, surveys the proceedings and finds them mystifying. Torres says that the monkey stands in for our forgotten innocence.

The black and white, grainy documentary news footage of the six projections packs a strong emotional punch for Torres. The news on the monitor is in real

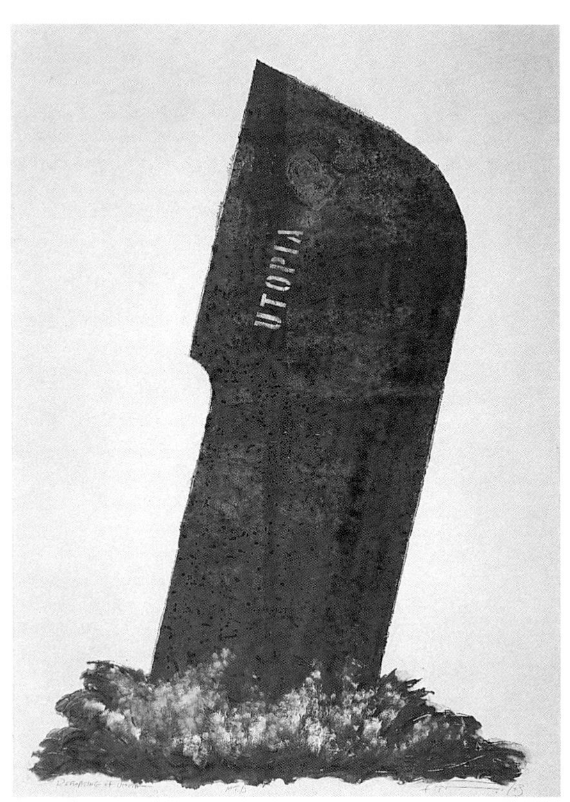

UTOPIA (SINKING OR REFLOATING?), 1993

los setenta adquirieron formas distintas, pero todas intentaban mejorar la situación de los desposeídos o de aquellos carentes de libertad, como el movimiento a favor de los derechos civiles —que dio ímpetu al movimiento a favor de los derechos de la gente de raza negra— y la lucha a favor de la igualdad de la mujer en la sociedad. Todos ellos se unieron contra la guerra de Vietnam, poniendo en práctica lo que habían aprendido sobre colonialismo tanto en un contexto nacional como imperialista. Los grupos, dispares y a veces opuestos, hallaron inspiración en diversas gradaciones del marxismo. El hecho de que, en los comunismos chino y soviético, el idealismo marxista se convirtiese en la práctica en represión no demostró el error de la teoría, sino los fallos cometidos en su aplicación. Las atrocidades de las purgas y los gulags no son exclusivas de esta ideología, sin embargo fueron el brutal modo de represión de Stalin para edificar y mantener su propio poder. Ahora que la Unión Soviética ya no existe y que el marxismo se ha visto insultado y abandonado por gran parte de la "intelligentsia", una de las grandes teorías utópicas de los tiempos modernos se ha visto suprimida. La parafernalia comunista es ahora coleccionable. La visión utópica que sirvió para inspirar multitudes en el tercer mundo se ha convirtido en diversas realidades políticas irrealizables. Quizás la nostalgia por el marxismo sea un sentimiento inadecuado, pero en el contexto del presente es inimaginable otra visión para una nueva sociedad. En términos políticos, con la excepción de Alemania, no ha surgido ninguna estructura democrática que sustituya a los represivos regímenes comunistas, e incluso en Alemania, con el resurgimiento del odio racial y de la xenofobia, se ha desatado el caos.

El intento de Gorbachev de liberalizar la Unión Soviética fue tanto su ruina como la de su país: ahora su sucesor, Boris Yeltsin, incapaz de hacer llegar a su pueblo incluso los bienes más básicos del capitalismo, se enfrenta a multitudes ceñudas, a caras grises bajo carteles que exigen la reinstauración

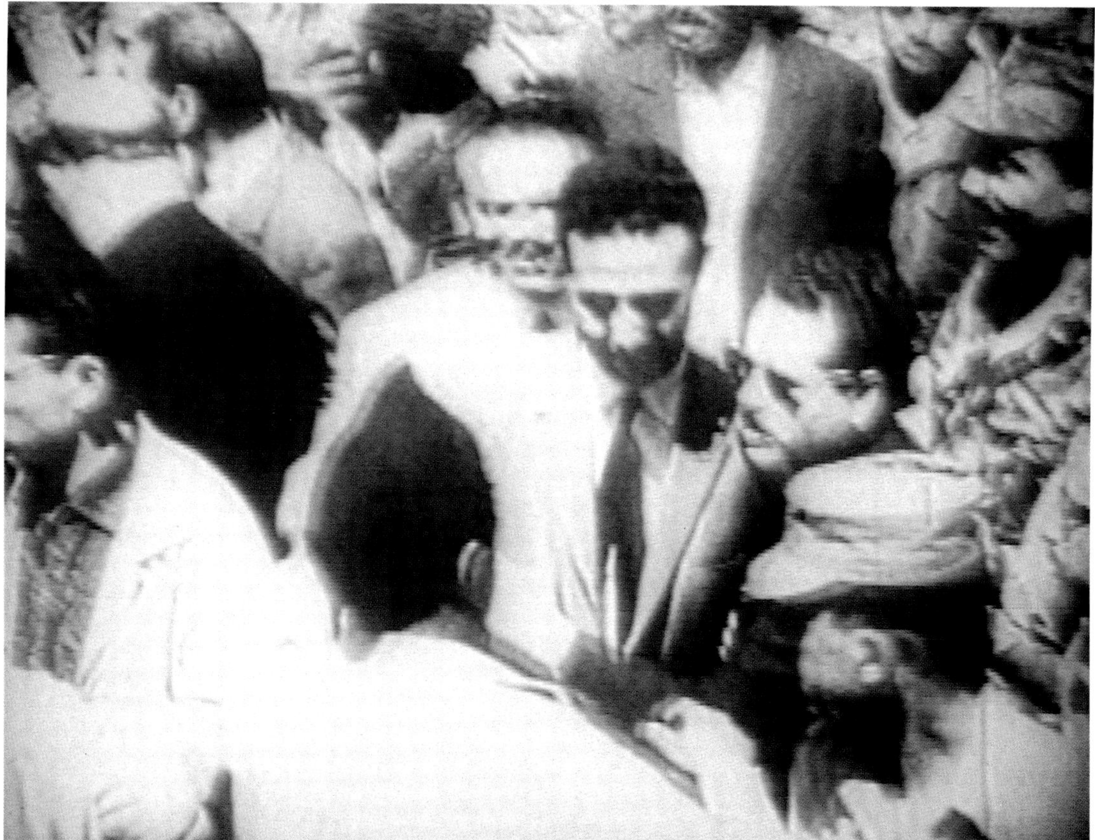

Too Late for Goya, 1993

de los malos y viejos tiempos de Stalin. Gorbachev es una de las figuras que aparece en el material histórico de **Too Late for Goya**. En retrospectiva, la expresión de su rostro es reflejo de su funesto destino. En **Triptych #28 (Newsweek Series) [Tríptico #28 (Newsweek Series)]**,[14] Torres muestra los disturbios que tuvieron lugar en Moscú a causa de la subida de los precios durante el mandato de Yeltsin. Las imágenes de malestar civil flanquean la figura de un saltador de trampolín en acción. El salto es elegante y realizado sin esfuerzo. Por contraste, la trayectoria de los acontecimientos en los paneles laterales hace prever un desenlace nada benigno.

[14] **Triptych #28 (Newsweek Series)**, *1992, Cibachrome, 65 3/4 x 150", colección de la Bohen Foundation.*

El concepto de una ideología utópica parece embarazosamente romántico, algo que requiere demasiada imaginación y determinación en un mundo empapado de malestar postmoderno. El modo en que Torres contempla la futura potencialidad de una sociedad que emana de una base ideológica nos viene sugerida en un grupo de monotipos cuya imagen es el casco de un buque de carga que forma un ángulo brusco y está medio sumergido en el mar.[15] La posición del barco de Torres puede ser interpretada como la de un barco que se hunde o que emerge. El nombre del barco es *UTOPIA*. La primera interpretación es, en la mayoría de los casos, la del barco que se hunde; sin embargo, si la interpretación del barco que emerge prevalece, la utopía surgirá, como Afrodita, renacida del fondo del mar. La imagen es una sucinta exposición del juego de Torres con un nivel múltiple de tensiones. Es lúgubre y divertida. Con el balance de interpretaciones en tan precario equilibrio, la obra delega la responsabilidad de imaginar cómo será el futuro a los ojos del espectador, como si dijera: "De tí depende que flotemos o que nos hundamos".

[15] **UTOPIA (¿Hundiéndose o emergiendo?)**, *1993, tinta sobre papel, 60 x 42". Parte de una serie de cuatro monotipos realizados en el taller Segura Publishing Co., en Tempe, Arizona, durante el mes de abril de 1993.*

Torres fue uno de los jóvenes del París de 1968. La experiencia de estar comprometido en política de participación, por decirlo de alguna manera, y en el debate que examina el marxismo de nuevo, es la

time, so to speak, captured by a satellite dish and delivered fresh. Like the periscope, the satellite keeps an ear to the outside world. The contrast in style between the historic and contemporary delivery of history reinforces awareness that all these images are prepared to convey a point of view. There is no such thing as (unvarnished) truth.

base de buena parte de su obra hasta la fecha. Si bien su obra tiene siempre un aire de precisión y de minuciosa atención hacia los detalles, también es evasiva. Torres ofrece ideas, sugiere una determinada interpretación; pero su obra no ofrece respuestas precisas. También las instalaciones dejan que el espectador decida si el barco se hunde o sale a la superficie.

La obra de Torres no está hecha para el transeúnte que cruza el museo. **Too Late for Goya** exige que el espectador agrupe elementos visuales y las asociaciones que éstos evocan para poder descifrar una hipótesis. En las seis proyecciones se exponen lentamente los acontecimientos históricos que han condicionado el presente, mientras que los problemas actuales aparecen a toda velocidad en la CNN. Un mono, sentado como un bobo en una silla alta, observa las acciones y las encuentra desconcertantes. Torres dice que el mono representa nuestra olvidada inocencia.

El documental informativo de las seis proyecciones, de imagen granulosa y filmado en blanco y negro, resulta de gran fuerza emotiva para Torres. Las noticias en el monitor son en tiempo real, por así decirlo, captadas por un satélite y emitidas cuando aún son recientes. Al igual que el periscopio, el satélite no pierde de vista el mundo exterior. El contraste de estilos entre cómo se difundía la historia antes y ahora refuerza la certidumbre de que todas estas imágenes están preparadas para transmitir un punto de vista determinado. La (pura) verdad es algo que no existe.

The History Book of Persistent Forgetfulness (Handwritten Notes at Page Margin)

Francesc Torres

There exists a fundamental difference between the amoeba and the human being. The amoeba is cognitively incapable of remembering that which it did the night before. So from this it follows that, for some, alcohol is an excellent tool for communing with the primitive; making up a story afterwards to fill the black hole of the unconscious. —Frank Towers, *The Idiot's Bliss*

To lean out of the window of the world in which we live is equivalent to confronting a mystery as profound as the Atlantic's abyss. The mystery is provided by a paradox implicit in the battle between rivals who desire to remember different things which therefore make them understand themselves and the external world in a form completely alien and antagonistic to each other. For some, historic memory constitutes a base from which to justify revenge or to correct the past. For others, it is a lifesaver of the human spirit at a time when we should be already tired of so many settlings of scores and so much compulsive repetition of horror.

The soldiers of vengeful and binary memory are pleased by the telluric. They compute genes and chromosomes and are moved by colorful rags. They suffer from an obsessive fixation in respect to the imaginary lines that can be drawn on a map. They maintain an exhaustive record of the insults and vexations—real or dreamed—inflicted on them by others; multitudes so similar to them that in order not to be confused, they force themselves to be publicly moved by a rag of a different color. The followers of this way of life have a selective memory; they only remember that which interests them, or that which proves them right.

The other group, the more fragile group, are those who want to remember everything. This way they do not forget the suffering caused to humanity by the delusions born in the absence of doubt, of possessing the absolute truth, of the certainty of manifest destiny, or of the monopoly of the divine favor and the indisputable ownership of history.

—Manuscript text found on the floor of the latrine of a bar in Coyoacan, Mexico, in October of 1992, two blocks away from the house where Trotsky lived and was assassinated.

El libro de historia del olvido empecinado (anotaciones manuscritas a márgin de página)

Francesc Torres

Existe una diferencia fundamental entre la ameba y el ser humano. La ameba es congénitamente incapaz de recordar lo que hizo la noche anterior. De esto se desprende que, para algunos, el alcohol sea un útil excelente para comulgar con lo primigenio; inventándose, de paso, un cuento con que llenar el agujero negro de la inconsciencia. —Frank Towers, *The Idiot's Bliss*

Asomarse a la ventana del mundo en que vivimos equivale a confrontar un misterio tan profundo como la fosa atlántica. El misterio viene dado por la paradoja implícita en una batalla entre contrincantes que desean recordar cosas distintas y que, por lo tanto, se entienden a sí mismos y al mundo externo de forma totalmente ajena y antagónica a la del otro. Para unos, la memoria histórica constituye la base para la justificación de la venganza, o para la corrección del pasado. Para otros, es el salvavidas del espíritu humano cuando ya tendríamos que estar cansados de tanto ajuste de cuentas y de tanta repetición compulsiva del horror.

Los soldados de memoria binaria y vengativa gustan de lo telúrico. Computan genes y cromosomas y se emocionan ante trapos de colores. Sufren de una fijación obsesiva respecto a las líneas imaginarias que pueden trazarse sobre un mapa. Mantienen una relación exhaustiva de las afrentas y vejaciones —reales o soñadas— de las que han sido objeto por parte de otras gentes, multitudes tan iguales a ellos mismos que, para no confundirse, se ven en la obligación de emocionarse públicamente ante un retazo pintado de otro modo. Los partidarios de esta manera de vivir tienen una memoria selectiva, sólo se acuerdan de lo que les interesa, de lo que les da la razón.

Al otro bando, en el bando más frágil, se encuentran aquellos que quieren acordase de todo para no olvidar el sufrimiento que le ha costado a la humanidad los espejismos nacidos de la ausencia de duda, de la posesión de la verdad absoluta, de la certeza en los destinos manifiestos, del monopolio del favor divino y de la propiedad indiscutible de la historia.

—Texto manuscrito encontrado en el suelo de la letrina de un bar en Coyoacán, México, en octubre de 1992, a dos cuadras de la casa donde vivió y fue asesinado Trotsky.

Entropy, the tendency of everything to move towards disorder, increases with time. The capability to remember the past and not the future coincides, according to Stephen Hawking, with the direction of the entropic process. When a memory is created in the brain—both artificial and organic—the minuscule quantity of energy necessary to activate a neuron or to move an electron transforms into heat. The heat augments the entropy. Memories, as such, generate heat which increases the disorder and this explains how the entropy increases from yesterday to tomorrow and how memories are originated in the past. Perhaps this could also explain why political power, in its anxieties of self-perpetuation, attempts to guarantee the order necessary for its stability through the control of collective memory and the shaping of its written records, this which we understand as History.

The works which thematically form a part of this book bring together something which has been developing in my work in a fragmented, although intense, manner during the last two years. It has fundamentally gravitated around forgetfulness as a shaping agent of history. It is not possible to manufacture history (nor, according to Chomsky, consensus) without the complicity of forgetfulness. As in the Balkan ethnic cleansing that is taking place in the former Yugoslavia even as I write these lines, it is necessary to eliminate from history all of the impure, clashing, and dreadful data which allow the calming certainty that things were, are and will be as we want them to be—as we wished they were or desired that they would have been.

Before elaborating on the exhibition's principal piece, **Too Late for Goya**, I wish to highlight three earlier pieces that deliberately attack collective amnesia and tackle many apparently unrelated historical landscapes by addressing time, place, culture and circumstances. I am concretely referring

La entropía, la tendencia de todo lo existente hacia el desorden, aumenta con el tiempo. La habilidad de recordar el pasado y no el futuro coincide, según Stephen Hawking, con la dirección del proceso entrópico: cuando un recuerdo se crea en un cerebro —tanto artificial como orgánico— la minúscula cantidad de energía necesaria para activar una neurona o mover un electrón se transforma en calor. El calor aumenta la entropía. Los recuerdos, por lo tanto, al liberar calor aumentan el desorden y esto explica que la entropía aumenta de ayer a mañana y los recuerdos se originan en el pasado. También podría, quizá, explicar por qué el poder político, en sus ansias de perpetuidad, intenta garantizar el orden necesario para su estabilidad y permanencia mediante el control de la memoria colectiva y el moldeo de su registro escrito, eso que entendemos por Historia.

Las obras que forman parte de este libro aglutinan temáticamente algo que ha estado desarrollándose en mi trabajo de manera fragmentada aunque intensa en los últimos dos años, y que ha gravitado fundamentalmente alrededor del olvido como agente modelador de la historia. No es posible manufacturar la historia (o según diría Chomsky, el consenso) sin la complicidad del olvido. Como en la limpieza genética balcánica que está teniendo lugar en la antigua Yugoslavia mientra escribo estas líneas, es necesario eliminar del campo de la memoria todo dato impuro, discordante, pavoroso, que amenace la sedante certeza de que las cosas fueron, son y serán como nosotros queremos que sean. Como nosotros quisimos que fueran o deseamos que hubieran sido.

Antes de comentar la pieza principal de la exposición, **Too Late for Goya**, deseo resaltar tres obras previas que atentan deliberadamente contra la amnesia colectiva; contra el deseo poco inocente de crear un vacío histórico para llenarlo de nadas. Piezas que abordan otros tantos paisajes históricos aparentemente ajenos entre sí por razones de tiempo, lugar, cultura y circunstancias. Me

[1] Gregorio Morán, El Precio de la Transición, *Editorial Planeta, Barcelona, 1991.*

[2] *I had already used this material in the work* **Plus Ultra**, *Kunstforum, Nationalgalerie, Berlin, 1988. For complete documentation of this project see the following catalogs:* Plus Ultra, *DAAD and Nationalgalerie, Berlin, 1988 and* La Cabeza del Dragón (The Head of the Dragon), *Museo Nacional Centro de Arte Reina Sofía, Madrid, 1991.*

[3] ETA, *Euzkadi Ta Askatasuna, an armed organization, similar to the Irish IRA, has been fighting for Basque independence for the past three decades. Basque radical nationalists consider them freedom fighters; the Spanish central government in Madrid considers them terrorists. Three members of this organization, posing as sculptors, rented a basement and*

to the installations **Fifty Rains** (1991), **Memorial** (1992), and **Chronicle of Getting Lost** (1992).

Fifty Rains (National Museum Center of Art Reina Sofia, Madrid, 1991) is a virulent reaction to the ideological and historical breeding ground that exists in Spain at the end of the political transition from Francoism to democracy. As Gregorio Moran explains so well in his book *The Price of the Transition,*[1] the success of the "Spanish model" of political change, which several Latin American and East European countries are trying to copy, was built over the ashes of a sacrifice: that of the country's historical memory. Disregarding the citizens, there was a tacit agreement between politicians to cleanse historical stains and to leave the past alone. For the right as much as the left, recalling the past meant confronting misery: those of the right had to confront their collaboration with the fascist regime and those of the left had to accept the embarrassment that their enemy, General Franco, had died of old age in his bed. The best thing was to throw dirt over the cadaver in the national closet and happily plunge into postmodern politics; to celebrate a democracy which was not representative but of representation, wherein gestures substitute for content, where ideological principles are a nuisance and power in a clinically pure state is the only thing worth fighting for. **Fifty Rains** is situated in the nebulous terrain of history—in the realm of banned histories.

The installation covered the past fifty years in Spain, emphasizing three years in particular: 1943, 1973 and 1993. Each year was represented by a room which had a linear communication with the other rooms. The 1943 room was replete with architectural remains, objects, furniture and documents from the ruins of what had been the Spanish Embassy in Berlin during the Reich.[2] Among the garbage, as if miraculously preserved, were little gold framed photographs which showed the building's interiors before it was bombed on November 23, 1943, by the British RAF. On one of the walls, a large framed

[1] Gregorio Morán, El Precio de la Transición, *Editorial Planeta, Barcelona, 1991.*

[2] *Este material había sido ya utilizado en la instalación* **Plus Ultra**, *Kunstforum, Nationalgalerie, Berlin, 1988. La documentación completa de esta pieza puede encontrarse en los siguientes catálogos:* Plus Ultra, *publicado conjuntamente por la DAAD y la Nationalgalerie, Berlin, 1988 y* La cabeza del dragón (The Head of the Dragon), *Museo Nacional Centro de Arte Reina Sofía, Madrid, 1991.*

[3] ETA, *Euzkadi Ta Askatasuna, organización armada similar al IRA irlandés, ha mantenido la lucha por la independencia del País Vasco durante casi treinta años. Los nacionalistas vascos radicales califican a los militantes etarras de libertadores; el Gobierno Español en Madrid los califica de terroristas. Tres miembros de esta organización, bajo pretexto de ser escultores, alquilaron una planta baja en la capital de España y*

refiero concretamente a las instalaciones **Cincuenta Lluvias** (1991), **Memorial** (1992) y **Crónica del Extravío** (1992).

Cincuenta Lluvias (Museo Nacional Centro de Arte Reina Sofía, Madrid, 1991) es una reacción virulenta ante el caldo de cultivo ideológico e histórico que vive España una vez finalizada la transición política del franquismo a la democracia. Como muy bien explica Gregorio Morán en su libro *El precio de la transición,*[1] el éxito del "modelo español" de cambio político que ahora intentan copiar algunos países latinoamericanos y del este de Europa, se erigió sobre las cenizas de un sacrificio: el de la memoria histórica del país. A espaldas de la ciudadanía, tuvo lugar un acuerdo tácito entre políticos de saldar con borrón y cuenta nueva los hechos del pasado. Tanto para la derecha como para la izquierda recordar el pasado significaba confrontar miserias; los de la derecha debían confrontar su colaboracionismo con el régimen fascista, y los de la izquierda debían aceptar la vergüenza de que su enemigo, el general Franco, se les hubiera muerto de viejo en la cama. Lo mejor era echarle tierra al cadáver del armario nacional y estrenar con alegría la posmodernidad política; celebrar una democracia no representativa, sino de representación, aquélla donde los gestos substituyen a los contenidos, donde los principios ideológicos son un engorro y el poder en estado clínicamente puro es lo único por lo que vale la pena luchar. **Cincuenta Lluvias** se sitúa en el terreno nebuloso de la historia, es decir, en el de los sedimentos no traducidos a relato escrito, en el terreno, resumiendo, de las historias proscritas.

La instalación cubría cincuenta años de la historia reciente de España enfatizando tres años singulares: 1943, 1973 y 1993. Cada año estaba representado por una sala comunicada linealmente con las otras. La sala del año 1943 estaba repleta de restos arquitectónicos, objetos, mobiliario y documentos provenientes de las ruinas de la Embajada de España en Berlín durante el Reich.[2] Entre la

photograph of the embassy's destroyed facade slowly turned on its central axis suggesting the chaos and the jumble of the objects in its interior produced by the hurricane of history.

The early years of post-war Spain, from 1939-1945, were those of the harshest political repression. The fervor of the Spanish fascists, nevertheless, was decreasing steadily since it was clear that the Axis forces (Germany, Italy and Japan) were losing the Second World War. The English bomb that destroyed the Spanish Embassy before they could even finish furnishing it sums up the verdict of history on the Spanish regime. It was a regime in complete moral bankruptcy, which, like a lizard's tail, continues to writhe for a long time even after being cut off from the body.

In the room of 1973 was an exact reproduction of the armored car in which the General Luis Carrero Blanco, Franco's political heir, was assassinated by ETA.[3] Beheading the regime's continuity, the assassination marks the beginning of Spain's political transition. On the walls surrounding the car were eight Cibachromes of various newspaper covers of the time which headlined the assassination. The images, however, were all out of focus, as if they had passed through the sieve of time and the erosion of memory, although there was enough information so that they could still be identified. For the installation in this room, I tried to convince the Spanish Ministery of Defense to lend Carrero's original destroyed car.[4] The idea was to utilize the historic remnants in their pure state and to transform them into art, just as had transpired in the room of the year 1943. For the very political reasons that the essence of the work questioned, it was not possible to obtain the real car. The alternative consisted of obtaining an identical car and restoring it to its original condition, including the license plate number. That is to say, turning back the clock of history to one second before Franco's heir was killed in the explosion. As a result, the room marked two opposite temporal

dug a tunnel and a vault under the street, which was filled with high explosive. On the assigned day, when Carrero Blanco was returning from attending Mass, his car was blown up. The explosion was such that the limousine went straight up, cleared a six story building and came to rest in the cloisters of a monastery while the monks were at prayer. Carrero, his bodyguard and his driver were killed. Amazingly, nobody else was hurt.

4 *Admiral Carrero Blanco's destroyed limousine was on display at the Museo del Ejército (Army Museum) in Madrid until very recently when it was transferred to the Alcázar in Toledo, a historic building that has special meaning for Spanish right wingers of both civilian and military ilk. Some officials at the Ministry of Culture in Madrid are trying to keep the Alcázar from becoming a glorified museum of fascism.*

basura, cual milagrosamente conservadas, se encontraban pequeñas fotografías de marco dorado mostrando interiores del edificio antes de ser bombardeado en la noche del 23 de noviembre de 1943 por la RAF inglesa. En una de las paredes, una fotografía grande de la fachada destruida del edificio de la Embajada, también enmarcada, giraba lentamente sobre su eje central sugiriendo el caos y la mezcolanza de los objetos de su interior producido por el vendaval de la historia.

Los primeros años de la posguerra en España, de 1939 a 1945, fueron los de más dura represión política. El celo de los fascistas españoles, no obstante, fue decreciendo a medida que quedaba claro que las fuerzas del Eje (Alemania, Italia y Japón) perdían la guerra mundial. La bomba inglesa que destruyó la Embajada española antes de que pudieran acabar de amueblarla, resume el veredicto de la historia sobre un régimen en completa bancarrota moral, pero que, como las colas de los lagartos, siguió retorciéndose por largo tiempo en España una vez cortado del resto del cuerpo al que pertenecía.

En la sala del año 1973 podía verse una reproducción exacta del automóvil blindado en el que fue asesinado por ETA[3] el almirante Luis Carrero Blanco, heredero político de Franco. Decapitada la continuidad del régimen, el asesinato marca el comienzo de la transición política española. En las paredes de la sala alrededor del automóvil, se encontraban ocho cibachromes con las portadas de otros tantos periódicos dando la noticia del atentado. Las imágenes, sin embargo, estaban todas ellas desenfocadas, como pasadas por el tamiz del tiempo y el desgaste de la memoria, aunque con suficiente registro para ser identificadas. Para la instalación de esta sala traté que el Ministerio de Defensa español prestara el coche real y destrozado de Carrero;[4] la idea era utilizar un sedimento histórico en estado puro y transformarlo en arte, lo mismo que sucedía en la sala del año 43. Por razones políticas que la índole del propio trabajo cuestionaba, no fue posible obtener el coche

perforaron un túnel y una bóveda bajo la calle, la cual llenaron de explosivos. En el día señalado, cuando Carrero Blanco se dirigía a su Ministrerio después de atender misa, volaron su automóvil. La explosión fue de tal fuerza que la limusina salió lanzada en vertical por encima de un edificio monacal de cinco pisos para caer en el claustro del monasterio mientras los monjes rezaban. Carrero, su guardaespaldas y su chófer murieron en el atentado. Milagrosamente, nadie más resultó herido.

4 *El automóvil destruido del Almirante Carrero Blanco estuvo expuesto en el Museo del Ejército en Madrid hasta muy recientemente cuando fue trasladado al Alcázar de Toledo, un edificio histórico de especial significación para la extrema derecha española, tanto civil como militar. Desde el Ministerio de Cultura, el organismo estatal bajo cuya jurisdicción se halla el Alcázar, se está intentando que dicho edificio no se transforme, de facto, en un museo del fascismo español.*

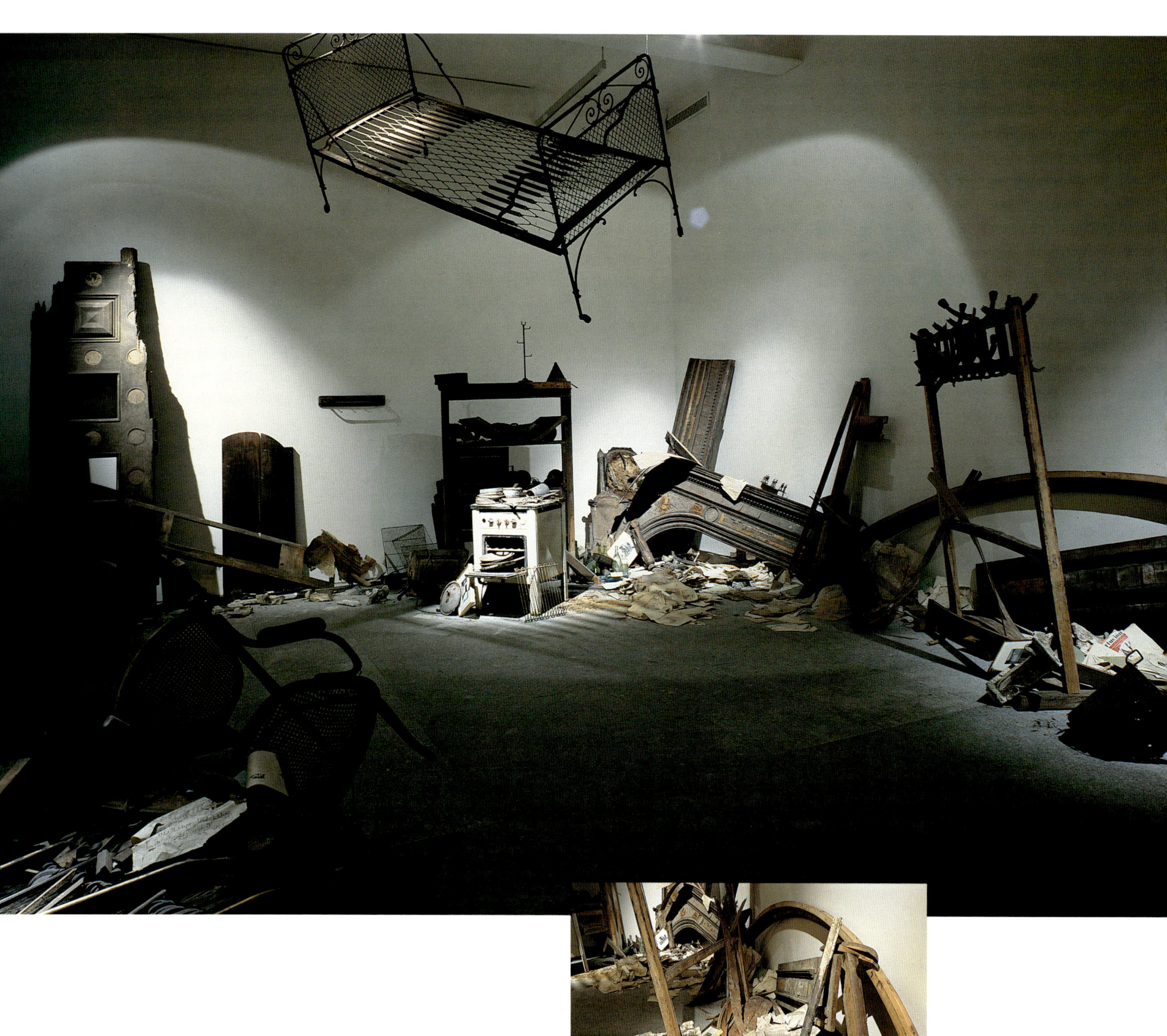

FIFTY RAINS, 1991

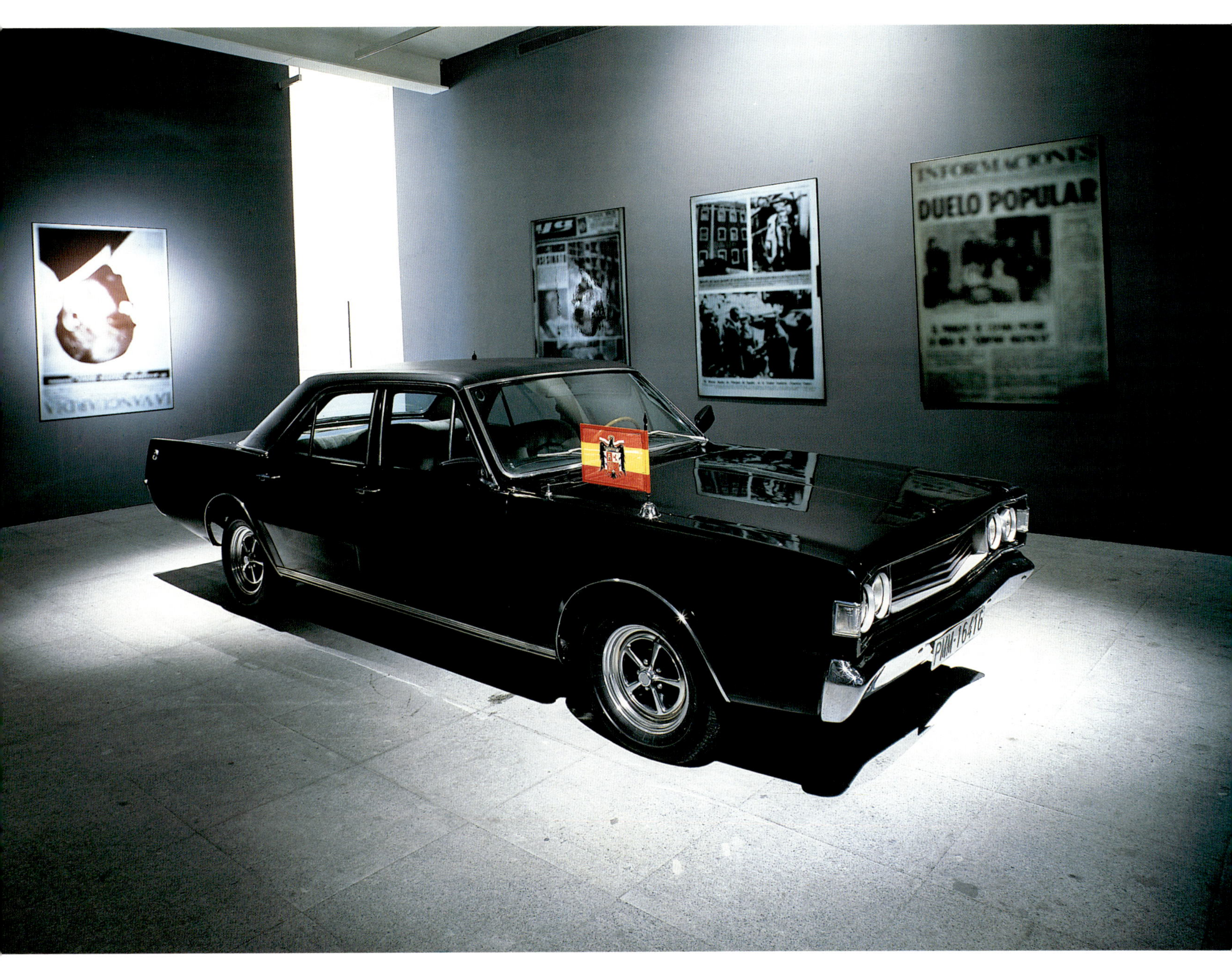
INFORMACIONES
DUELO POPULAR
PMM-16416

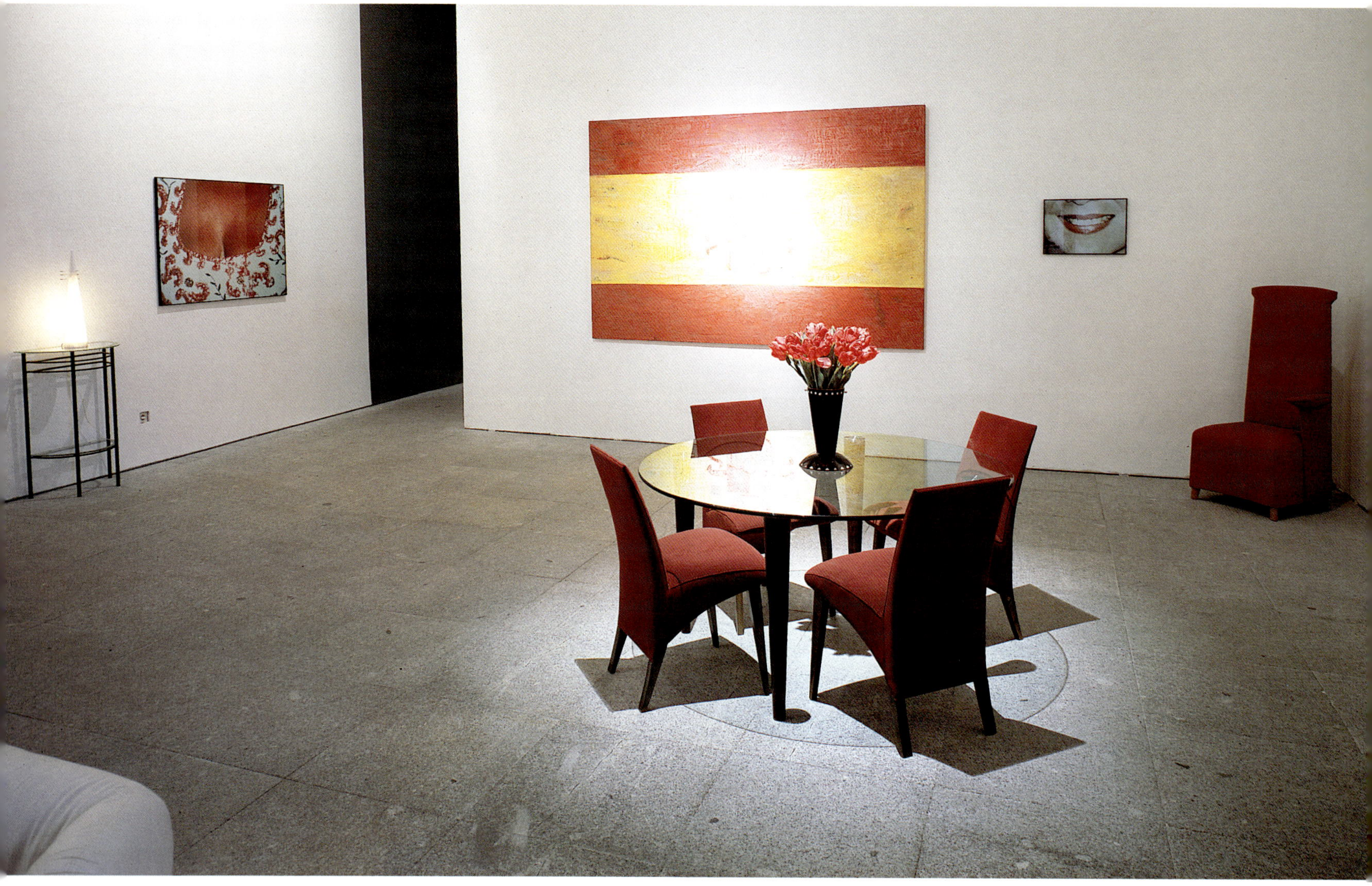

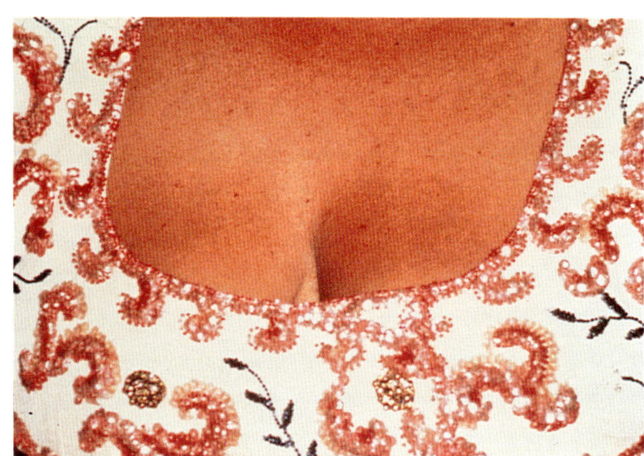

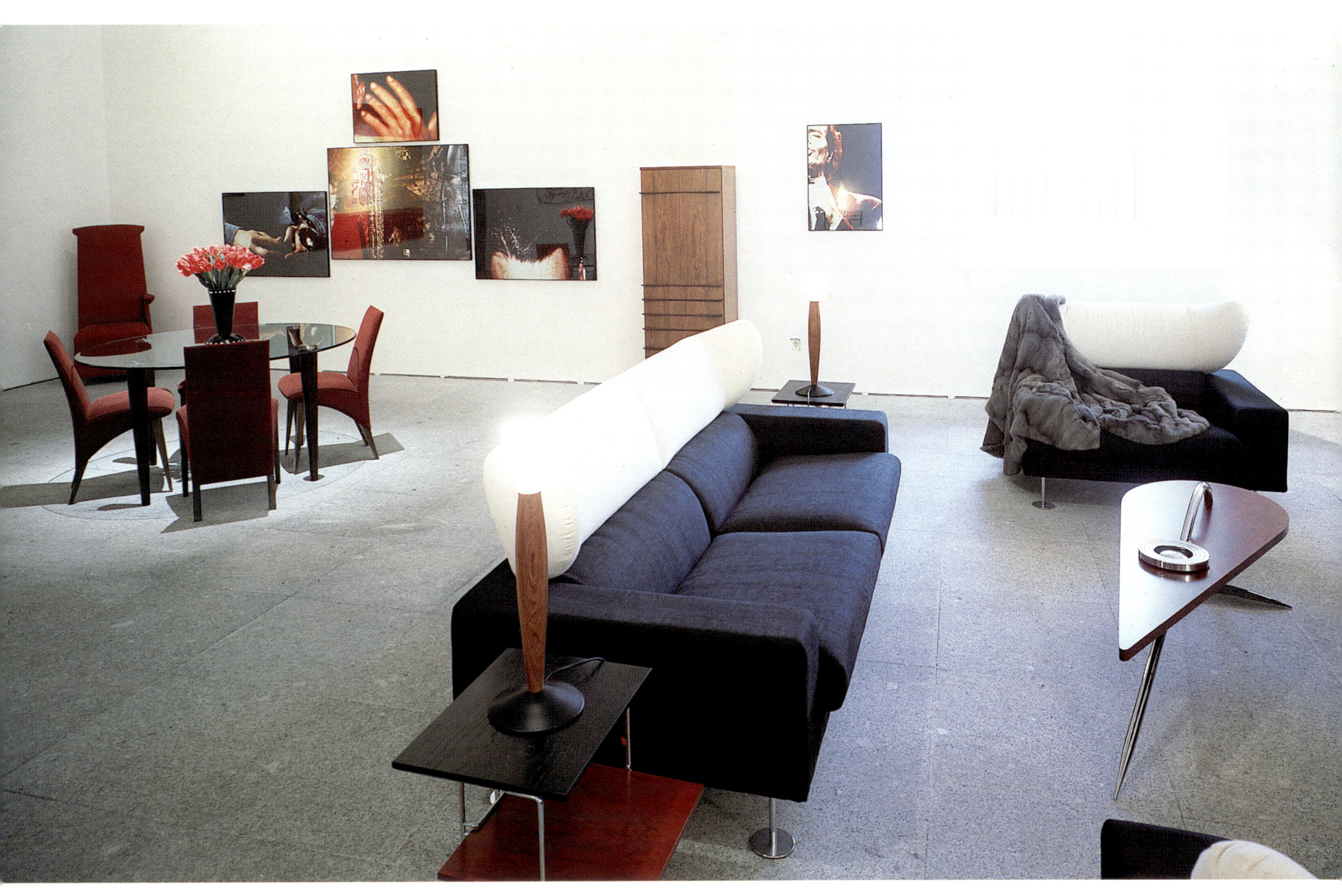

directions: the moments immediately before and after the event, the intact car and the news of its blasting.

In the last room, that of 1993, one found the reproduction of the interior of a refined house. The interior followed the guidelines of the most influential style magazines. All of the furniture was expensive and exclusive, made by name-brand designers, implying a taste that was both bold and vanguard. A fur coat valued at fifty thousand dollars hung over an arm chair. The books on the shelves catalogued those read by the enlightened and rich new classes which govern the country (books by authors such as Habermas, Keynes, Fukuyama, the "new" French philosophers). There was no lack of art on the walls. These works were precisely what informed the matter of such a sublime interior. In the dining area was a large encaustic painting of the Spanish flag in the style of Jasper Johns' painting **Flag**. This referenced the mirage of Spain's role in modern art, a country from which some of the giants of twentieth century art have come (expatriates, educated or recognized out of the country for the most part) and yet has been only marginally integrated into the modern movement. The rest of the art on the walls parodied appropriation. They are enlargements of small fragments of images which had appeared in print media (the earring of Franco's granddaughter, the president's sideburn, the bust of a famous flamenco singer, the handcuffed wrists of an ETA member, etc.). Together they formed a constellation of Spain's social reality, a reality which, as laid out in weekly magazines, appears intermixed without any discernible criteria between the relevant and the totally banal. The only thing which separates the arrest of a terrorist from a sports star's wedding is the advertisement for a luxury car. Everything is worth the same and nothing seems to be too important.

Fifty Rains was shown in 1991, one year before 1992, the Year of Spain. The room for 1993 is that

---

verdadero. La alternativa consistió en obtener un automóvil idéntico y restaurarlo, devolviéndolo a su estado original, incluyendo la reproducción de la matrícula; es decir, retrasar el reloj de la historia hasta un segundo antes de la explosión que costó la vida al heredero franquista. Como resultado, la sala demarcaba dos direcciones temporales opuestas; los momentos inmediatos antes y después del acontecimiento: el automóvil intacto y la noticia de su voladura.

En la última sala, la de 1993, se hallaba reproducido el interior de una casa refinada siguiendo las pautas de las revistas de estilo más influyentes. Todos los muebles eran de diseño de firma, caros y exclusivos pero que denotaban un gusto osado y vanguardista. Sobre una butaca reposaba un abrigo de pieles valorado en cincuenta mil dólares. Los libros de las estanterías eran un catálogo de lo que lee la nueva clase dirigente del país, ilustrada y rica (Habermas, Keynes, Fukuyama, los "nuevos" filósofos franceses, etc.). Las obras de arte no faltaban en las paredes y éstas eran, precisamente, las que ponían en contexto la lectura de tan sublime interior. En el espacio del comedor una gran pintura en encáustica reproducía la bandera española a la manera de la pintura **Flag** de Jaspers Jones, una referencia al espejismo del papel jugado dentro del arte moderno por España, un país que ha dado gigantes del arte del siglo veinte (expatriados, formados o reconocidos en el extranjero en su mayor parte) pero que ha estado sólo tangencialmente integrado en el movimiento moderno. El resto del arte en las paredes parodiaba el apropiacionismo, mostrando ampliaciones de pequeños fragmentos de imágenes que habían aparecido en los medios de comunicación impresa (el pendiente de la nieta de Franco, la patilla del Presidente del gobierno, el busto de una famosa tonadillera, las manos esposadas de un etarra, etc.) y que constituían en conjunto una constelación de la realidad social de España. Una realidad que, como en las revistas semanales de actualidad, aparece mezclada sin ningún criterio

of the unknown and the hangover now that the party is over. Many people are now perplexed as they face an exhausted economy and a Europe with very little sense of community as it looks on like an indolent spectator at a war based on ethnic cleansing in its own backyard. The installation's sound system, common to all three rooms, reinforced the sensation of suspended time: one heard a far off storm and the sound of uninterrupted rainfall. Seen altogether, **Fifty Rains** unfolded like an unstable equilibrium composed of two interiors—one destroyed and the other in suspension, sustained by the fulcrum of an assassination.

Memorial (Hirshhorn Museum and Sculpture Garden, Washington, DC, 1992) follows along the same line of recovering "disappeared" history; disappeared in the Argentine sense of the word. This installation coincided with the first anniversary of the Gulf War. That is the war which, according to Baudrillard,[5] was not going to happen while they were preparing, was not taking place while it was occurring, and had not taken place after it was over. A year after the Allied victory, nobody in the West seemed to remember what had happened. It was a war which had the aesthetic quality of a Paramount Studios back lot and the unreal quality of the first Apollo landing on the moon. The largest air transport mobilization in history and the largest land offensive since World War II did not even dent the emotional consciousness of the Western societies involved in this enormous exploit. With the same speed with which it ignited the television set of the First World War, the technological war was banished from passing into history and dismissed to that dungeon of solitary confinement which is forgetfulness. Maybe we could not believe what we were seeing; maybe we suspected that, just like the televised moonscapes from a quarter century ago, everything could have

[5] *Jean Baudrillard*, La Guerre du Golfe n'a pas eu Lieu, *Editions Galilèe, Paris, 1991.*

discernible entre lo relevante y lo absolutamente banal. Lo único que separa el arresto del terrorista de turno de la boda de una estrella del deporte es el anuncio de un automóvil de lujo. Todo vale por igual, nada parece importar demasiado.

Cincuenta Lluvias se expuso en 1991, un año antes del Año de España, 1992. La sala del '93 es, pués, la de la incógnita y la resaca ahora que la fiesta ha terminado, perplejos muchos ante una ecomomía desvencijada, una Europa muy poco comunitaria, espectadora indolente de una guerra de limpieza étnica en su propio patio. La sensación de tiempo suspendido se veía reforzada por la pista de sonido de la instalación que era común a las tres salas: una tormenta lejana y el sonido de la lluvia cayendo ininterrumpidamente. Vista en conjunto, **Cincuenta Lluvias** se revelaba como el equilibrio inestable de dos interiores, uno destruido y otro en suspensión expectante, sostenidos por el fulcro de un asesinato.

Memorial (Hirshhorn Museum and Sculpture Garden, Washington, DC, 1992) sigue en la línea de recuperación de la historia "desaparecida", en el sentido argentino de la palabra. Esta instalación coincidió con el primer aniversario de la Guerra del Golfo; aquella guerra que, según Baudrillard,[5] no iba a suceder mientras se preparaba, ni tenía lugar mientras estaba ocurriendo, ni había sucedido después de terminada. Al año de la victoria aliada en una guerra que había tenido la calidad estética de las atracciones de patio trasero de los estudios Paramount y la irrealidad de los primeros alunizajes del programa Apolo, nadie en Occidente parecía acordarse de lo sucedido. La mayor mobilización aerotransportada de la historia y la mayor ofensiva terrestre desde la Segunda Guerra Mundial no había dejado el menor rastro emocional colectivo en las sociedades occidentales involucradas en tan gran hazaña. Con la misma rapidez con que había iluminado las pantallas de televisón del Primer Mundo, se desvaneció del lago primigenio de rayos catódicos aquella guerra tecnológica para pasar, no a la

[5] *Jean Baudrillard*, La Guerre du Golfe n'a pas eu Lieu, *Editions Galilèe, Paris, 1991.*

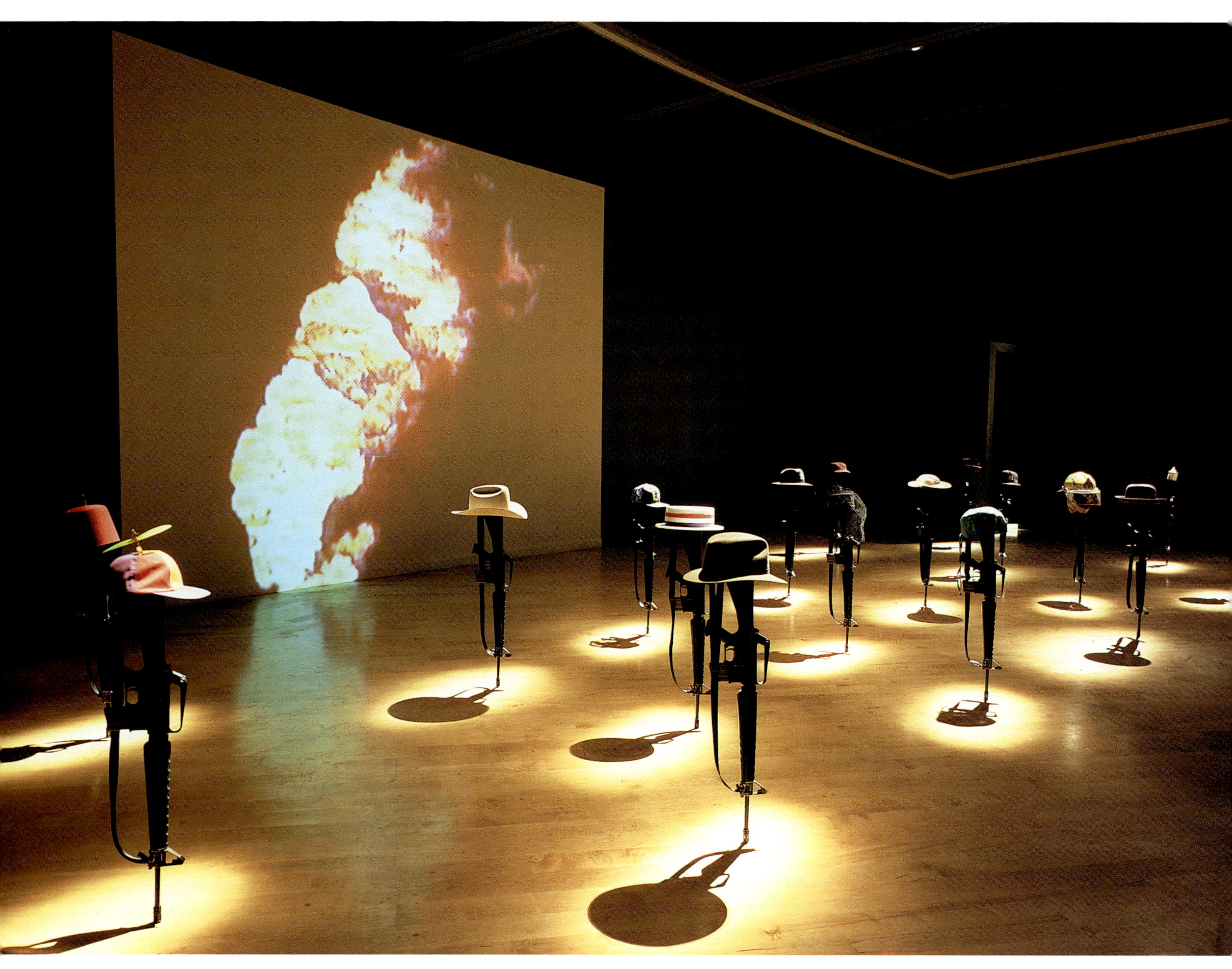

Memorial, 1992

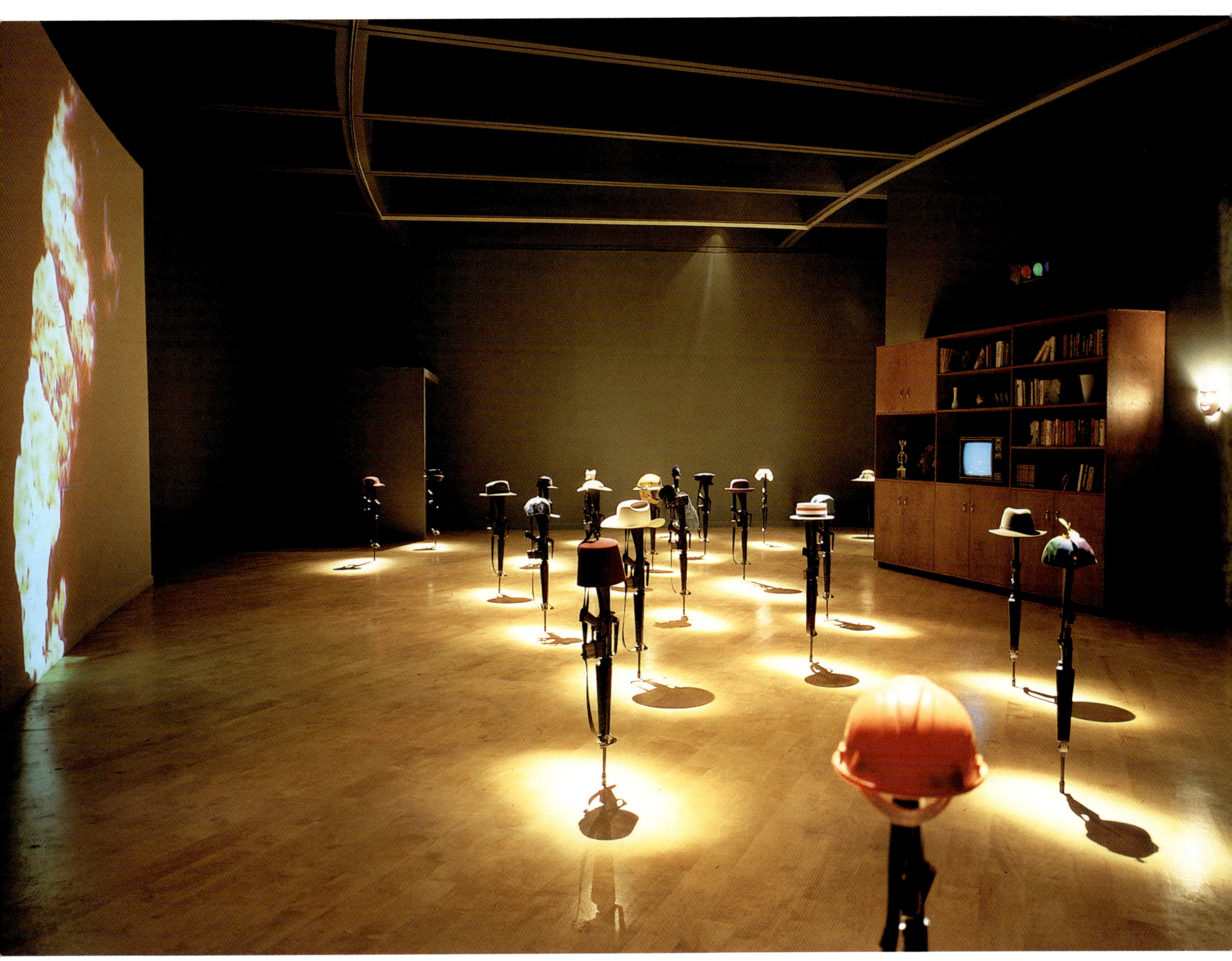

been a stage design, a scenography, made to galvanize the battered moral soul of the market-based societies. Armstrong was not on the moon, Desert Storm took place in the Arizona desert, and the Iraqi tanks were really Egyptian T-72 tanks captured by the Israelis during the Yom Kippur War and handed over much to the Pentagon's curiosity.

As such, the talking heads on the television screen went hoarse repeating time and time again that the weapons used were technological marvels; so marvelous that they documented their own work "neutralizing" the enemy, relegating the correspondents in Saudi Arabia to the inane exercise of interviewing meandering rearguard soldiers. Anyone who had seen the reports from Vietnam knew that war is something else; that it is not a green and grainy landscape filled with fireflies; nor is it the bluish image of a building which is transformed into a blinding glow; nor is it the flight of one eye that ends up slipping through a window, all mute, without screams, without blood, without blackish, broken bodies. The harsh reality escaped from the cage a few times. For instance, when a missile not as intelligent as the others blew up a bomb shelter filled with Iraqi civilians, or when the television cameras finally arrived at the Highway of Death in order to show us cadavers of hundreds of automobiles—blackened receptacles of absent and tangible bodies. When images of broken bodies began to trickle out to remind us that it had been a serious adventure, because, officially, there is no victorious fighter without dead enemies, all sheen of reality had been stolen from the orgy. The Gulf War, so frighteningly banal, was so easy to forget.

Memorial is a reminder of an electronic mirage and a *memento mori* for those who spiritually died while seated in front of the television screen, losing their capacity to discern between truth and lies, silence and screams, life and its simulacra, spectacle and death. The space of the installation was

---

historia, sino a la mazmorra de reclusión en solitario que constituye el olvido. Quizá no nos creíamos lo que estábamos viendo; quizá teníamos la sospecha de que, al igual que con los alunizajes televisados de hace un cuarto de siglo, todo pudiera ser un montaje de bambalinas para galvanizar el alicaído ánimo moral de las sociedades de mercado. Armstrong no estuvo en la Luna; la Tormenta tuvo lugar en el desierto de Arizona; los tanques iraquíes eran en realidad tanques T-72 egipcios capturados por los israelíes durante la guerra de Yom Kippur y entregados a la curiosidad del Pentágono. Entre tanto, las cabezas parlantes en la pantalla de televisión se desgañitaban repetiendo una y otra vez lo tecnomaravillosas que eran las armas utilizadas; tan maravillosas que documentaban su propio trabajo de "neutralización" del enemigo, relegando los reporteros destacados en Arabia Saudí al inane ejercicio de entrevistar a soldados despistados en retaguardia. Cualquiera que hubiera visto los reportajes del Vietnam sabía que la guerra es otra cosa; que no es un paisaje verdoso y granulado repleto de luciérnagas; ni es la imagen azulada de un edificio que se tranforma en resplandor; ni es el vuelo de un ojo que acaba colándose por una ventana, todo ello mudo, sin gritos, sin sangre, sin cuerpos negruzcos, rotos. La realidad fiera se escapó de la jaula algunas veces, como cuando un misil menos inteligente que los otros dió en un refugio de civiles iraquíes o cuando las cámaras de televisión llegaron por fin a la Autopista de la Muerte para mostrarnos los cadáveres de centenas de automóviles, recipientes ennegrecidos de cuerpos ausentes y tangibles. Cuando empezaron a gotear imágenes de muñecos rotos para que no cupiera duda de que la aventura había ido en serio y porque, al fin y al cabo, no hay guerrero vencedor sin enemigos muertos, ya se había hurtado al aquelarre de todo viso de realidad. La Guerra del Golfo, de tan aterradoramente banal, fue de fácil olvido.

Memorial es el recordatorio de un espejismo electrónico y un *memento mori* para aquéllos que

situated around the intersection of three ritual fields: the field of the imaginary cemetery where they provisionally bury the fallen soldiers prior to transporting them to their definitive tomb; the national cemetery, like Arlington in the United States or Verdun in France; and a living room like that of a middle class house. Occupying the space were two dozen M-16 assault rifles standing in equilibrium on their nozzles, a different civilian hat, like the helmet of an unfortunate soldier, hanging over the butt of each rifle. The rifles were arranged in a radial formation oriented towards a generic cabinet of shelves, complete with books and generic domestic objects. Among the objects was a television, switched on, but without a video signal; pure "snow", electronic texture without content, sister of the few tenths of a second prior to the impact of a missile, equipped with a television camera, a one-eyed cyclops fond of entering through the windows like moonlight, mosquitoes and assassins.

Diametrically opposite to the cabinet, a large video projection showed a Kuwaiti oil well burning like the proverbial eternal flame of all military cemeteries, in all the tombs of all the unknown soldiers, although in this case germane to the volcano. The sound of the flames spat out by pressure was done in such a way that it resonated in the viewers' guts more than in their ears; more than a sound, it was a dark and profound vibration. On both sides of the cabinet were two wall lamps whose screens reproduced the two masks of classic theater, making a reference to an event that began as farce and ended as tragedy. Or was it the other way around? Or was it both things at the same time?

The light from the lamps flickered with the same frequency as the vibrations of the sound system. It was as if the flickering were a consequence of the hurricane of fire, a frozen photogram of the last image produced by the storm of steel in the desert.

murieron espirirtualmente sentados frente al televisor, dejando disolver su capacidad de discernimiento entre la verdad y la mentira, entre el silencio y el grito, entre la vida y su simulacro, entre el espectáculo y la muerte. El espacio de la instalación se configura mediante el cruce de tres ámbitos rituales: El cementerio militar de campaña o de emergencia, allí donde se entierra provisionalmente a los soldados caídos hasta el traslado a su tumba definitiva; el Cementerio Nacional, como el de Arlington en Estados Unidos o el de Verdún en Francia; y la sala de estar de una casa particular de clase media. El espacio queda ocupado por dos docenas de fusiles de asalto M-16 apoyados en equilibio sobre su bocana; un sombrero distinto de civil, cual yelmo de soldado menguado en fortuna, reposa sobre la culata de cada uno de ellos. Todos los fusiles se encuentran en disposción radial orientados hacia un mueble-estanteria genérico, repleto de libros y objetos domésticos también genéricos entre los que no falta el televisor, encendido, pero sin señal de vídeo; pura "nieve", textura electrónica sin contenido, hermana de las pocas décimas de segundo posteriores al impacto del misil televisivo, ciclópeo, monocular, aficionado a entrar por las ventanas como los rayos de luna, los mosquitos y los asesinos.

Diametralmente opuesta al mueble, una gran proyección de vídeo muestra un pozo petrolífero kuwaití ardiendo como la proverbial llama eterna en todo cementerio militar, en toda tumba de soldado desconocido, aunque en este caso emparentada con el volcán. El sonido del fuego escupido a presión está trabajado para que funcione más en las entrañas del espectador que en su oreja; más que un sonido es una vibración oscura y profunda. A ambos lados del mueble se encuentran dos lámparas de pared cuyas pantallas reproducen individualmente las dos máscaras del teatro clásico, haciendo referencia a lo que, comenzando como farsa, acabó como tragedia. ¿O fué al revés? ¿O fue ambas cosas al mismo tiempo?

If the two previous works, **Fifty Rains** and **Memorial**, dealt with memory's death by starvation, **Chronicle of Getting Lost** (Church of San Luis de los Franceses, Seville, 1992) made an indirect reference to the assassination of history in order to be able to substitute it for another history. It was like a double imposter in charge of covering the embarrassments and masking the villainies of the family, of transforming the butcher knives hidden under the tiles of the dining room into elegant silverware.

Within the immediate context of the World Expo in Seville in 1992, anchored by the the hysterical and historical commemoration of the fifth centenary of the "discovery" of America, the program of art exhibitions was considered more as decoration than as a part of a dialogue with the Expo's content. There existed a general nervousness about avoiding discordant notes and the fear of demonstrations against the version of the Columbian voyage as an "encounter between cultures" (without noting that some had to pay for such a fatal encounter with their existence) hung over the heads of the organizers like the sword of Damocles. When, thanks to the courage of a few,[6] I was asked to do a project in such a charged atmosphere, my first reaction was to refuse. The danger of fighting against twisted discourses is that it is difficult to avoid giving a twisted response because of the contrived context one faces. It was not easy to maintain a cool head in the face of the intellectual dishonesty and the stupidity of the official attitude surrounding the decaffeinated celebrations of 1992. After ruminating about the matter, I decided to go ahead, convinced that any little act of resistance to what was brewing was worth the effort. Explosive situations can be deactivated, perhaps even reconciled, with a good dosage of the spiritual and rational exercise that is art.

To the disillusionment of my political adversaries, I left the statistics of the genocide at home. In its place, I opted for a work which was going to be the contrary of the unconscionable stammering of our

[6] *Mar Villaespesa was the curator of the series of exhibitions under the title of* PLUS ULTRA, *commissioned by the Government of Andalucía. She withstood political pressure to exclude me from the show by threatening to resign and take the entire project with her.*

La luz de las lámparas parpadea con la misma frecuencia que la vibración de la pista de sonido, de manera que parece que el parpadeo sea consecuencia de la tormenta de fuego, fotograma congelado de la última imagen producida por la tormenta de acero en el desierto.

Si las dos obras precedentes, **Cincuenta Lluvias** y **Memorial**, trataban de la muerte por inanición de la memoria, **Crónica del Extravío** (Iglesia de San Luis de los Franceses, Sevilla, 1992) hacía referencia indirecta al asesinato de la historia para poderla substituir por otra historia; una especie de doble impostora encargada de cubrir las vergüenzas y enmascarar las villanías de la familia, de transformar en cubertería de plata los cuchillos de verdugo ocultos bajo las tablas de la biblioteca.

Dentro del contexto inmediato de la Exposición Universal de Sevilla de 1992, anclada histérica e históricamente por la conmemoración del quinto centenario del "descubrimiento" de América, la programación de exposiciones de arte estaba pensada más como decoración del evento que como parte de un diálogo con su contenido. Existía un cierto nerviosismo generalizado por evitar notas discordantes y el temor a manifestaciones contra la versión del viaje colombino como "encuentro entre culturas" (sin añadir que algunas de ellas pagaron con su existencia tan fatal casualidad), planeaba como una espada de Damocles sobre las cabezas de los organizadores. Cuando, gracias al coraje de unos pocos,[6] se me propuso hacer un proyecto en tan cargada atmósfera, mi primera reacción fue negarme. El peligro de pelear contra discursos torcidos es que es difícil no acabar dando una respuesta también torcida por lo forzada. No era fácil mantener la cabeza fría ante la deshonestidad intelectual y la tontería de la actitud oficial ante las celebraciones descafeinadas de 1992. Después de rumiar el asunto, decidí dar el salto, convencido de que cualquier pequeño acto de

[6] *Mar Villaespesa fue la comisaria de la serie de proyectos especiales bajo el título de* PLUS ULTRA, *encargado por la Junta de Andalucía (gobierno autónomo). La Sra. Villaespesa resistió fuertes presiones institucionales en contra mía amenazando con abandonar el proyecto si no se aceptaba mi participación.*

leaders; definitively, for a meditation protected by art, for something which could serve as a final point to five hundred years of half-truths which are, in fact, more insidious than lies.

The Church of San Luis de los Franceses is a jewel of Andalusian Baroque which, because of a series of historical sweepstakes, is not used for religious services. This circumstance gave me the opportunity to utilize it as an installation space completely incorporated into the piece's content. The majority of Sevillian churches are a consequence of Seville's richness, a wealth which is a direct result of the colonization of the Americas. Seville was the port of entry and center of distribution for the spoils of overseas pillaging and, although this booty was consumed in Europe's imperial wars of religion, that which remained in Seville was sufficient to make the city very economically powerful. As such, a church in Seville, more than in any other place, represents a point of confluence of that which was exported to the Americas (the culture of Spain's Counter-reform) with that which was imported from the Americas (the gold, in its literal and metaphorical aspects—solar symbol of masculinity, intelligence, purity, power, richness, etc.).

The Church of San Luis offers unusual acoustic qualities thanks to the enormous quantity of wood and the profusion of textures and nooks. It seemed logical to take advantage of this characteristic so that the sound system became the nucleus of the installation. The rest of the elements would not fight with the architecture but would become allied with them.

I began by uncovering the reliquary in the base of the altar, removing the wooden cover which had been painted like *faux marbre*. The reliquary was composed of dozens of little receptacles in which teeth, finger phalanges, hair and other remains of saints were placed under glass, identified by minuscule handwritten labels. In the center, there was a niche which had sheltered a crystal urn

resistencia valía la pena ante lo que se avecinaba, y de que situaciones explosivas pueden desactivarse, quizá incluso reconciliarse, con el bálsamo del espíritu y de la razón que es el arte.

Para desilusión de mis adversarios políticos, dejé en casa las estadísticas del genocidio. Opté en su lugar por una obra que iba a ser lo contrario de la inconsciencia gagá de nuestros líderes; opté, en definitiva, por una meditación protegida por el arte, por algo que pudiera servir de punto final a quinientos años de medias verdades que son, de hecho, más insidiosas que las mentiras.

La iglesia de San Luis de los Franceses es una joya del barroco andaluz que, por una serie de avatares históricos, no está dedicada al culto. Esta circunstancia me dio la oportunidad de utilizarla como espacio de instalación totalmente incorporado al contenido de la pieza. La mayoría de las iglesias sevillanas son, huelga decirlo, consecuencia de su riqueza, pero de una riqueza muy particular y resultado directo de la colonización de las américas. Sevilla fue el puerto de recibo y distribución del expolio de ultramar, y aunque dicho botín fue consumido en las guerras imperiales de religión en Europa, lo que quedó en Sevilla fue suficiente para hacerla una ciudad económicamente poderosa. De ahí que una iglesia en Sevilla, más que en cualquier otra parte, represente el punto de confluencia de lo que se exportó a las américas, la cultura de la España de la Contrarreforma, con lo que se importó de ellas, el oro, en su aspecto literal y metafórico (símbolo solar de masculinidad, inteligencia, pureza, poder, riqueza, etc.).

La iglesia de San Luis, gracias a la ingente cantidad de maderas y a la profusión de texturas y recovecos, ofrece unas cualidades acústicas fuera de lo corriente, y me pareció lógico aprovechar esta característica para que la pista de sonido fuese el núcleo de la instalación. El resto de los elementos no iban a pelear con la arquitectura sino a aliarse con ella.

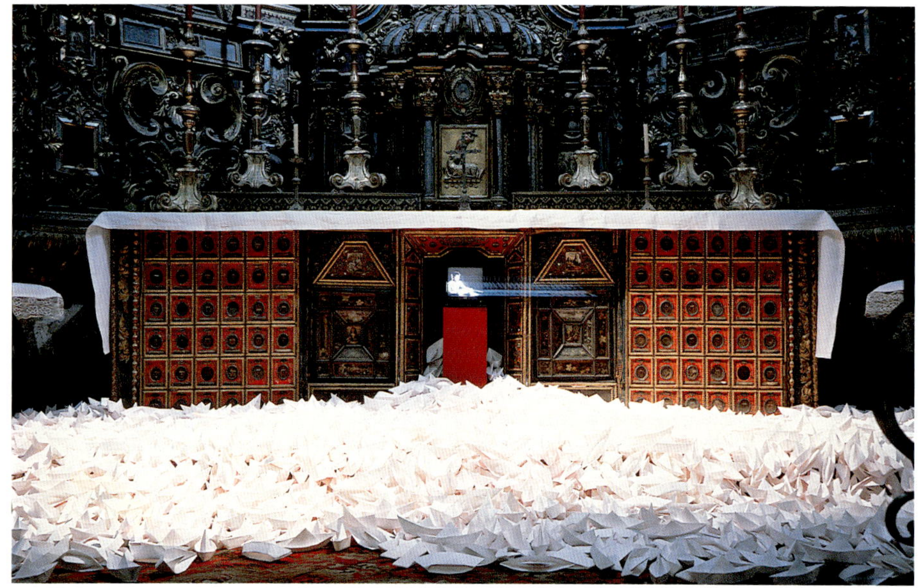

Chronicle of Getting Lost, 1992

containing the remains of some important saint. There I placed a small 8" video monitor on which one could see a short sequence of a boy, easily identifiable as a Native American, seated at a table and reading a heavy book from the sixteenth century. At a given moment, the top of the table would turn into a miniature sea upon which three little paper ships sailed toward the boy. When he noticed them, he lifted his head, and with one blow of his breath, he made them disappear. The stormy blow was synchronized and integrated into the general sound system. The small lit point of the monitor, the young boy reading history as written by the conquerors, seemed to sustain the massive bulk of the main altar. From behind the base of the small monitor, a cascade of little paper boats fell—all swept away by the breath—invading the altar and the greater part of the church's nave. These boats (perhaps all of those which crossed the Sea of Darkness laden with riches or hungry for gold) were made by children from several schools in Seville, and amounted to approximately 20,000 vessels which created a whiteness of sea foam. They surrounded a lone seated figure on one of the church pews. It was the figure of Columbus, in a pensive mood, holding a paper

---

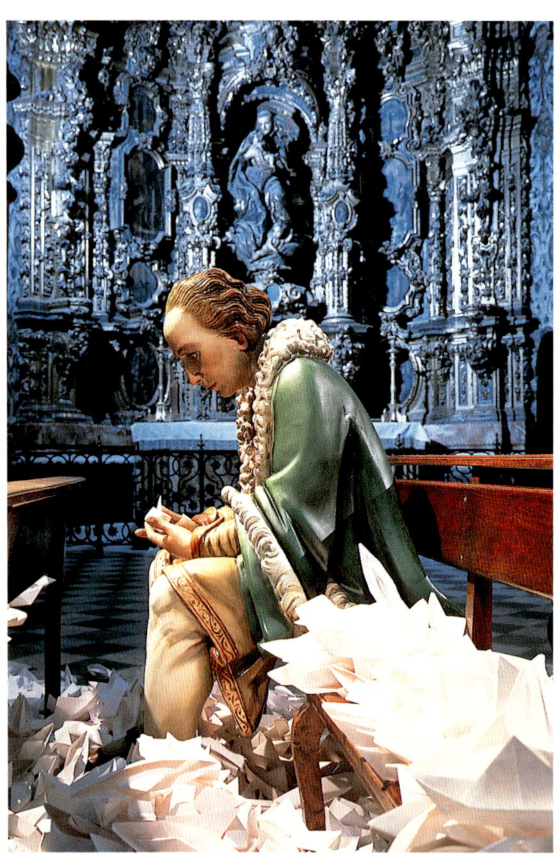

Chronicle of Getting Lost, 1992

Empecé por descubrir el relicario en la base del altar sacándole la cobertura de madera pintada como *faux marbre*. El relicario estaba compuesto de docenas de pequeños receptáculos en los que, bajo cristal, se guardaban dientes, falanges de dedo, pelo y otros restos de santos, identificados por una minúscula etiqueta manuscrita. En el centro se encontraba una hornacina que había albergado una urna de cristal con los restos de algún santo importante. Ahí coloqué un pequeño monitor de vídeo de 8" en el que podía verse una corta secuencia de un muchacho, fácilmente identificable como nativo americano, sentado a una mesa y leyendo un pesado libro del siglo XVI. En un momento determinado, la superficie de la mesa se transformaba en un mar en miniatura en el que aparecían, navegando hacia el muchacho, tres barquitos de papel. Cuando el chico se apercibía de ellos, levantaba la cabeza y de un soplo los hacía desaparecer. El soplo tormentoso estaba sincronizado e integrado a la pista de sonido general. El pequeño punto luminoso del monitor, el joven muchacho lector de la historia escrita por sus conquistadores, parecía sostener la imponente mole del altar mayor. De detrás de la base del pequeño monitor caía una cascada de barquitos de papel (todos los arrastrados por el soplo huracanado) que invadía el altar y la mayor parte de la nave de la iglesia. Dichos barquitos, ¿todos los que cruzaron el Mar Tenebroso cargados o hambrientos de riquezas?, realizados por los niños de varias escuelas sevillanas, sumaban alrededor de veinte mil y creaban una blancura de espuma marina que

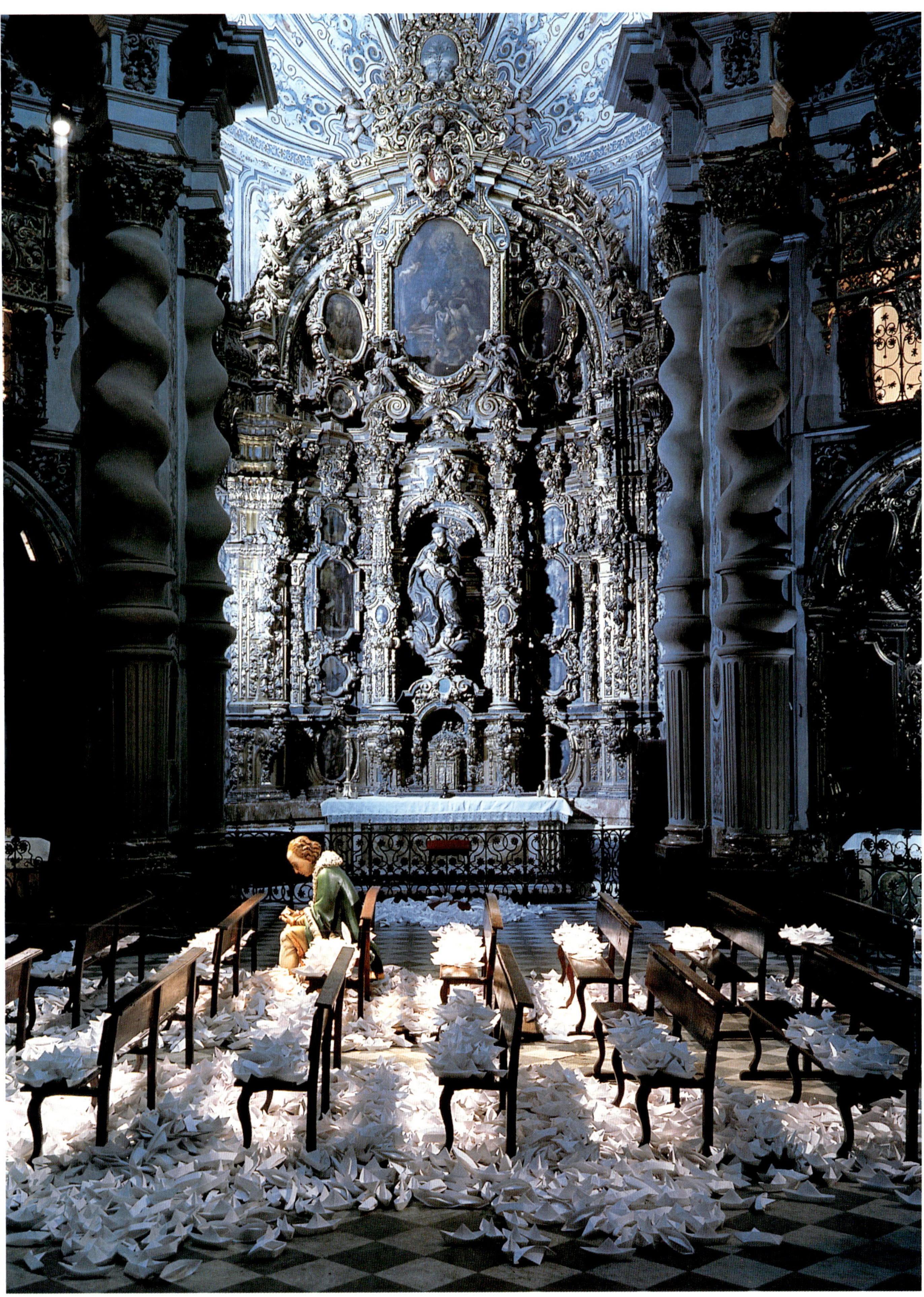

boat in his hands. The polychrome figure incorporated elements of the Columbus found in school textbooks with the veneer of a Baroque image, like those of the extolled saints in the surrounding altars.

All of this was visual support for the soundtrack which floated over the church's space, repeating on a half-hour cycle. This soundtrack contained a dialogue between Columbus, spread out and split in time (the triumphant navigator and able courtesan on the one hand and the decrepit and senile Columbus, incapable of following the thread of his own story, on the other) and a feminine character with a strong Caribbean accent, who forced him to remember as she questioned his words, fantasies, and intentions.

Chronicle of Getting Lost was a work realized with rage, fury, sadness, and compassion for those who believe that history is controllable, that history can be rewritten when the results are too terrible for a beatific spiritual peace or too eloquent for the time at which we seek to portray what we are.

I will go on, now, to comment on the installation **Too Late for Goya**. This installation constitutes the axis of the exhibition which generated this book while also presenting a condensation of the discursive line of my latest works, all of which are camouflaged as an epilogue to a century. The installation binds together a two-fold discourse. Behind the formal veil of a reflection on historic representation, the installation offers a political portrait of the passionate and stormy twentieth century which is now nearing its end. This century has seen the most brutally accelerated changes in all of humankind's history. There have been other such fundamental moments in humanity's parade, like the appearance of agriculture, the creation of cities or the Renaissance, to cite a few examples. But none of them can compare, in intensity at least, with the century that believed in the possibility of Utopia and burned its eyes and soul on the shining of Hiroshima.

---

rodeaba a una figura solitaria sentada en uno de los bancos de la iglesia. Se trataba de la figura de Colón, en actitud pensativa, sosteniendo entre sus manos uno de los barcos de papel. Dicha figura, policromada, incorporaba a partes iguales al Colón de las ilustraciones de los libros escolares y al acabado de una imagen barroca como las de los santos encaramados en los altares que la rodeaban.

Todo lo descrito era el soporte visual de la pista de sonido, de media hora de ciclo, que flotaba por el espacio de la iglesia. Dicha banda sonora contenía un diálogo entre un Colón desdoblado y escindido en el tiempo (el navegante triunfador y hábil cortesano por un lado, y el Colón decrépito y senil, incapaz de seguir el hilo de su propia historia, por el otro) y un personaje femenino de fuerte acento caribeño que le fuerza a recordar mientras le cuestiona sus palabras, entelequias e intenciones.

Crónica del Extravío fue un trabajo realizado con grandes dosis de rabia, tristeza y compasión por aquellos que creen que la historia es controlable hasta el extremo de llegar a reescribirla cuando sus resultados son demasiado terribles para la paz beatífica del espíritu, o demasiado elocuentes a la hora de retratar lo que somos.

Paso a comentar ahora la instalación **Too Late for Goya**, que constituye el eje de la exhibición que ha generado este libro y que presenta una condensación de la línea discursiva de mis últimos trabajos, camuflado todo ello de punto final de un siglo. Se trata de una instalación enlazada en un discurso a dos bandas: bajo el envoltorio formal de una reflexión sobre la representación histórica se ofrece un retrato político de este apasionante y atormentado siglo veinte, ya casi fenecido, que ha visto los cambios más brutalmente acelerados de toda la historia de la especie humana. Ha habido otros momentos fundamentales en el andar de la humanidad, como la aparición de la agricultura, la creación

The conceptual framework of the piece consists of crossing the classic and traditional strategy of historical representation—narrative painting with the electronic image; that which unites the aspect of historic residue implicit in television with the artistic dimension provided by video (art). The objective is to create a historic-electronic salon in which the exhibited images simultaneously share the static quality of a painted image with the kinetic quality of an electronic image in movement.

The video projections show the six most important political events of the century: the Russian Revolution (1917), Hitler's rise to power (1933), the Yalta Conference (1945), the creation of the State of Israel (1948), the process of decolonization exemplified by Algeria's war of independence (1963) and Gorbachev's rise to power (1985). These events were selected after several academic consultations which weighed importance on the basis of the events' subsequent consequences and their universal historic dimensions. Hiroshima, as an example of an event which is not included, was really an act of military technological character which ushered in a new generation of arms with such destructive potential that it effectively affected the political decisions for the duration of the Cold War; however, without the component of absolute terror, one can also say the same about aeronautics or computer technology applied to military ends and the corresponding political decisions to use them in anger. The Jewish Holocaust during World War II, as another example, was a tragedy of indescribable dimensions that served, without doubt, as an impetus to create Israel. In and of itself, however, it did not leave a political legacy which conclusively affected the possibility of repeating the barbarism, neither transforming the nature of power relations nor eliminating racism. As evidence of what I am saying, one could take the genocide in Cambodia during the seventies or the inter-ethnic war in the Balkans which goes on

de las ciudades, o el Renacimiento, por citar algunos ejemplos, pero ninguno de ellos puede compararse, en intensidad al menos, con el siglo que creyó en la posibilidad de la Utopía y abrasó sus ojos y su alma en el resplandor de Hiroshima.

El marco conceptual de la pieza consiste en cruzar la estrategia clásica y tradicional de representación histórica —la pintura narrativa— con la imagen electrónica, la cual aúna el aspecto de sedimento histórico directo implícito en la televisión, con la dimensión artística dada por el vídeo(arte). El objetivo es crear un salón histórico-electrónico en el que las imágenes expuestas comparten simultáneamente la calidad estática de la imagen pintada con la calidad cinética de la imagen electrónica en movimiento.

Las proyecciones de vídeo muestran los seis eventos políticos más importantes de este siglo, a saber: la Revolución Rusa (1917), la subida de Hitler al poder (1933), la Conferncia de Yalta (1945), la creación del Estado de Israel (1948), el proceso de descolonización ejemplificado por la guerra y la independencia de Argelia (1963), y la subida de Gorbachov al poder (1985). Los eventos fueron escogidos, después de varias consultas académicas, en función de sus consecuencias posteriores y de su dimensión histórica mundial. Hiroshima, como ejemplo de evento no incluido, fue en realidad un hecho de carácter tecnológico-militar que abrió una nueva generación de armas de tal potencia destructora que afectó efectivamente las decisiones políticas durante los cuarenta años de guerra fría; no obstante, sin el componente del terror absoluto, también puede decirse lo mismo de la aeronáutica o la informática aplicadas a fines militares y a las correspondientes decisiones políticas de su utilización en el uso de la fuerza. El Holocausto judío durante la Segunda Guerra Mundial, por poner otro ejemplo, fue una tragedia de indescriptibles dimensiones que sirvió, sin duda, para dar impulso a la

even as I write this text. The criteria reside in the decisions, accords or conflicts of a character that is strictly political—and also ideological—with sufficient impact over time to have changed the century's topographic history.

It is possible that, for the majority of people, some events like the Algerian War (I did not know whether to use this example or that of the Congo), seem surprising because of their obscurity as political paradigms in the twentieth century. Also, the images might not appear to be particularly compelling. It should be enough to have in mind that decolonization, of which Algeria's independence is particularly representative because it was obtained in the face of a first rate metropolis, very quickly multiplied the number of countries in the world. The impact was of tremendous magnitude as it affected the politics of the opposing blocks during the Cold War. In regard to the possibility of incorporating images which are not spectacular in an epic fashion, I am satisfied that it is this way; it is an efficient way to emphasize the image on film or video with its higher "reality index." Although readily manipulated, newsreel images are tougher to pin down than a painted image, which is more ductile and, as such, more suitable for exaltation.

For each of the cited events, six seconds of original material were imprinted on a videodisc. A computer extends these six second segments into half an hour of playing time in such a way that the changes can only be detected when observed for an extensive period. When it arrives at the last videogram, it goes backwards to the beginning and successively continues. The image is virtually static (pictorial) and objectively kinetic (videographic). The advance of all of the projections is synchronized in such a way that every ten seconds a pulsation is produced in each of them which coincides with the advance of the videogram.

---

creación del Estado de Israel; en sí misma, sin embargo, no dejó un legado político que afectase de forma concluyente la posibilidad de la repetición de la barbarie, transformase la naturaleza de las relaciones de poder o eliminase el racismo, valgan como prueba de ello el genocidio en Camboya en los años setenta o la guerra interétnica que tiene lugar actualmente en los Balcanes. El criterio, repito, reside en decisiones, acuerdos o conflictos de carácter estrictamente político —y también ideológico— con suficiente impacto en el tiempo como para haber cambiado la topografía histórica del siglo. Es posible que, para la inmensa mayoría de la gente, algunos hechos como la guerra de Argelia (estuve dudando entre ésta y la del Congo) parezcan algo sorprendentes por su oscuridad como paradigmas políticos del siglo XX, y que incluso las imágenes no les parezcan particularmente arrebatadoras. Baste con tener en cuenta que como resultado del proceso de descolonización, del cual la independencia de Argelia es estandarte por haber sido obtenida frente a una metrópolis de primera fila, se multiplicó el número de países del mundo en poquísimo tiempo, con un impacto de primera magnitud dentro de la política de bloques enfrentados. En lo referente a la posible poca espectacularidad épica de alguna imagen, me satisface que así sea; es una forma eficaz de enfatizar el hecho de que la imagen filmada o videografiada, debido a su más elevado "índice de realidad", aunque manipulable, es más cerril que la imagen pintada, que es a su vez, más dúctil y por lo tanto más idónea para la exaltación.

De cada uno de los eventos citados se tomaron seis segundos de material original y se imprimieron en videodisco. Un ordenador se encarga, en tiempo real, de extender a media hora la duración de dichos seis segundos, de manera que los cambios sólo se aprecian con un dilatado tiempo de observación. Al llegar al último videograma, vuelve hacia atrás hasta llegar al principio y así

Perched over a stylized steel chair, a realistic figure of a chimpanzee is lost in thought observing the political icons deposited throughout the century; the fading traces of events which, like seismic movements, have dragged about innumerable human beings, destroyed cities, raised mountains, moved boundaries and created and erased beliefs. The steel chair is mounted upon a base which spins in a 120 degree arc, aiding the sweep of the perplexed chimpanzee's innocent gaze. The chimp is the lucky relative, free of fault by the grace of a single chromosome of difference between that which distinguishes the genetic code of his species and our own.

In the corner of the room, a television, turned to the news station CNN, continuously spits out events of the present, the embryonic history devoid of time's patina, a historical plasma which is more allied with biology than with consciousness, an almost organic residue of the species' body.

Julian Beck, co-founder with Judith Malina of the Living Theater, once said that in order to know the truth, one must have the courage to confront the horror. If this is certain, there is no doubt that in his last epoch Goya must have known the truth by taming horror (history?) with art. It remains to be known how he would have done it had he been born later; late enough to be a son of the terrifying century of the prodigies and of the failed redemption, on the earth and in the heavens, of the impatient primate, victim and deluded maker of his own existence.

sucesivamente. La imagen es virtualmente estática (pictórica) y objetivamente cinética (videográfica). El avance de todas las proyecciones está sincronizado, de modo que cada diez segundos se produce una pulsación en todas ellas que coincide con el avance del videograma.

Encaramado sobre una estilizada silla de hierro, una figura realista de un chimpancé observa ensimismado los iconos políticos sedimentados por el siglo, trazas de otros tantos hechos que, como los movimentos sísmicos, han arrastrado a incontables seres humanos, destruido ciudades, levantado montañas, movido fronteras, creado y borrado creencias. La silla de hierro está montada, a su vez, sobre una base que gira en un arco de 120 grados, ayudando el paseo de la inocente mirada perpleja del chimpancé, pariente afortunado, libre de culpa gracias al único cromosoma de diferencia entre el código genético de su especie y la nuestra.

En un rincón de la sala, un televisor sintonizado con la cadena de noticias CNN escupe sin parar el presente, la historia aún embrionaria sin pátina temporal, más aliada de la biología que de la consciencia, un residuo casi orgánico del cuerpo de la especie.

Julian Beck, co-fundador con Judith Malina del Living Theater, dijo una vez que para conocer la verdad hay que tener el coraje de enfrentarse al horror. Si eso es cierto, no cabe duda de que Goya debió conocer en su última época la verdad, mediante la doma del horror (¿la historia?) con el arte. Quedará por saber cómo lo hubiera hecho de haber nacido más tarde, lo suficiente para ser hijo del pavoroso siglo de los prodigios y de la fallida redención, en la tierra y en los cielos, del primate impaciente, víctima y artífice alucinado de su existencia.

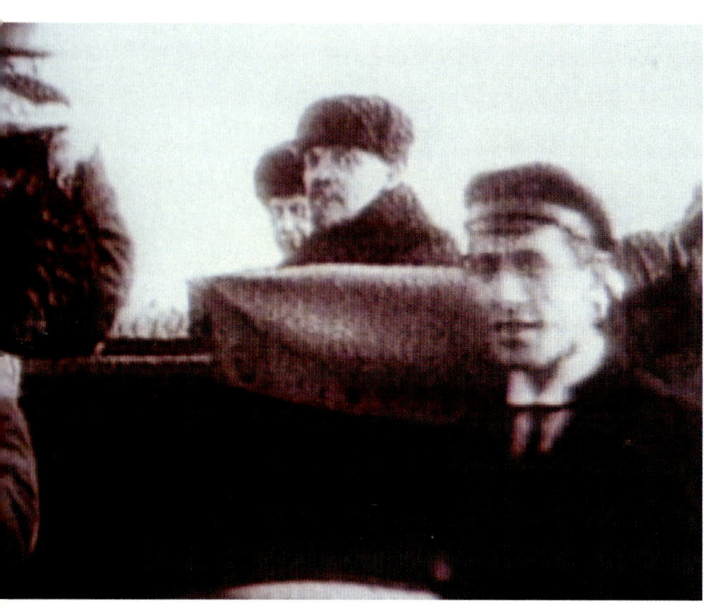

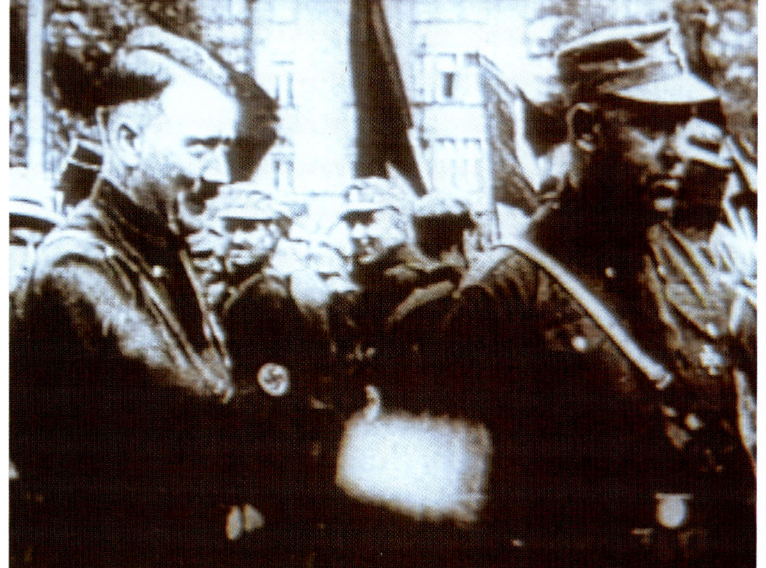

The projected images are, from left to right:

The Russian Revolution, 1917
Vladimir Ilyich Ulyanov (Lenin)

German General Elections, 1933
Adolf Hitler

Yalta Conference, 1945
Winston Churchill,
Franklin Delano Roosevelt,
Joseph Stalin, Francesc Torres

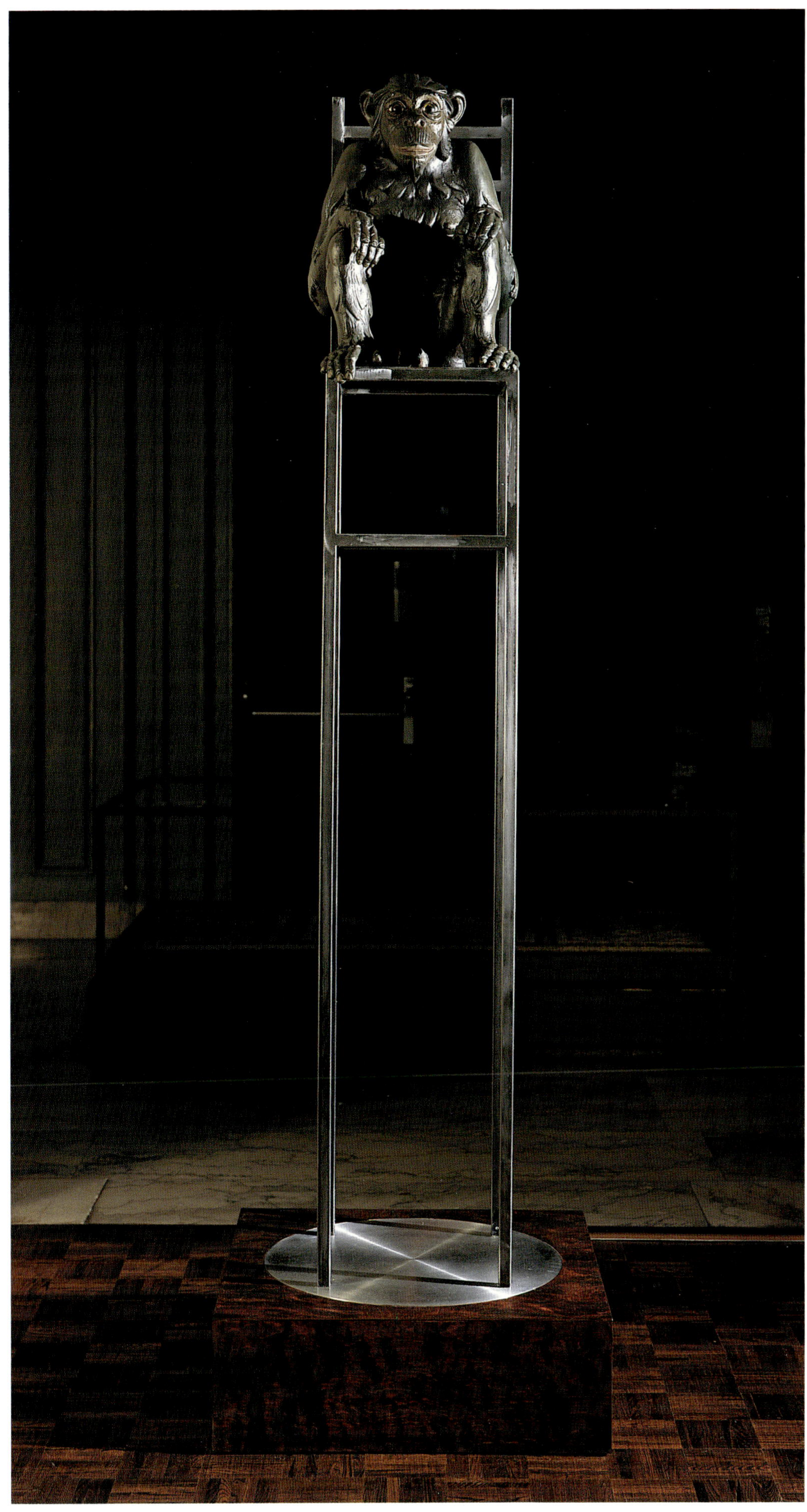

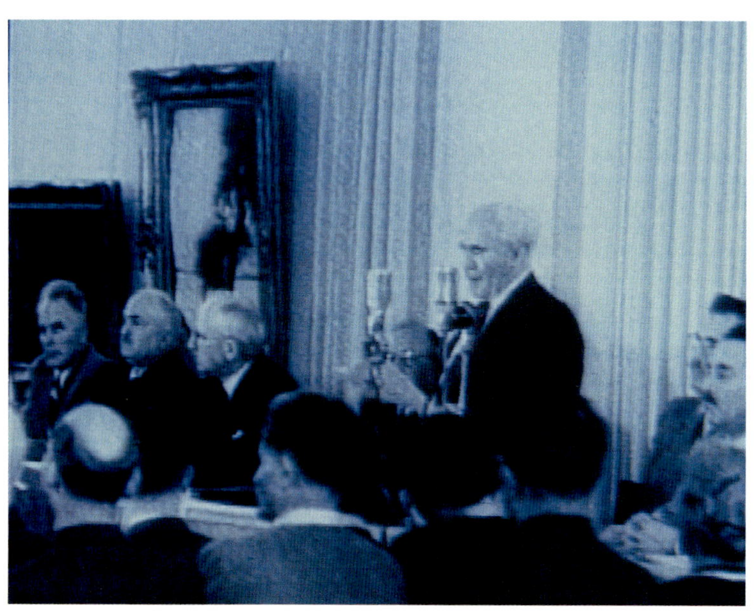

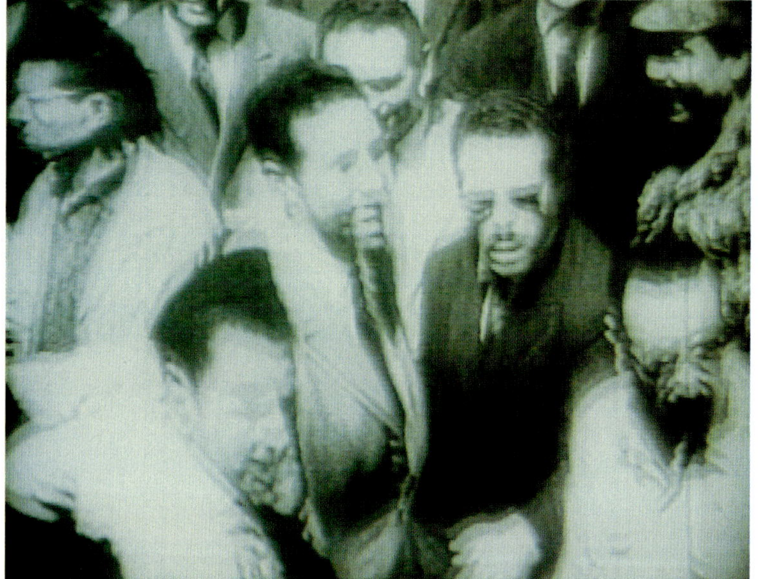

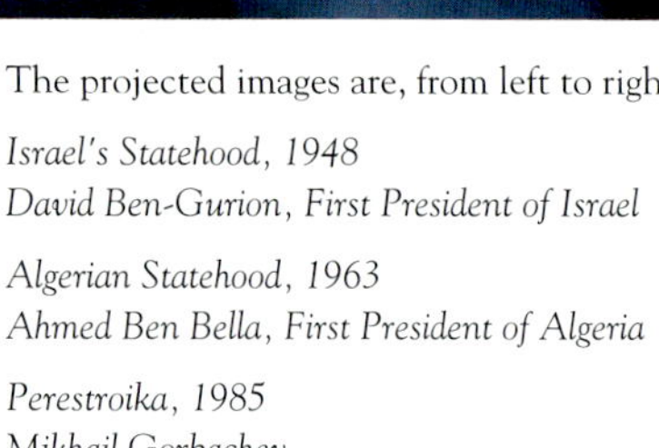

The projected images are, from left to right:

Israel's Statehood, 1948
David Ben-Gurion, First President of Israel

Algerian Statehood, 1963
Ahmed Ben Bella, First President of Algeria

Perestroika, 1985
Mikhail Gorbachev

Far right:

Francisco de Goya y Lucientes
Subir y bajar (To Rise and to Fall),
from Los Caprichos, *1797-1799*
Etching and aquatint, 7 1/4 x 5 inches
Courtesy of Memorial Art Gallery, Rochester, New York

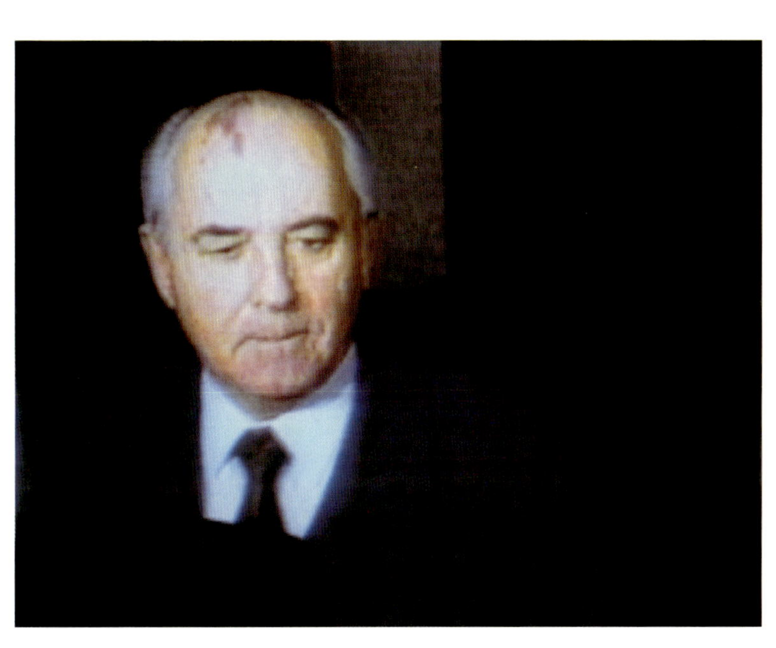

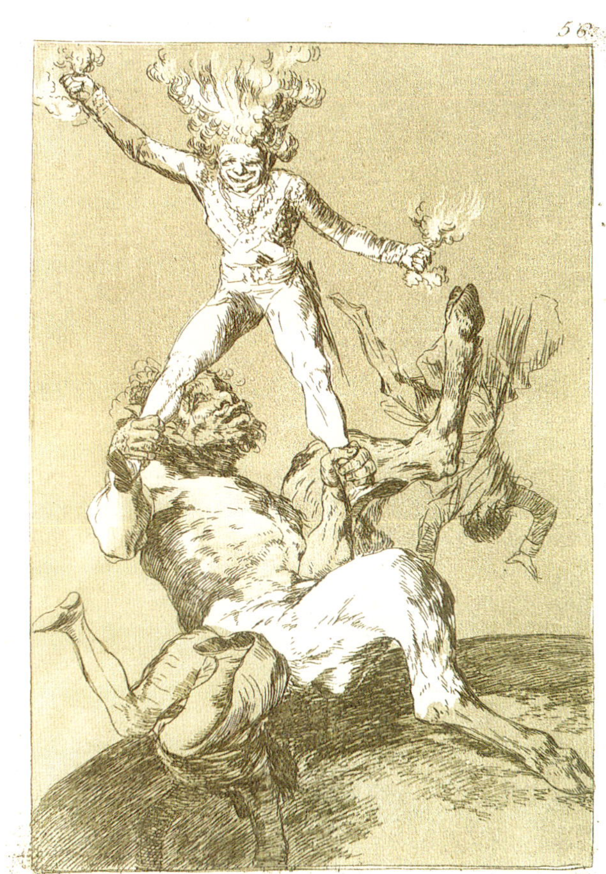
56.
Subir y bajar.

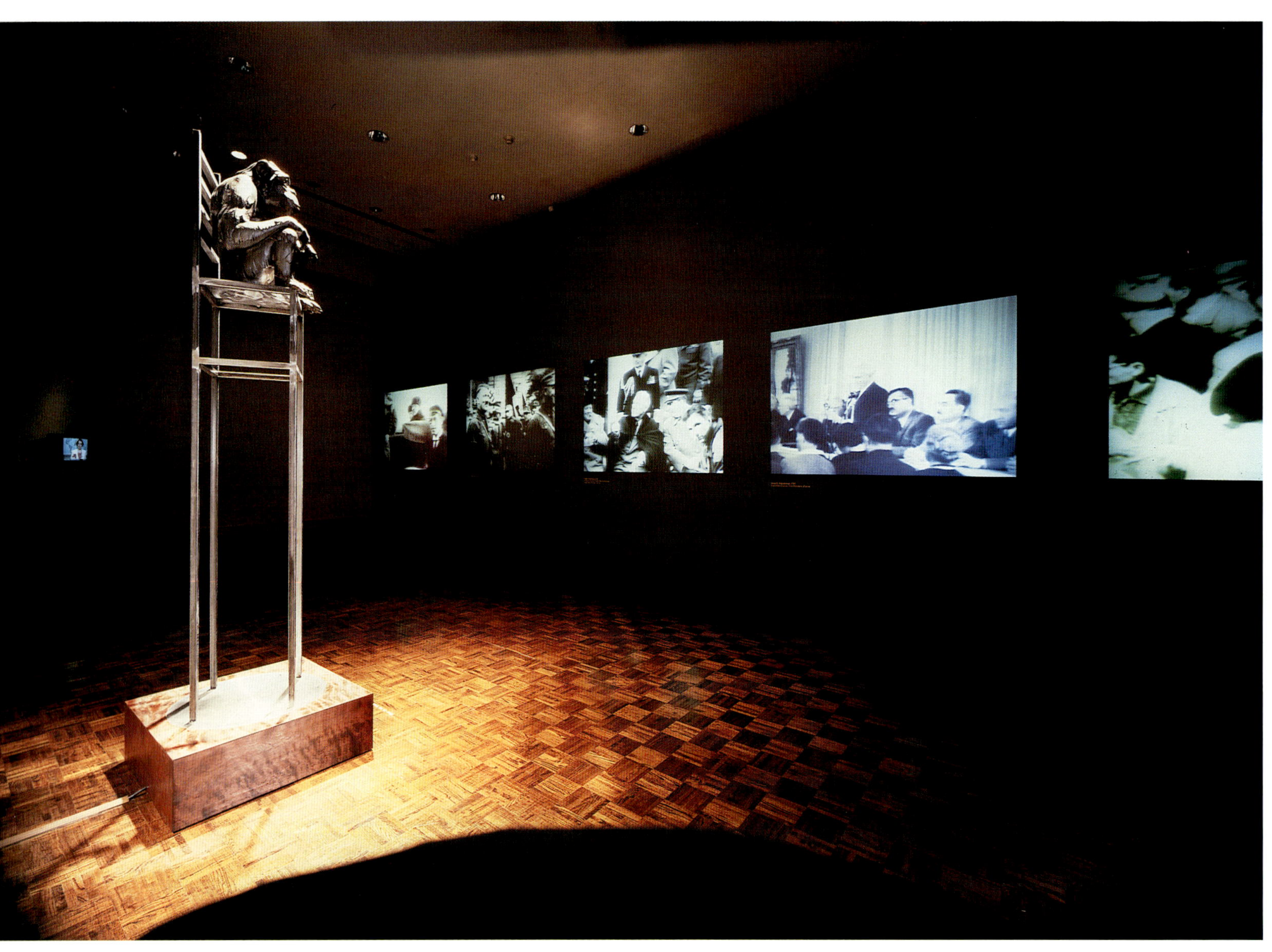

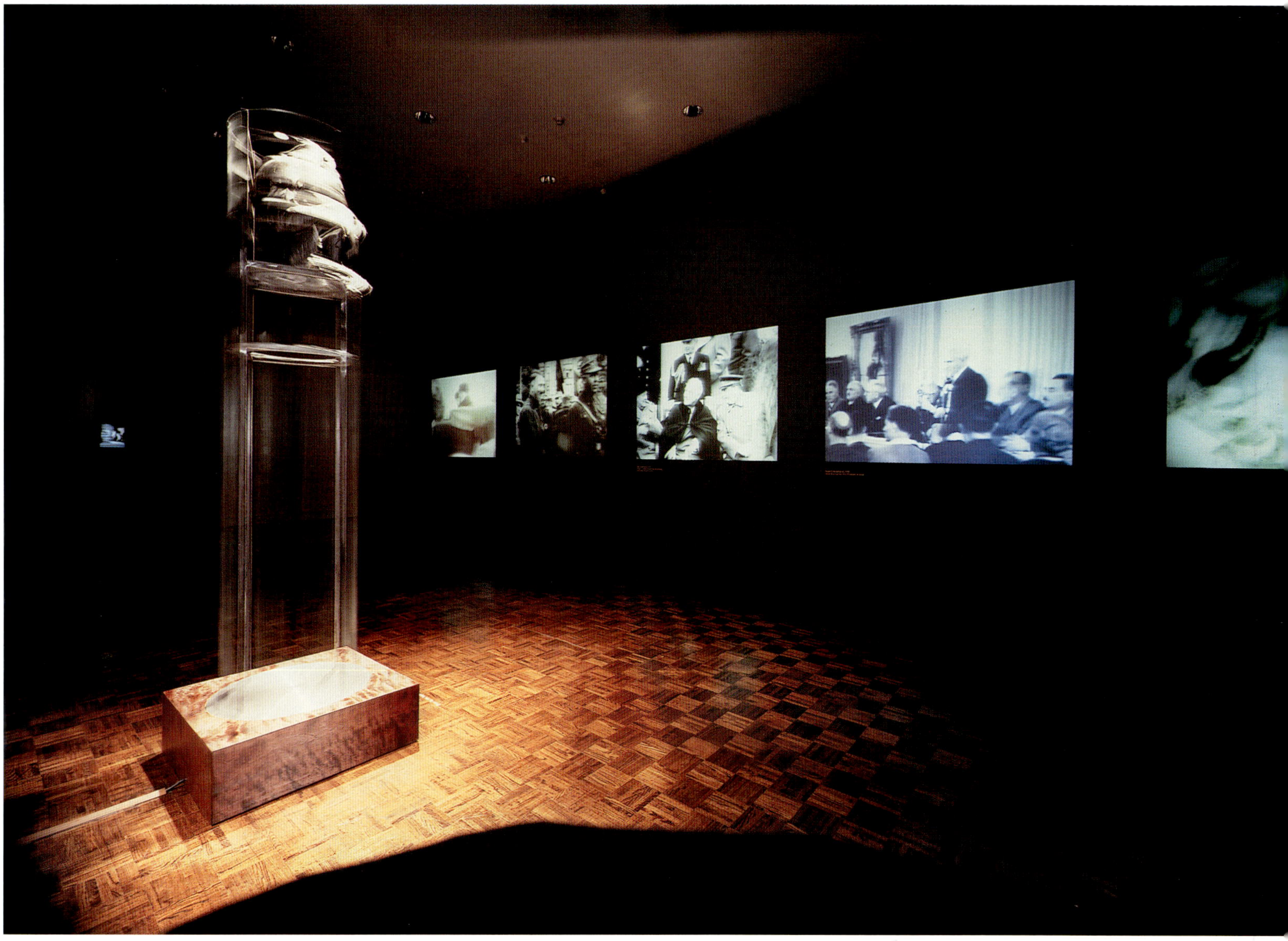

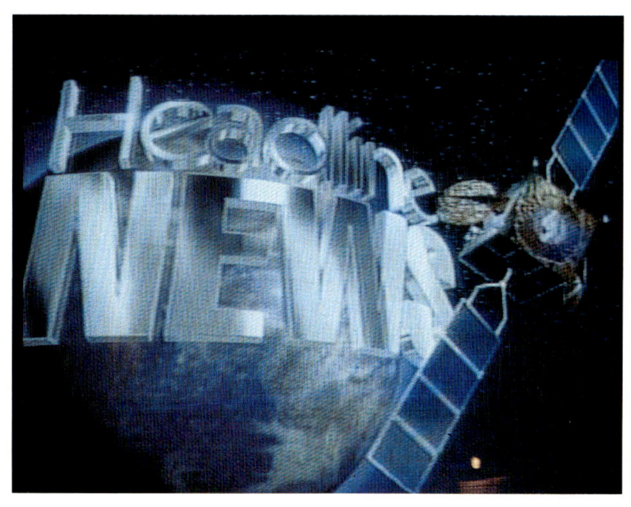
Headline
NEWS

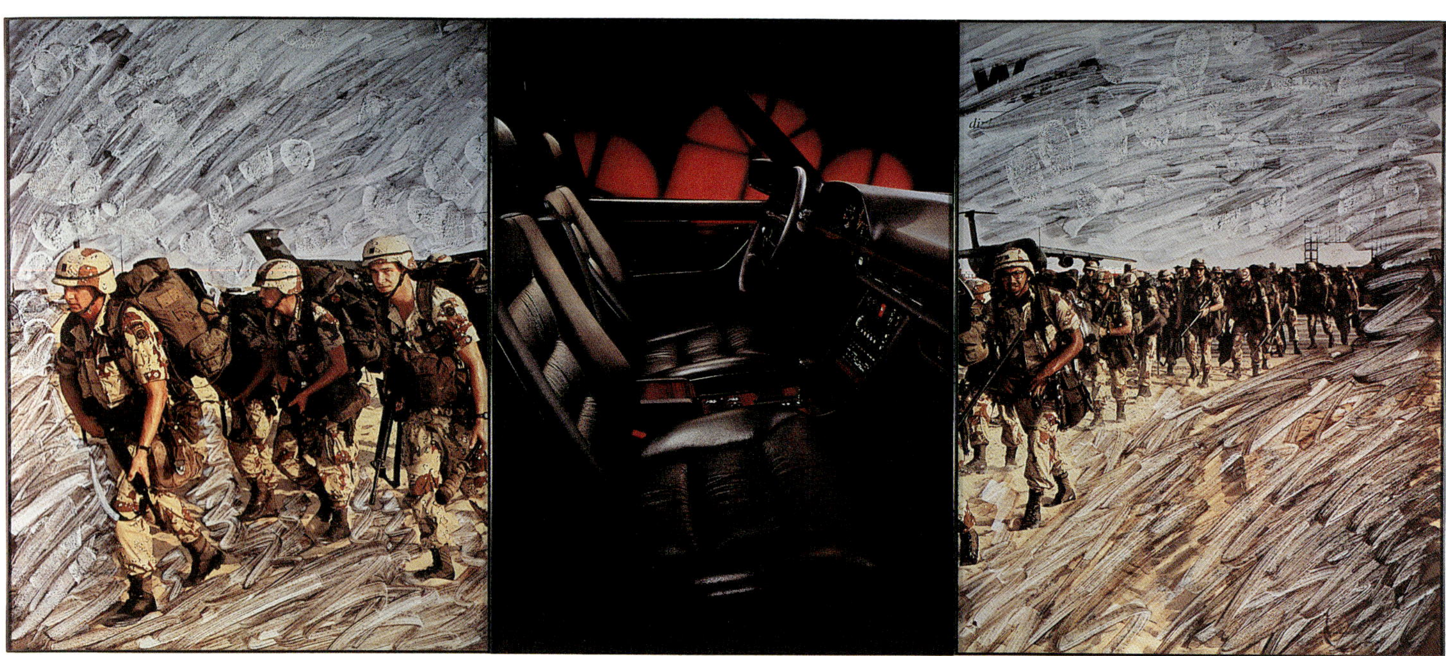

Newsweek Series #27, 1990-92

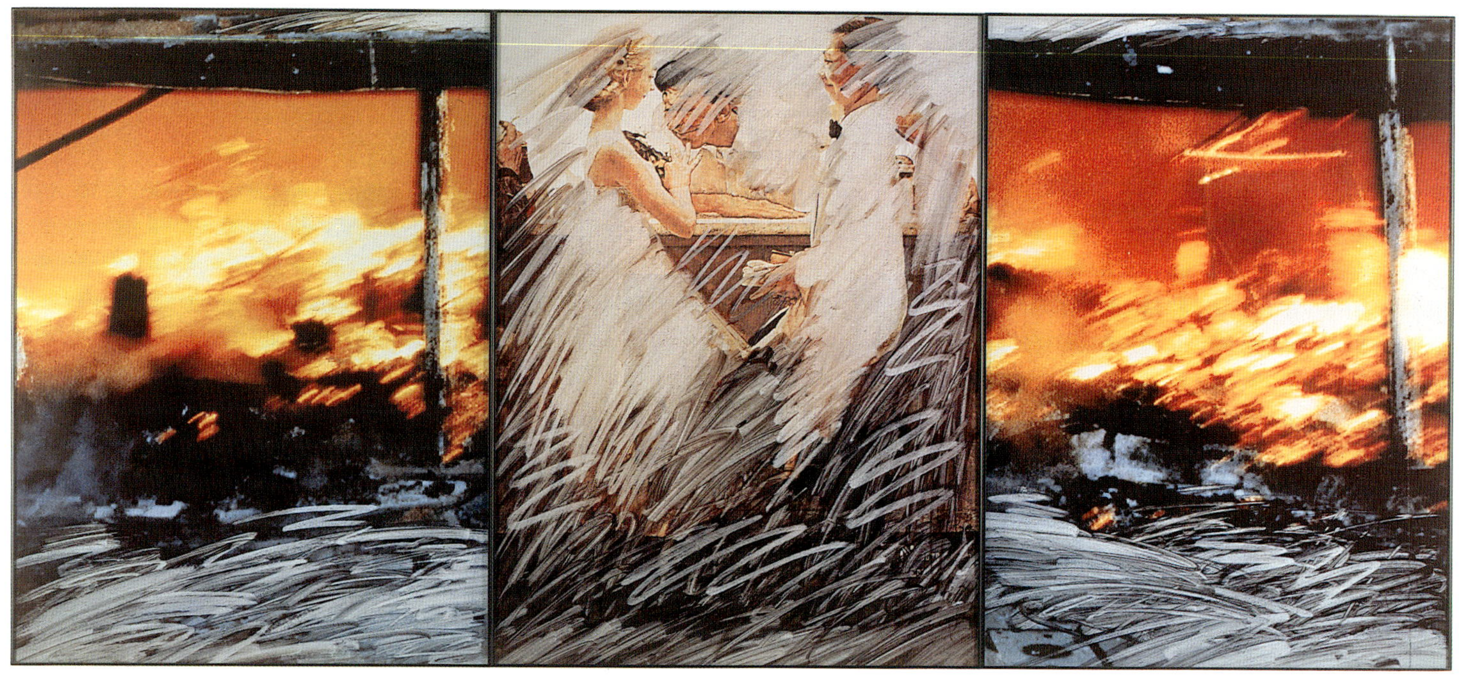

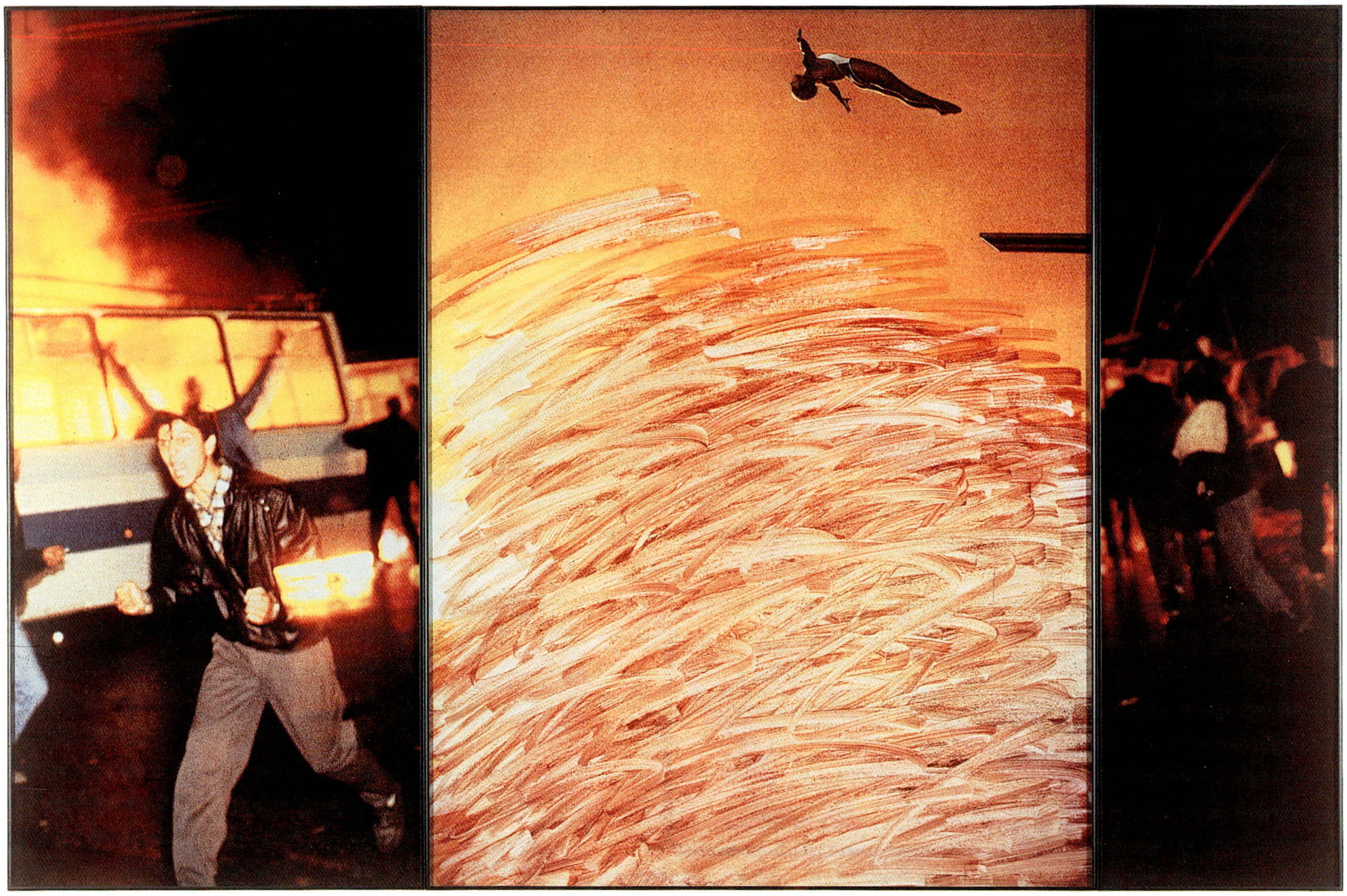

Newsweek Series #28, 1990-92
Newsweek Series #29, 1990-92

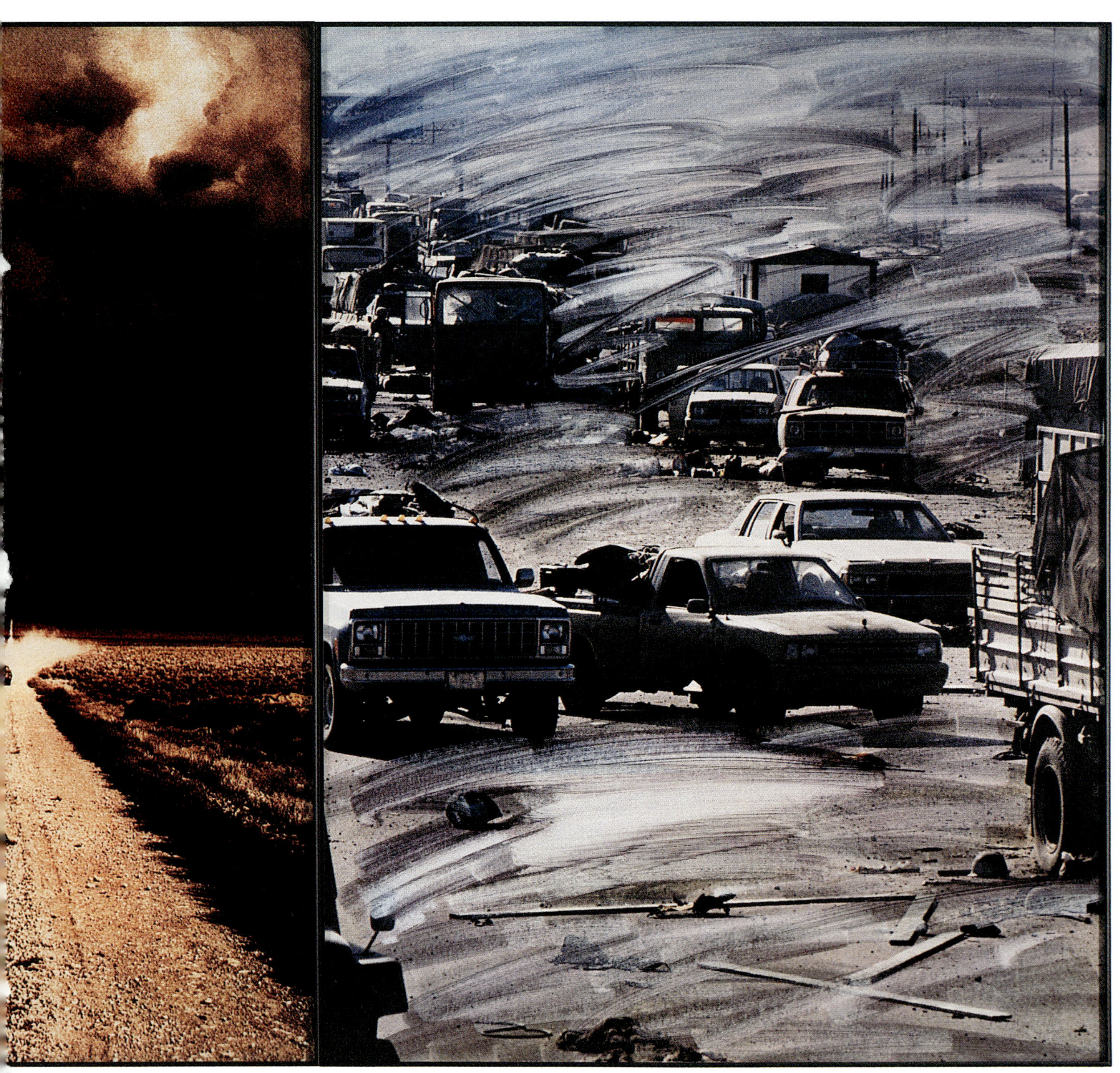

Newsweek Series #30, 1990-92

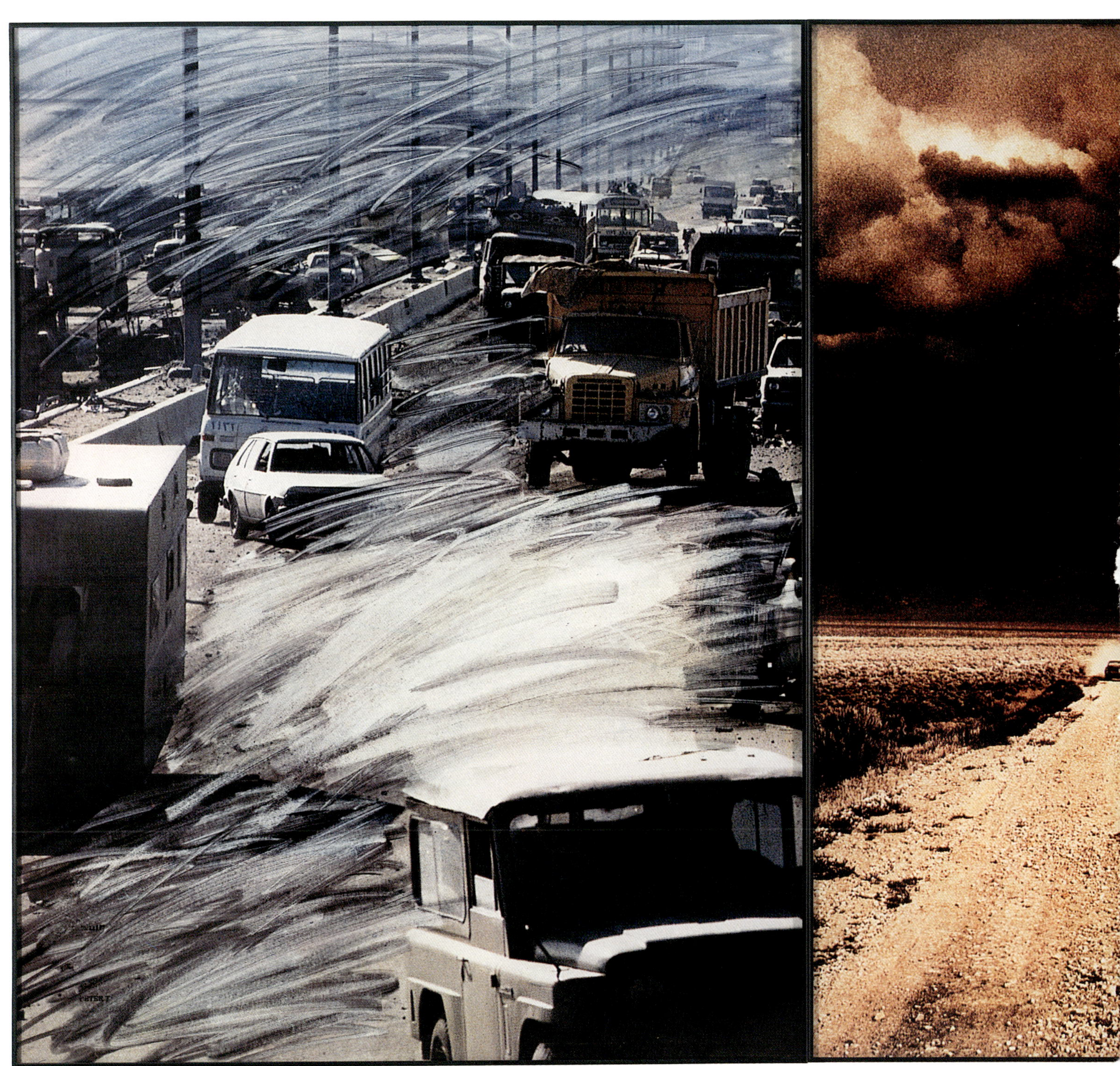

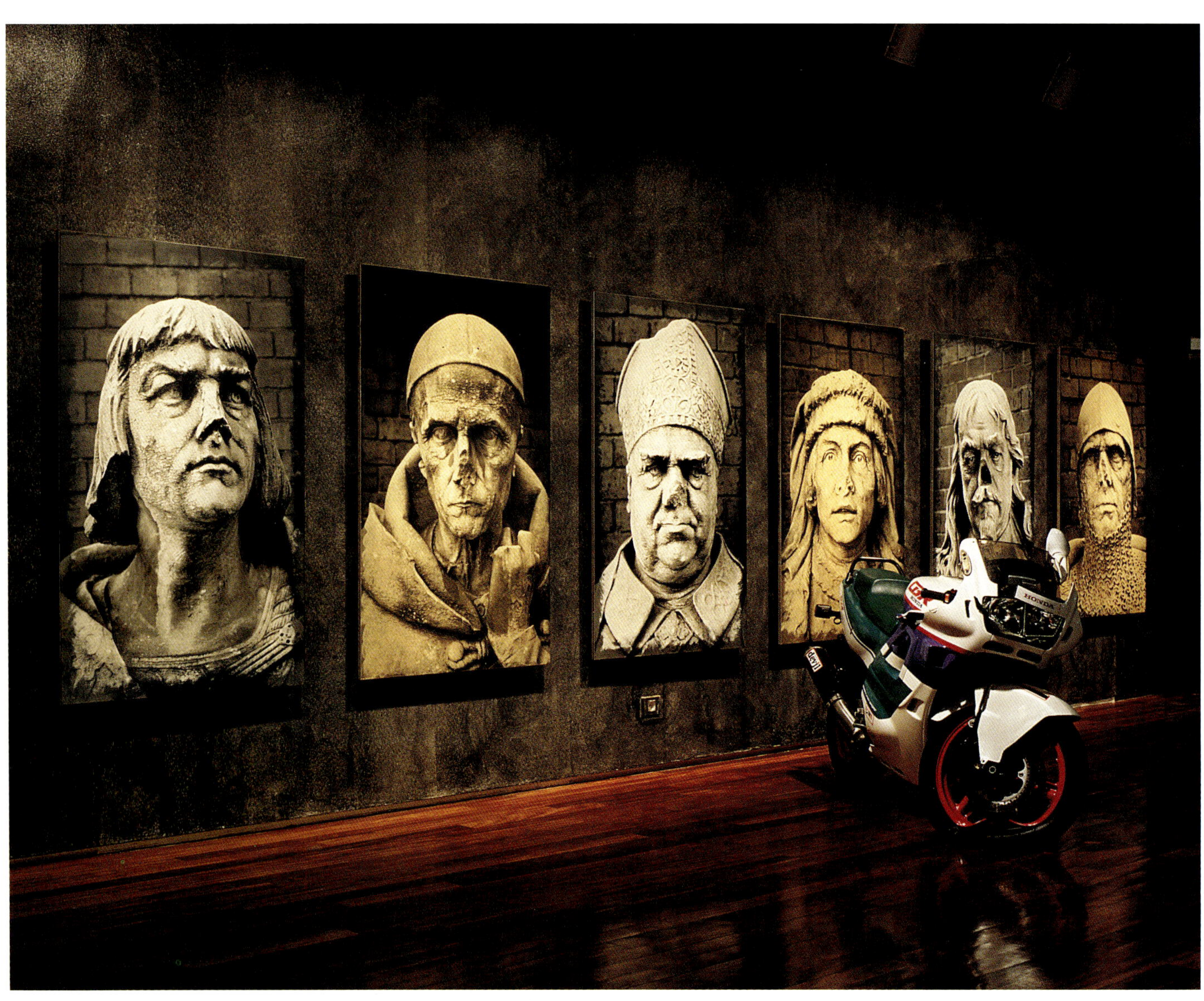

Destiny, Entropy, and Junk /2, 1991

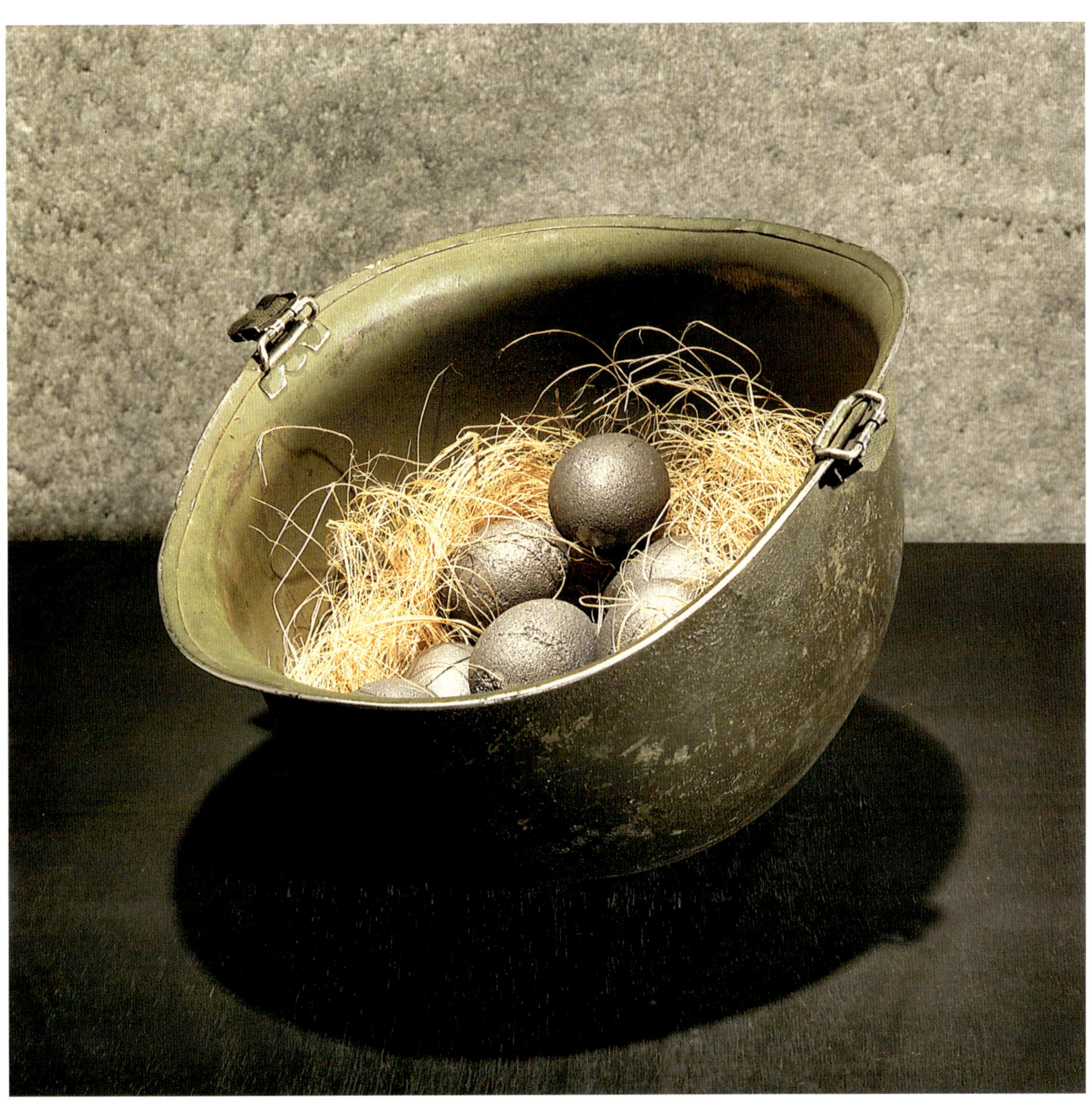

Soldier's Complaint, 1991

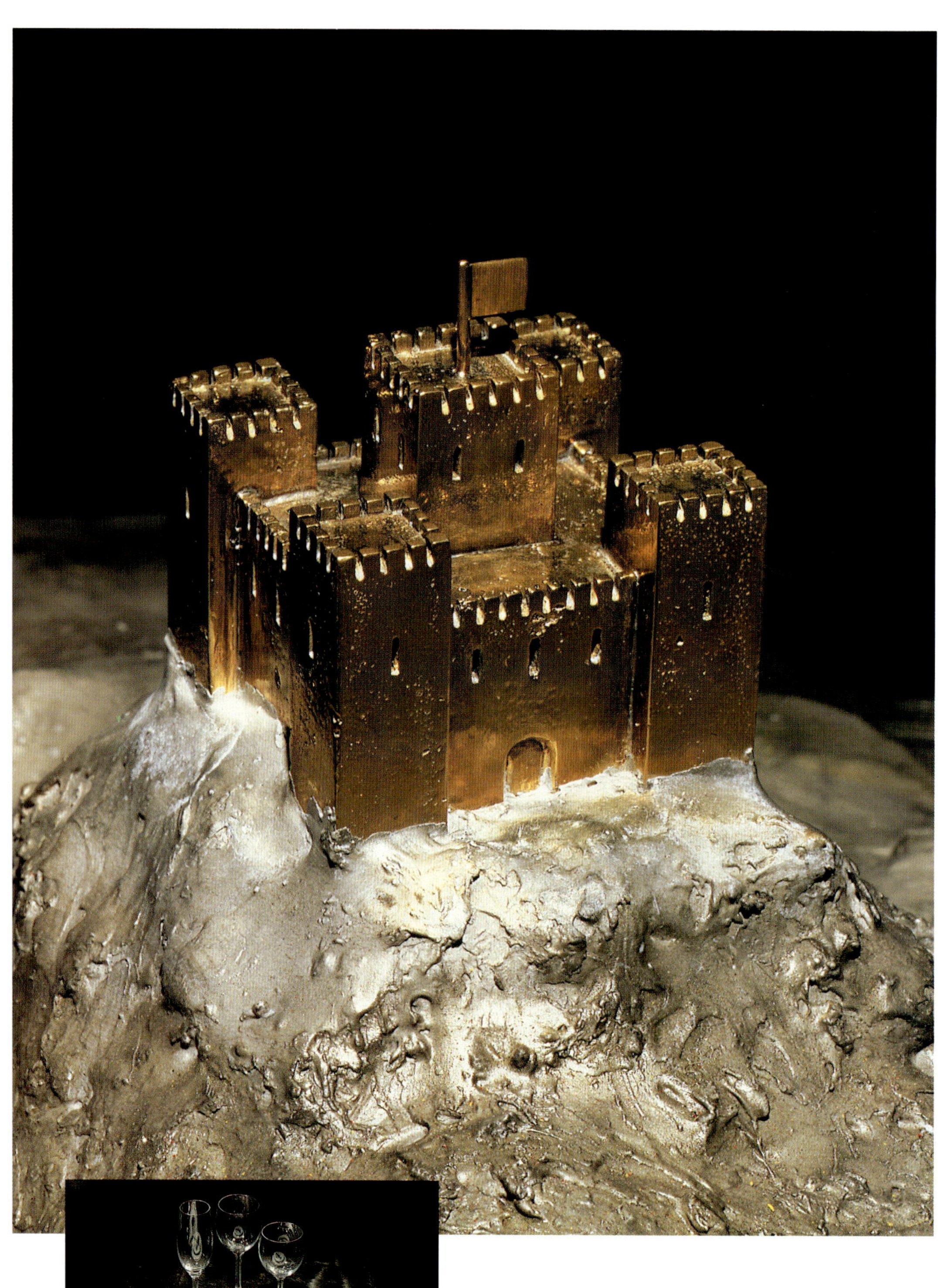

Table for Hegelian Heroes at a Business Lunch; Dining Room Storm Also Applicable to the Domestic Front, 1991

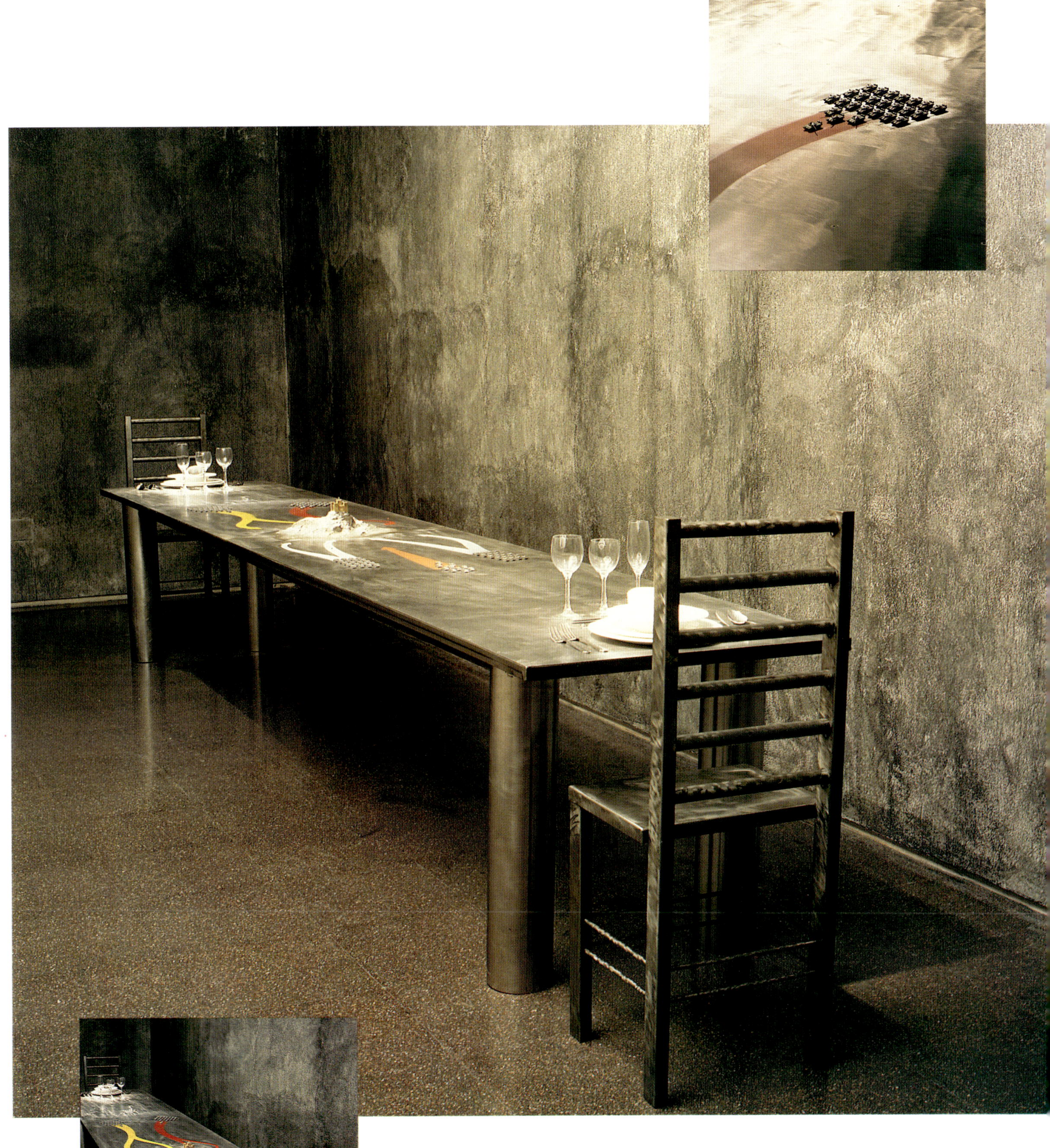

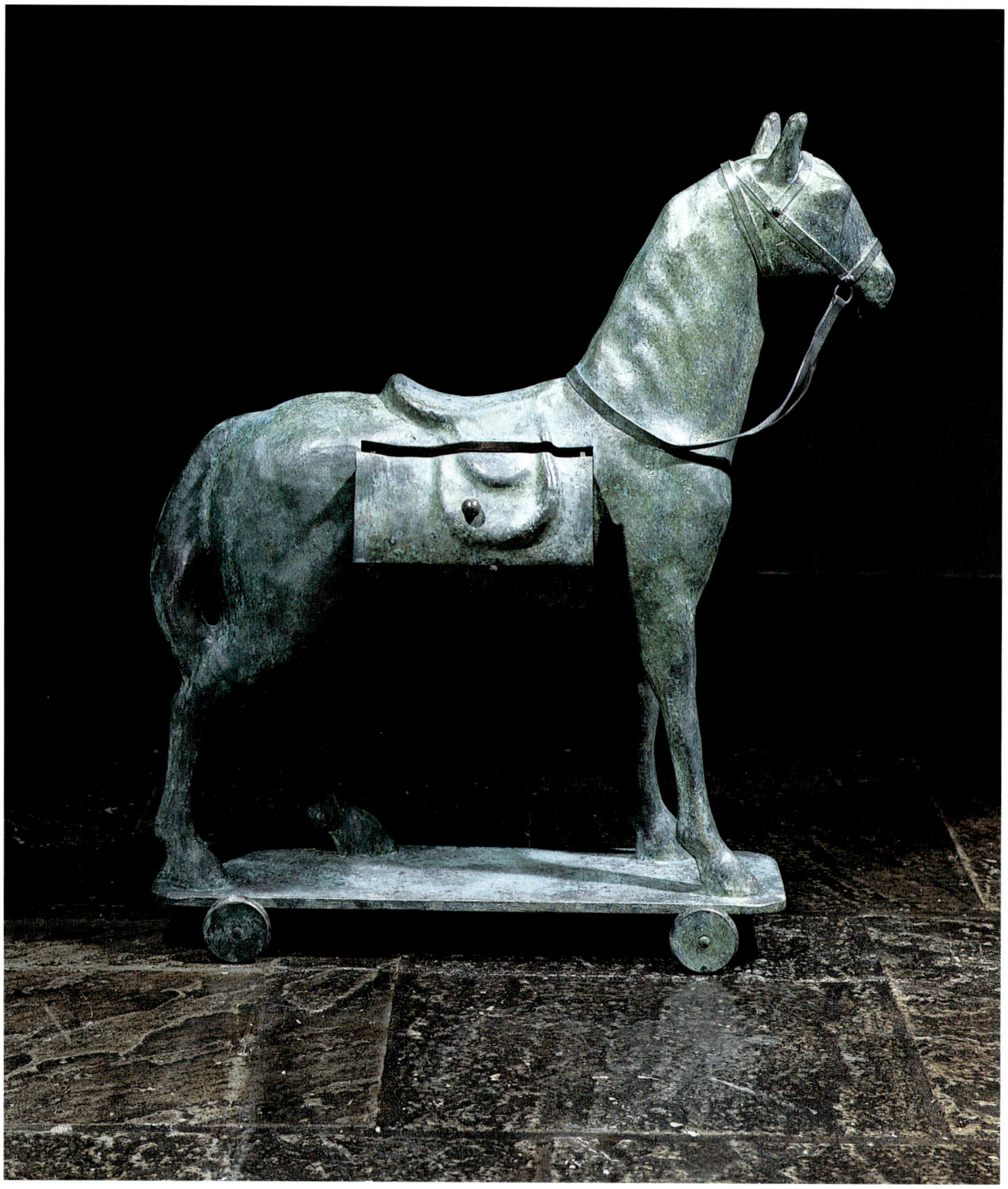

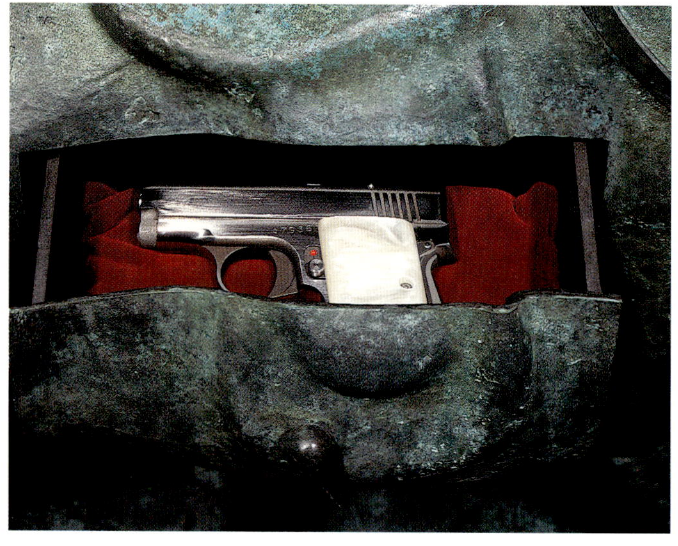

Model for a Trojan Horse, 1993

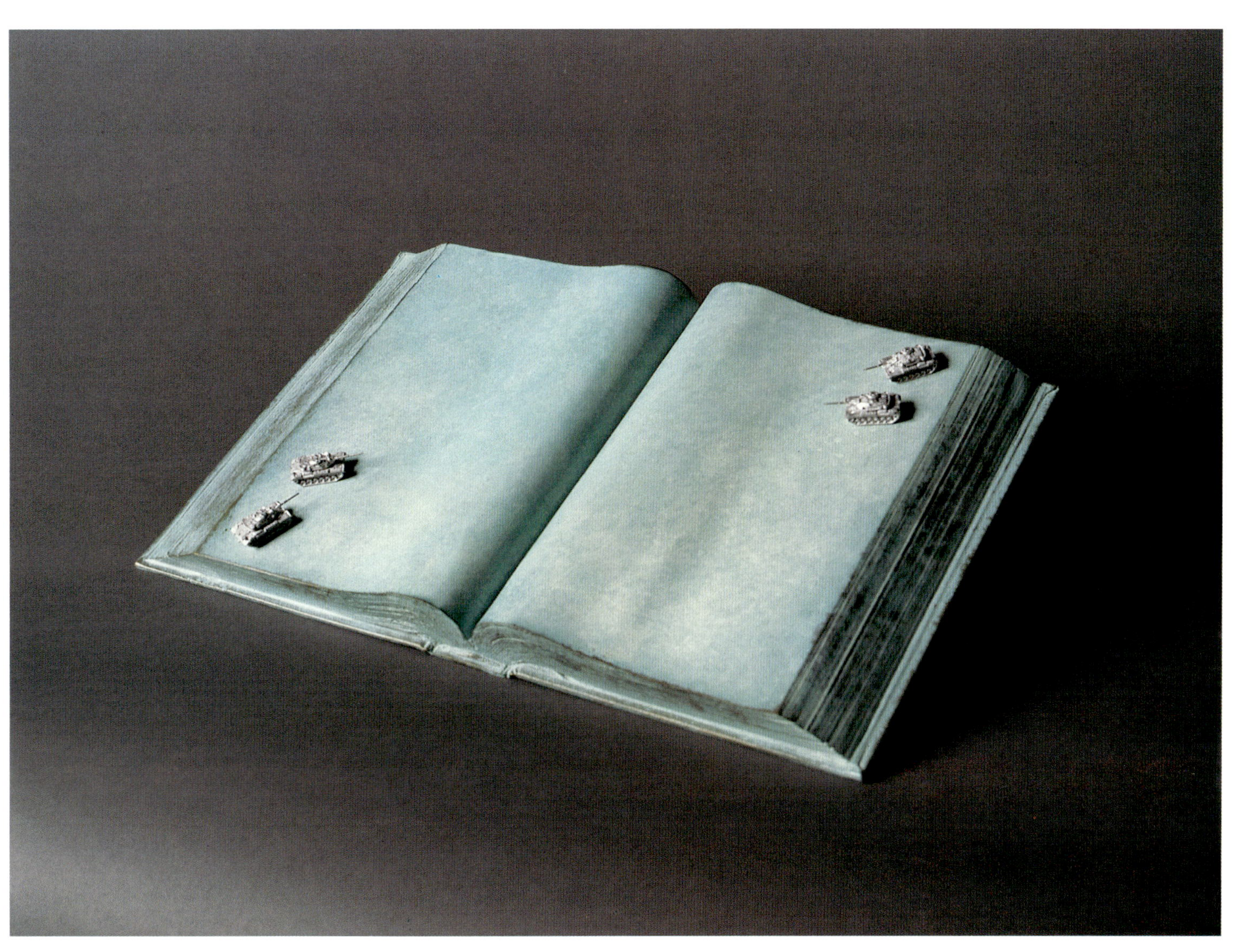

The History Book of Persistent Forgetfulness, 1992

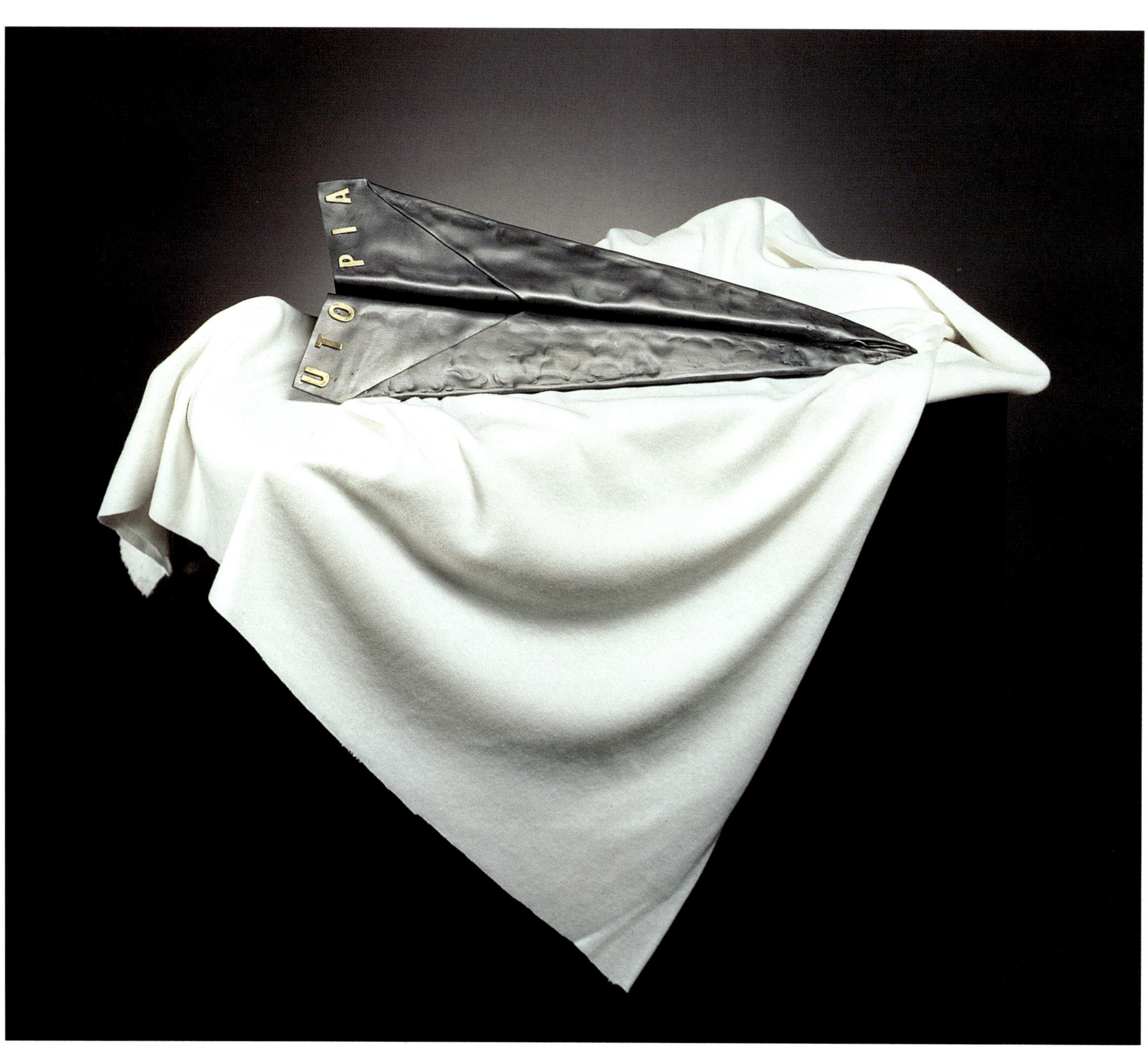

UTOPIA, 1992

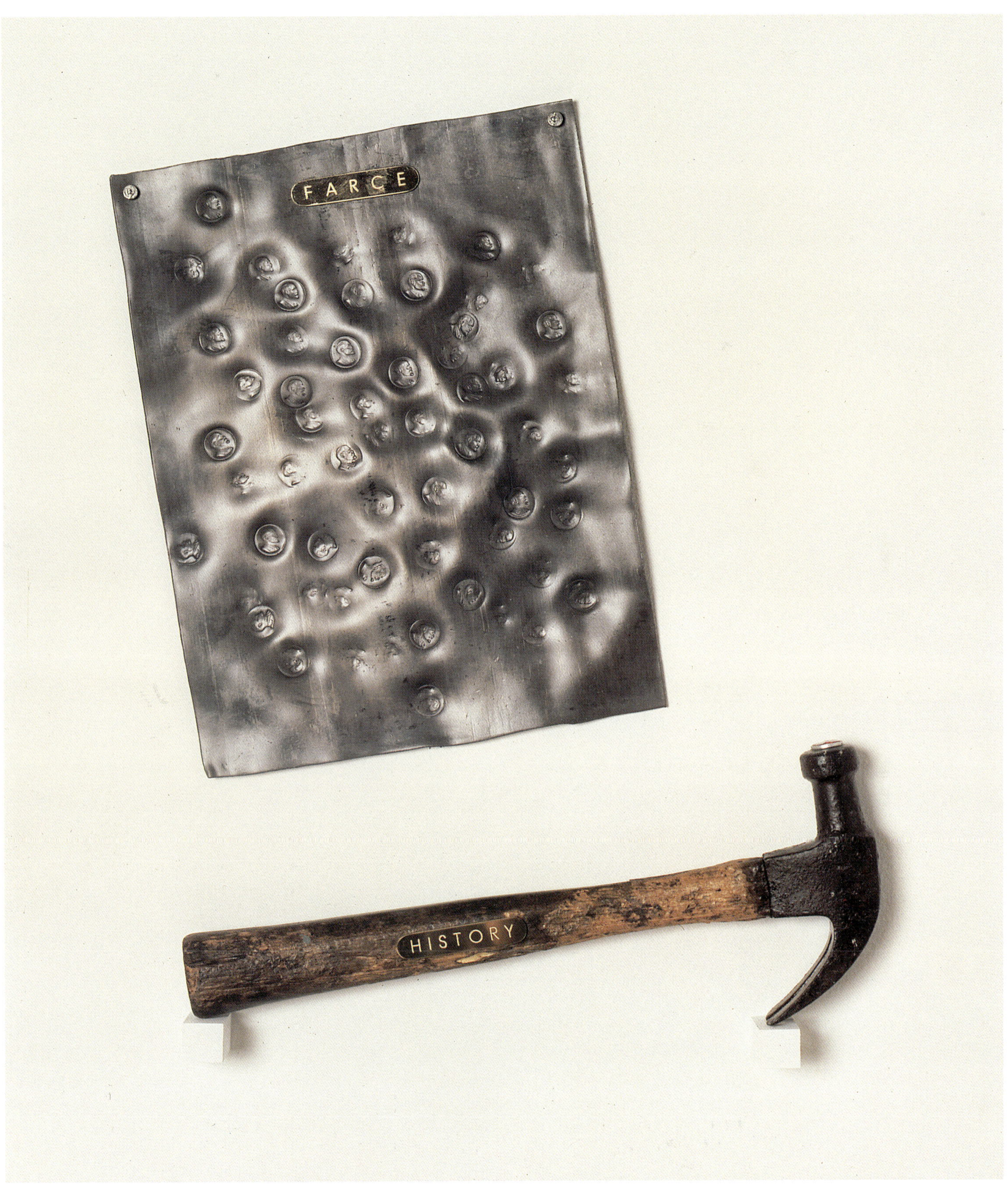

History and Farce, 1992

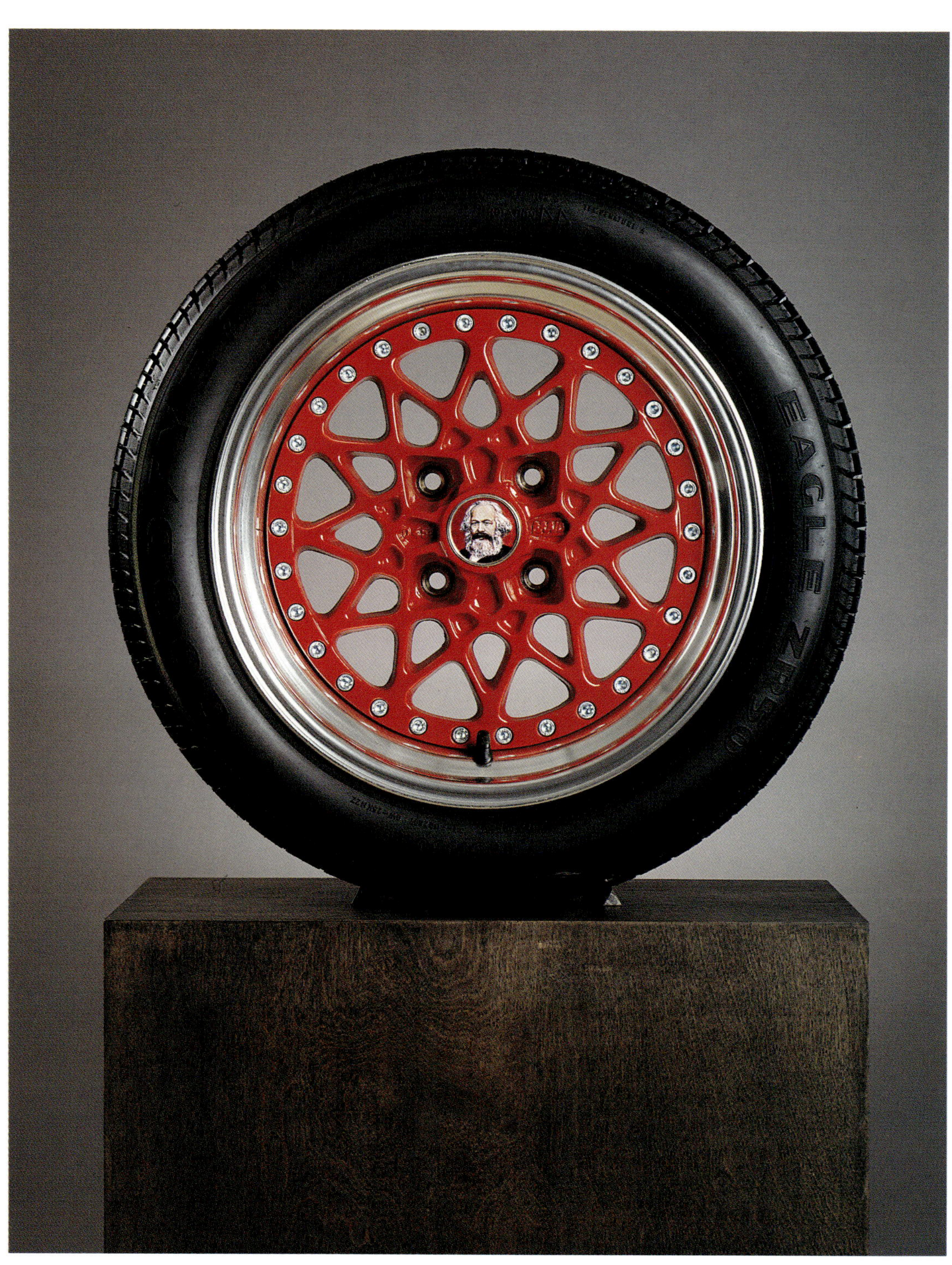

European (Historic) Competition Wheel, 1991

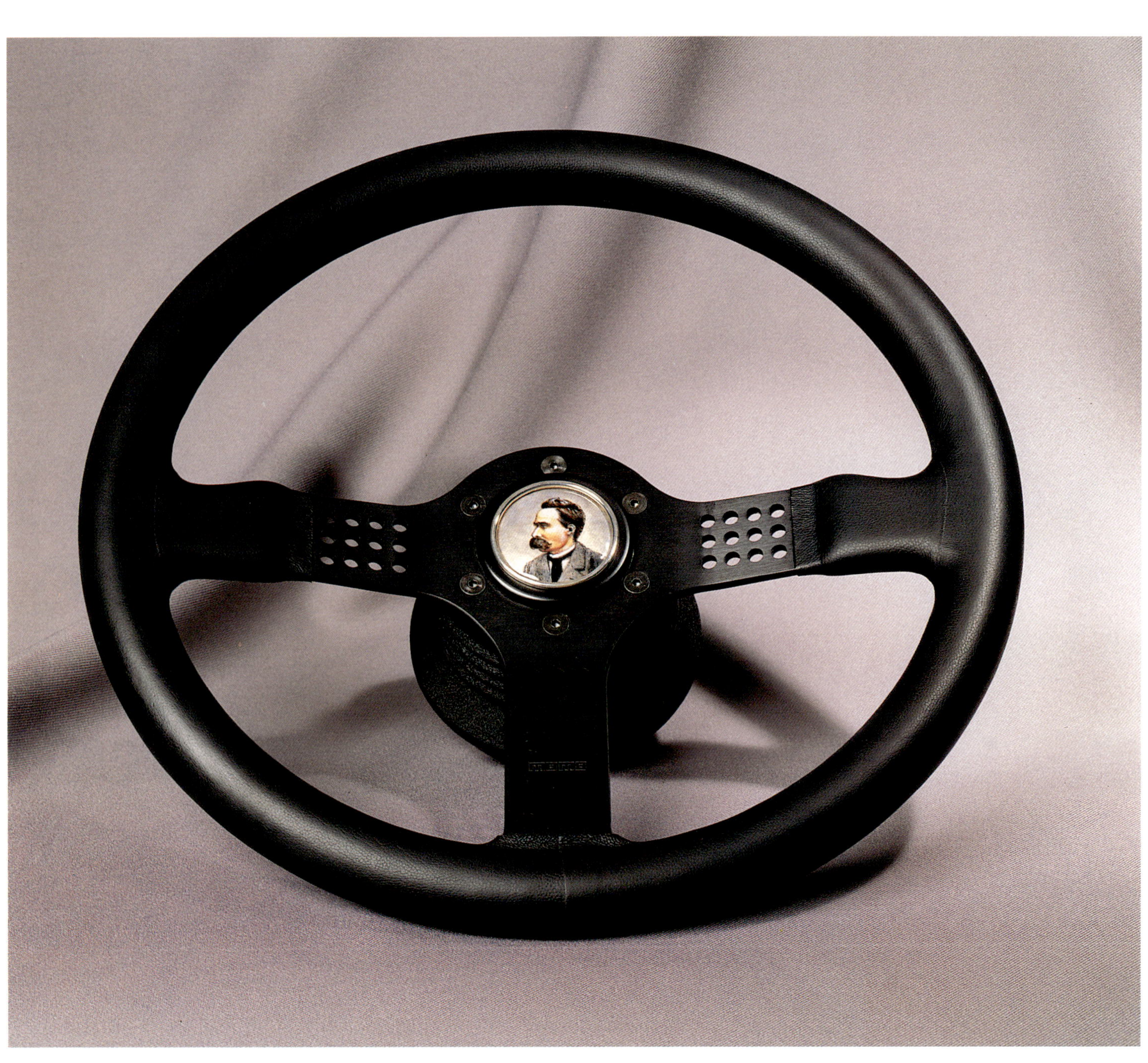

Nietzsche by MOMO, 1993

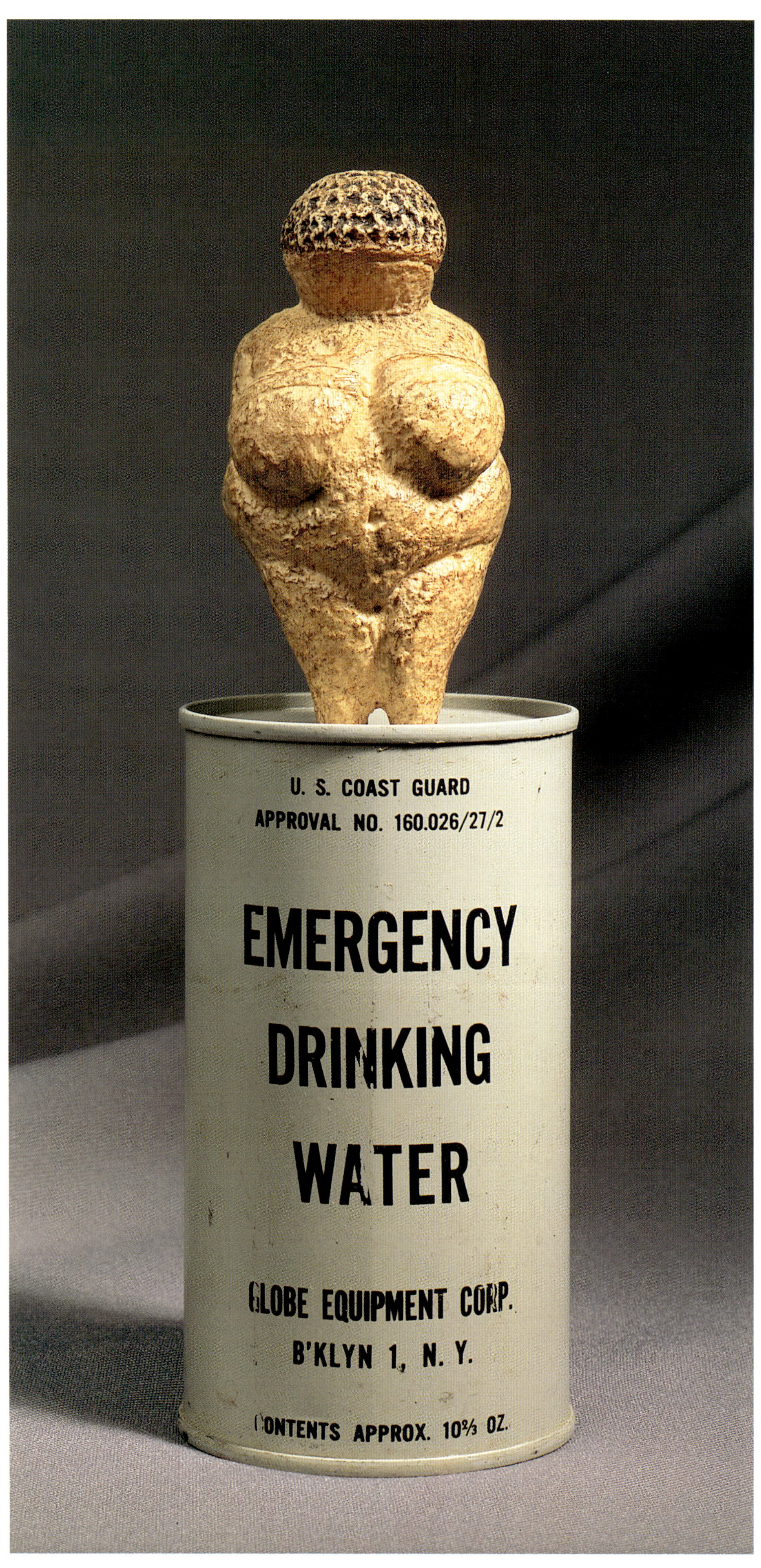

Emergency Drinking Water, 1992

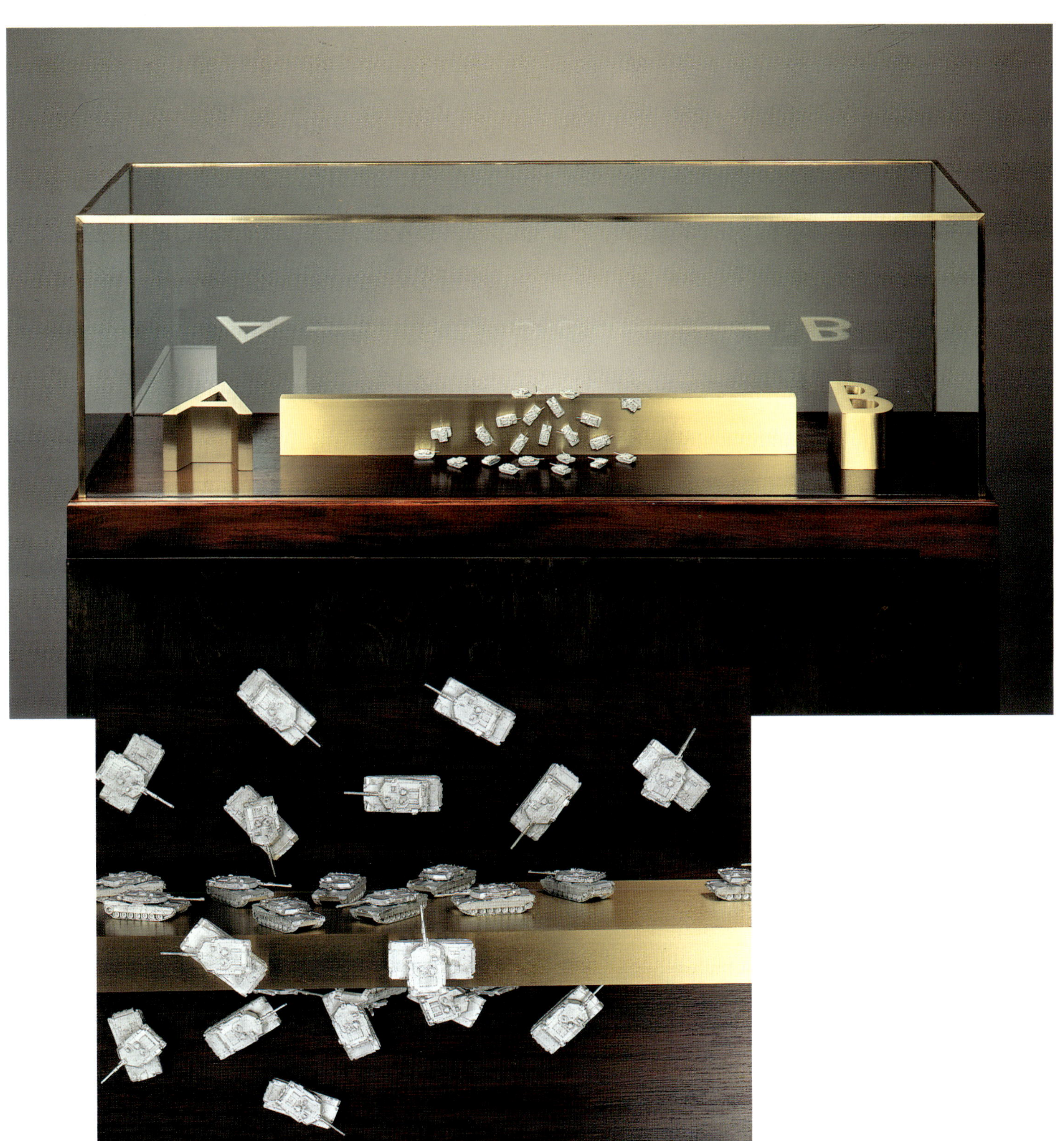

Logic and the Termites, 1992

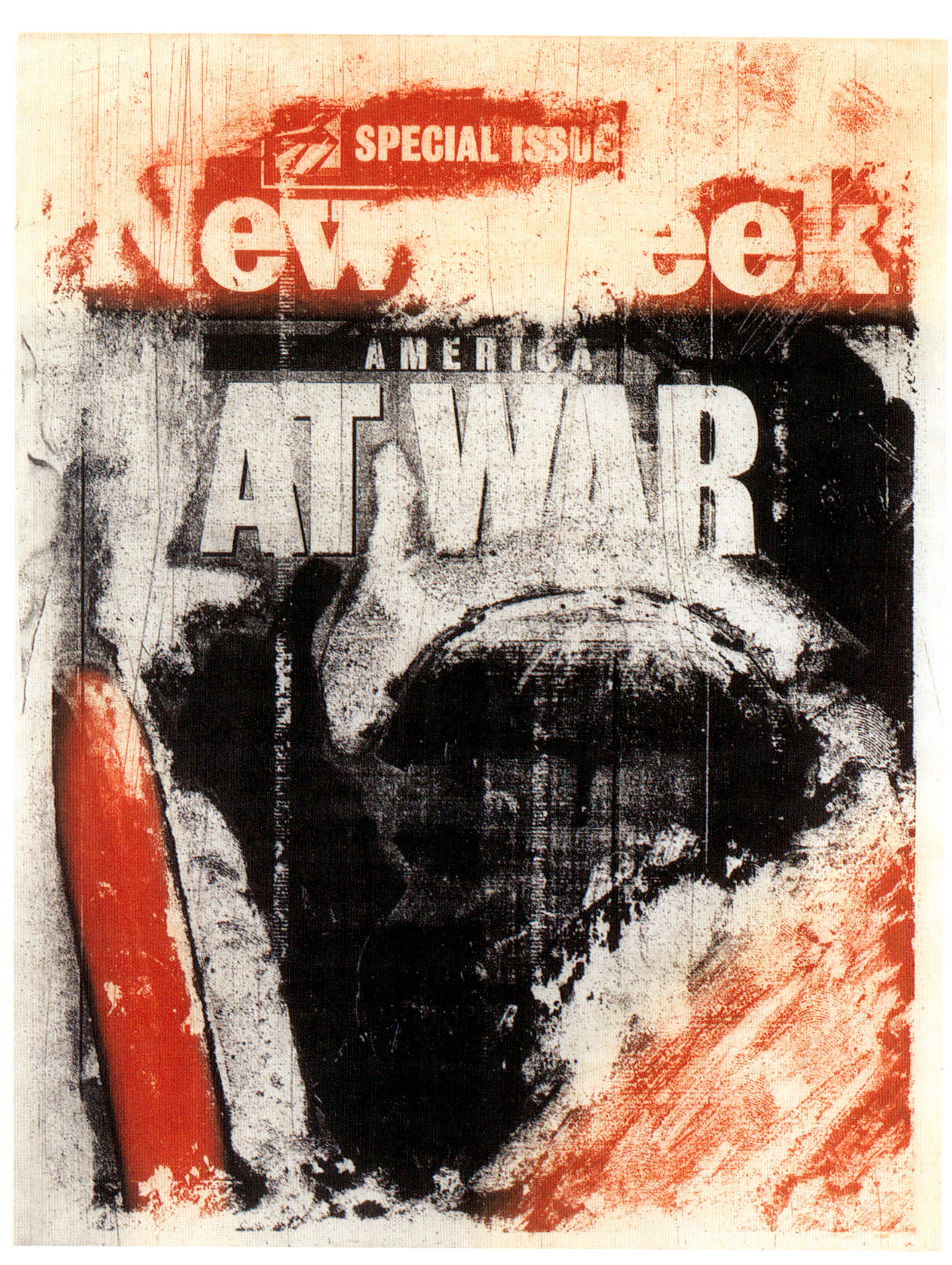

FORGET EVERYTHING I-III, 1991

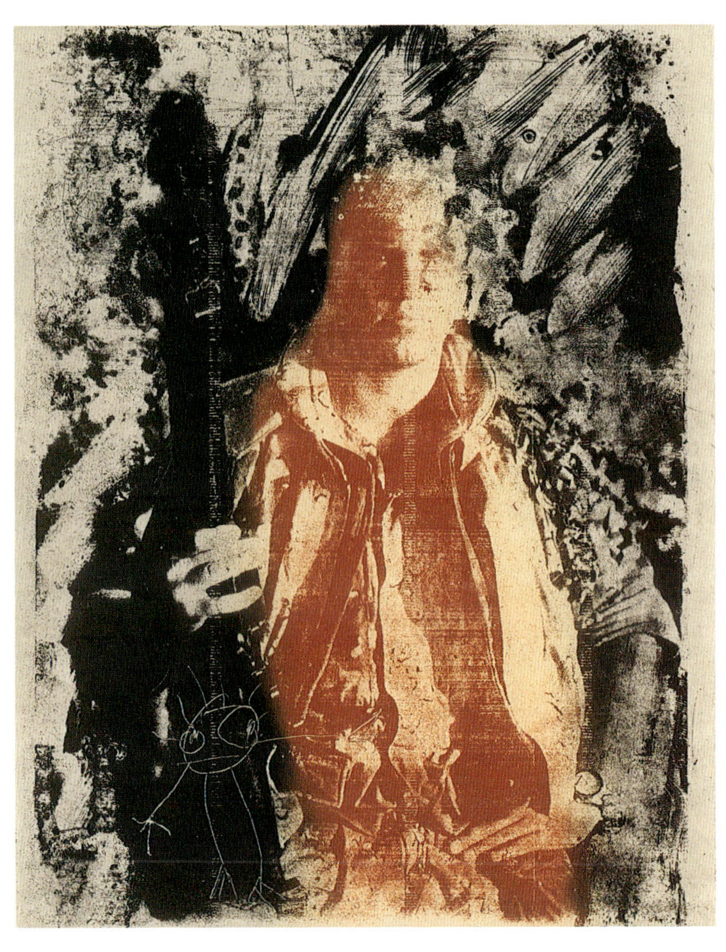

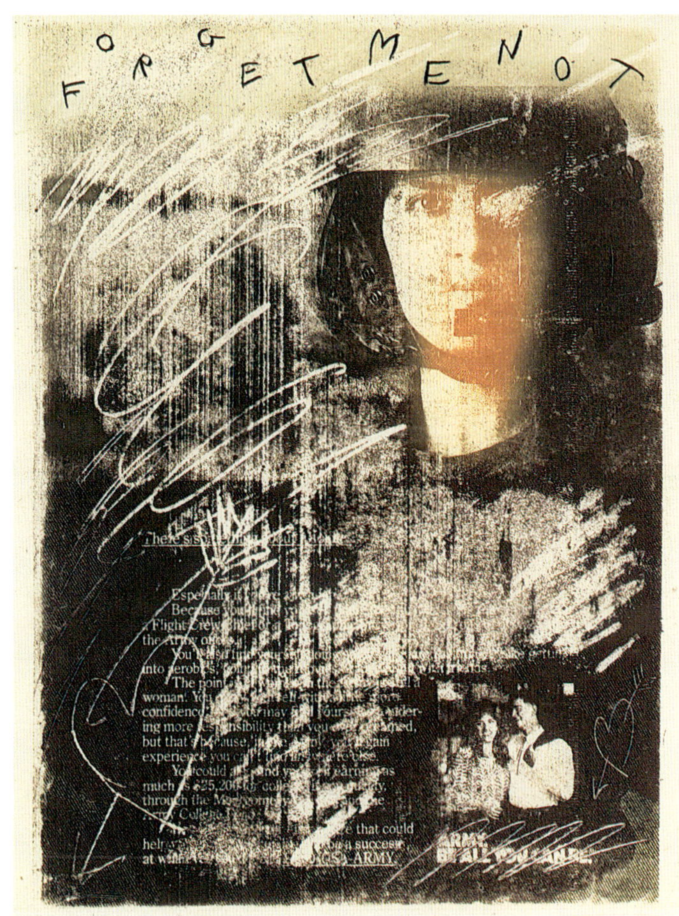
FORGET ME NOT

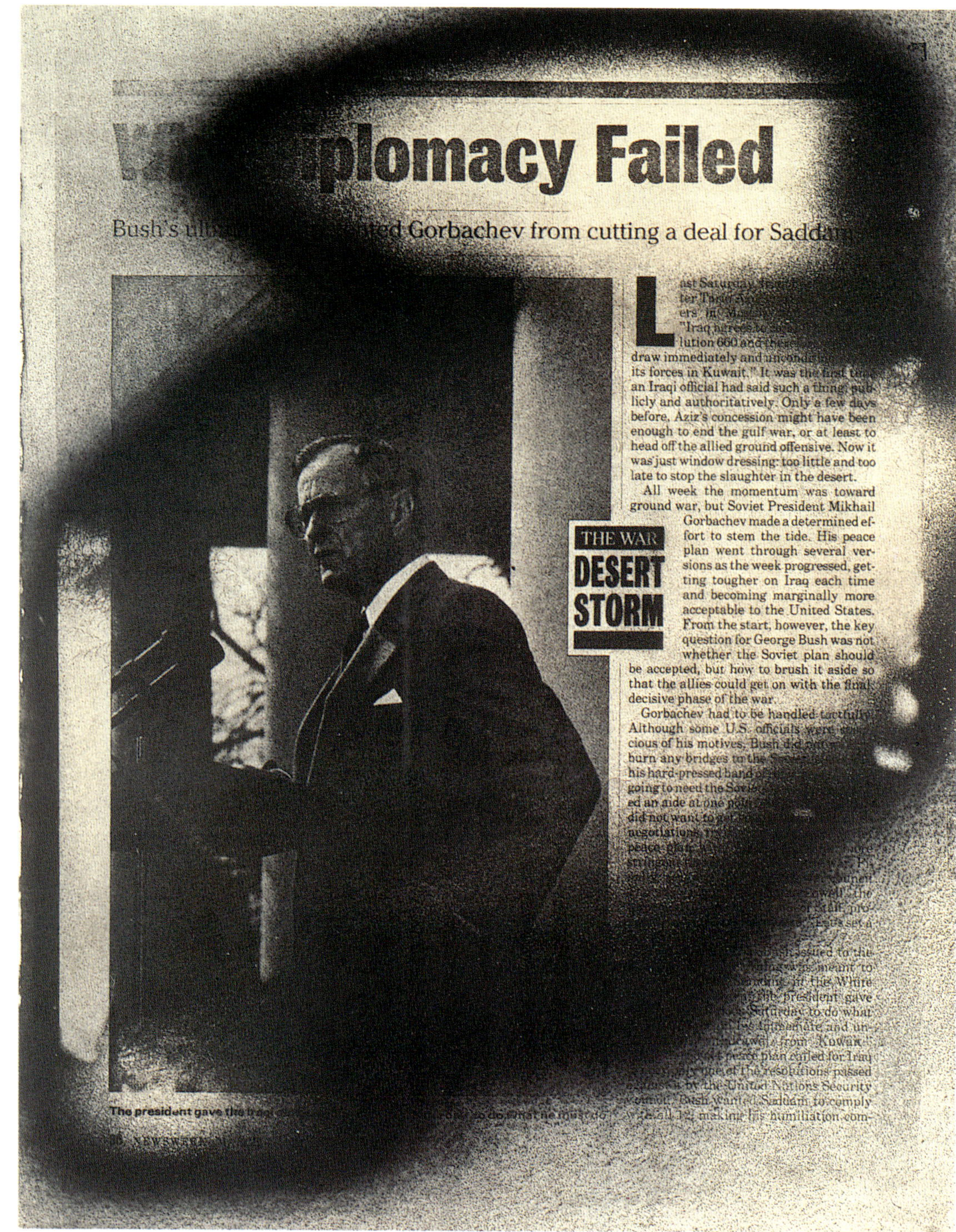

[illegible] plomacy Failed

Bush's ul[illegible]ted Gorbachev from cutting a deal for Sadda[illegible]

Last Saturday [illegible] ter Tariq [illegible] ers in Mo[illegible] "Iraq agrees [illegible] lution 660 and the[illegible] draw immediately and uncondi[illegible] its forces in Kuwait." It was the first [illegible] an Iraqi official had said such a thing, pub- licly and authoritatively. Only a few days before, Aziz's concession might have been enough to end the gulf war, or at least to head off the allied ground offensive. Now it was just window dressing: too little and too late to stop the slaughter in the desert.

All week the momentum was toward ground war, but Soviet President Mikhail Gorbachev made a determined ef- fort to stem the tide. His peace plan went through several ver- sions as the week progressed, get- ting tougher on Iraq each time and becoming marginally more acceptable to the United States. From the start, however, the key question for George Bush was not whether the Soviet plan should be accepted, but how to brush it aside so that the allies could get on with the final decisive phase of the war.

Gorbachev had to be handled tactfully. Although some U.S. officials were [illegible] cious of his motives, Bush did not [illegible] burn any bridges to the [illegible] his hard-pressed band [illegible] going to need the Sovie[illegible] ed an aide at one poi[illegible] [illegible]

THE WAR

DESERT STORM

The president gave the Iraqi [illegible]

[illegible] NEWSWEEK

FORGET EVERYTHING IV-VI, 1991

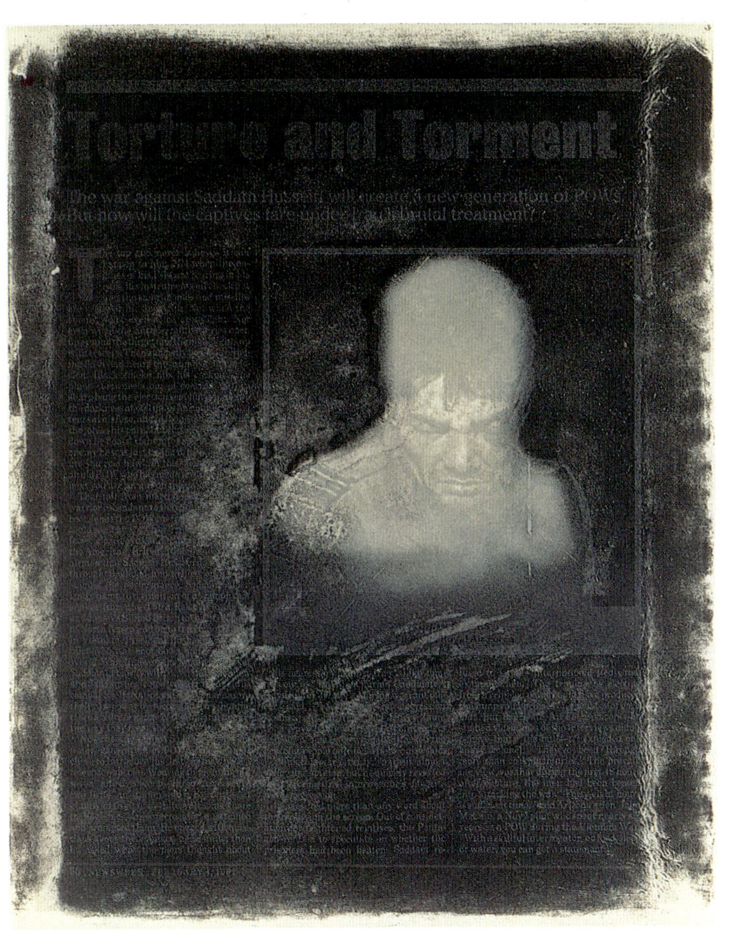
Torture and Torment
The war against Saddam Hussein will create a new generation of POWs

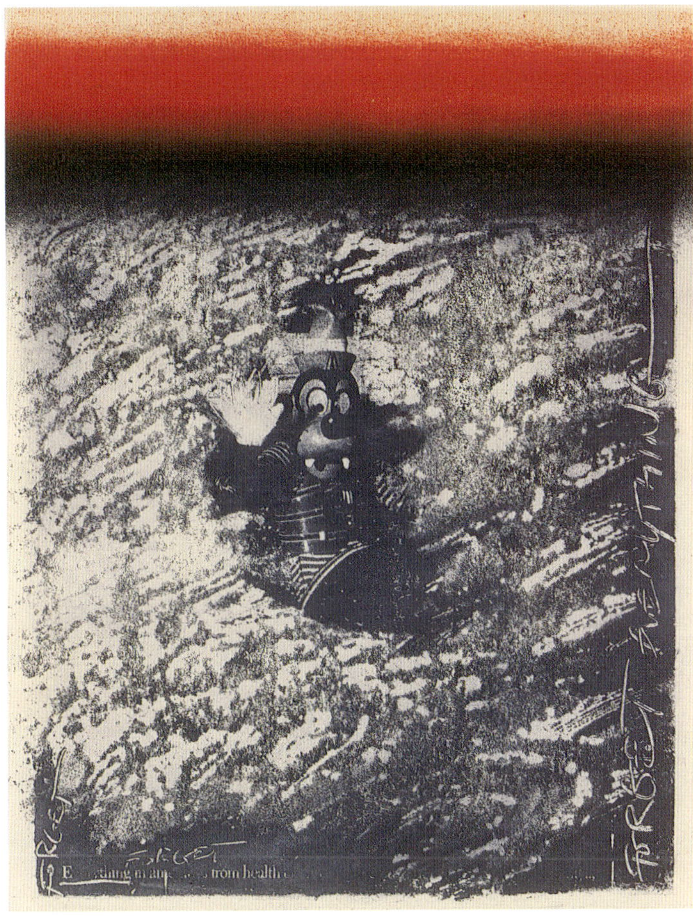

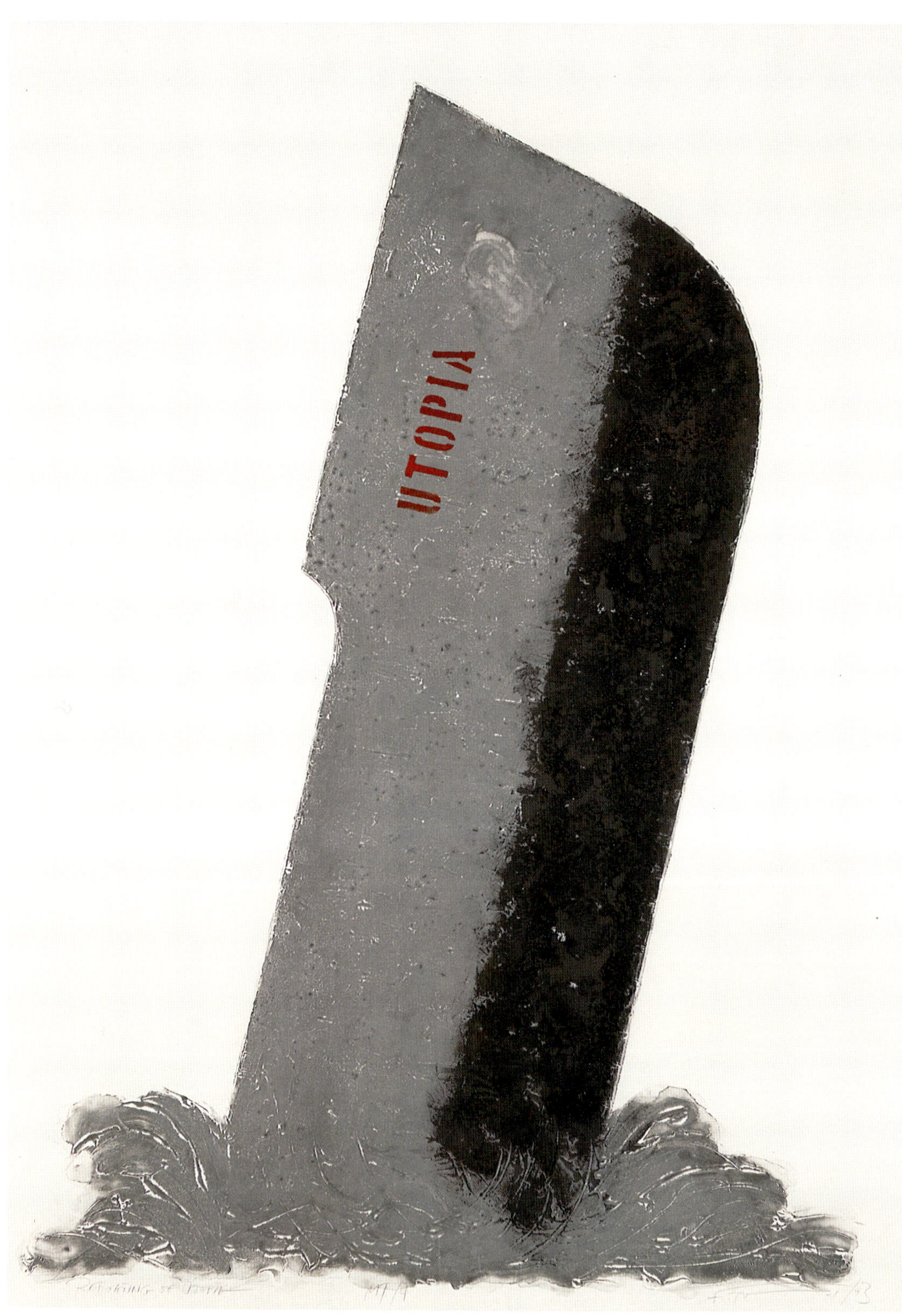

UTOPIA (Sinking or Refloating?), 1993

Catalogue to the Exhibition

Francesc Torres Curriculum Vitae

Bibliography

Board of Directors and Staff
Arizona State University Art Museum

Credits

Catalogue to the Exhibition

Dimensions are given in inches followed by centimeters: height precedes width precedes depth.

Installations

Too Late for Goya, *1993*
Seven-channel media installation:
video, sound, fiberglas sculptural figure,
television, special digital sound box,
satellite dish and a reproduction of a Goya print
30 x 60 feet (9 x 18 meters)
Courtesy of the artist

Destiny, Entropy, and Junk/2, *1991*
Six silk-screens on aluminum,
each 60 1/2 x 39 1/2 inches (154 x 100 cm),
and wrecked motorcycle
Courtesy of the artist

Photographic Works

Newsweek Series #26, *1990-92*
Cibachrome triptych
65 3/4 x 150 inches (170 x 375 cm)
Courtesy of The Bohen Foundation, New York

Newsweek Series #27, *1990-92*
Cibachrome triptych
65 3/4 x 148 inches (167 x 374 cm)
Courtesy of The Bohen Foundation, New York

Newsweek Series #28, *1990-92*
Cibachrome triptych
65 3/4 x 99 3/4 inches (167 x 253.5 cm)
Courtesy of The Bohen Foundation, New York

Newsweek Series #29, *1990-92*
Cibachrome triptych
65 3/4 x 143 inches (167 x 363 cm)
Courtesy of The Bohen Foundation, New York

Newsweek Series #30, *1990-92*
Cibachrome triptych
63 x 133 1/2 inches (160 x 339 cm)
Courtesy of Arizona State University Art Museum,
Tempe, Arizona

Prints

Forget Everything I-VI, *1991*
Six aquatints and photogravure on copperplate etching
Each 22 1/8 x 29 inches (56 x 74 cm)
Courtesy of The Bohen Foundation, New York

UTOPIA (Sinking or Refloating?), *1993*
Ink on paper
60 x 42 inches (150 x 105 cm)
Courtesy of the artist

Table for Hegelian Heroes at a Business Lunch; Dining Room Storm Also Applicable to the Domestic Front, *1991*
Painted steel table finished with Sculpmetal, cast iron tanks, brass castle, two table settings and two steel chairs
32 x 192 x 32 inches (80 x 480 x 80 cm)
Courtesy of the artist

European (Historic) Competition Wheel, *1991*
Aluminum, rubber and enamel paint
23 x 23 x 9 inches (58 x 58 x 23 cm)
Courtesy of the artist

Soldier's Complaint, *1991*
Steel helmet, twelve cast iron eggs and esparto grass
14 x 14 x 8 inches (35.5 x 35.5 x 20.4 cm)
Courtesy of the artist

Emergency Drinking Water, *1992*
Resin, tin and water
8 1/2 x 2 11/16 inches diameter (21.6 x 6.8 cm diameter)
Courtesy of the artist

History and Farce, *1992*
Lead panel, hammer and brass
13 3/8 x 16 3/4 inches (34 x 42 cm)
Courtesy of Terry Berkowitz, New York

The History Book of Persistent Forgetfulness, *1992*
Cast bronze and zinc
13 7/8 x 9 1/4 x 1 1/4 inches (35.2 x 23.5 x 3 cm)
Courtesy of the artist

Logic and the Termites, *1992*
Brass, zinc, glass and wood
47 9/16 x 13 6/16 x 17 7/16 inches (110 x 34 x 44 cm)
Courtesy of the artist

Utopia, *1992*
Lead and brass
15 6/8 x 6 1/4 x 4 1/4 inches (39 x 16 x 11 cm)
Courtesy of the artist

Model for a Trojan Horse, *1993*
Bronze
30 x 30 x 10 inches (76 x 76 x 25 cm)
Courtesy of Arizona State University Art Museum, Tempe, Arizona

Nietzsche by MOMO, *1993*
Rubber, metal and enamel paint
4 3/4 x 13 3/4 inches diameter (12 x 34.9 cm diameter)
Courtesy of the artist

Curriculum Vitae
Francesc Torres

Born in Barcelona, Spain, in 1948, Torres worked and lived in Paris from 1967 through 1969. He came to the United States in 1972 and has lived in New York City since 1974.

Solo Exhibitions

1973

Two Exercises, Illinois Center, Chicago.
Elemental Considerations, Francis Parker School, Chicago.
Two Hundred Steps, Evanston Arts Center, Evanston, Illinois.

1974

Galería Redor, Madrid, Spain.
Behaving, Vehicle Art Inc., Montreal, Canada.

1975

Almost Like Sleeping, Artists Space, New York.
Personal Intersections, 112 Greene Street Gallery, New York.

1976

Synchronic Attempts, 112 Greene Street Gallery, New York.
Installation Piece, Galerie St. Petri, Lund, Sweden.
Installation Piece, Galeria Akumulatory 2, Poznan, Poland.
ICA, Friedrichsfehn, West Germany.
Kleine Galerie, Oldenburg, West Germany.
La Casa De Tothom (es crema)/Everybody's House (is burning), Galeria "G", Barcelona, Spain.

1977

Behavioral Works, Channel C Manhattan Cable TV, New York.
Repetition of the Novelty, PS 1, Long Island City, New York.
CEAC, Toronto, Canada.
Accident, 112 Greene Street Gallery, New York.
Scenography of Labor, in an abandoned textile factory, sponsored by Galería Tres, Sabadell, Spain.

1978

Profane History, Tot Art, Spanish Television, Barcelona, Spain.
Three Books, Franklin Furnace, New York.
Residual Regions, Whitney Museum of AmericanArt, New York.

1979

Look, Look, Look At It!, Autonomous University of Barcelona, Spain.
Aquesta és Una Instal.lació Que Té Per Títol.../This Is An Installation That Has As A Title..., Fundació Joan Miró, Barcelona, Spain.
John Doesn't Know What Paul Does, The Everson Museum, Syracuse, New York.

1980

Rock-Solid-Thin-Air, The Planetarium at the Hudson River Museum, Yonkers, New York.
Seen Elsewhere, Watson Gallery, Wheaton College, Norton, Massachusetts.
The Assyrian Paradigm, Williams College Museum of Art, Williamstown, Massachusetts.
Residual Regions, Los Angeles Institute of Contemporary Art, Los Angeles.
Running Speech, Elise Meyer Gallery, New York.

1981

The Head of the Dragon, Whitney Museum of American Art, New York.

1982

Drawings, Elise Meyer Gallery, New York.
Field of Action, Herbert F. Johnson Museum of Art, Cornell University, Ithaca, New York.
Airstrip, Hartford School of Art, University of Hartford, Hartford, Connecticut.

1983

Tough Limo, Anderson Gallery, Virginia Commonwealth University, Richmond, Virginia.
Masters of Contemporary Drawings: Francesc Torres, Anderson Gallery, Virginia Commonwealth University, Richmond, Virginia.

1984

Tough Limo, Washington Project for the Arts, Washington, DC.
Warriors Have Funny Heads, Damon Brandt Gallery, New York.
When Boys Play Rough..., Electronic Billboard at Times Square, New York.
Some Machines Work Better Than Others, Metrònom, Barcelona, Spain.

1985

Tough Limo, Museum of Art, Carnegie Institute, Pittsburgh, Pennsylvania.
Paths of Glory, Fine Arts Center, State University of New York at Stony Brook, New York.
Drawings, PPOW Gallery, New York.

1986

The Dictatorship of Swiftness, La Jolla Museum of Contemporary Art, La Jolla, California.

1987

The Dictatorship of Swiftness, Long Beach Museum of Art, Long Beach, California.

1988

Belchite/South Bronx, Fine Arts Center, University of Massachusetts, Amherst, Massachusetts.

Belchite/South Bronx (single-channel video), The Museum of Modern Art, New York.

Name Any City, The Queens Museum, Long Island City, New York.

Plus Ultra, Kunstforum, Nationalgalerie, West Berlin.

1989

Belchite/South Bronx, Contemporary Arts Center, Cincinnati, Ohio.

The Assyrian Paradigm for Indiana, Herron Center for Contemporary Art, Indianapolis.

Dromos Indiana, Indiana State Museum, Indianapolis.

1990

Belchite/South Bronx, Knight Gallery, Spirit Square Center for the Arts, Charlotte, North Carolina.

Belchite/South Bronx, Walter Phillips Gallery, The Banff Center, Banff, Alberta, Canada.

Plus Ultra (single-channel video), Círculo de Bellas Artes, Madrid, Spain.

Dromos Indiana (single-channel video), Galeria Alfons Alcolea, ARCO, Madrid, Spain; Wexner Center for the Visual Arts, The Ohio State University, Columbus, Ohio; Pacific Film Archives, University Museum, Berkeley, California.

Belchite/South Bronx and **Plus Ultra** (single-channel video), College of the Arts, The Ohio State University, Columbus, Ohio.

Destiny, Entropy and Junk, Capp Street Project, San Francisco, California.

1991

La cabeza del dragón/The Head of the Dragon, (retrospective), Museo Nacional Centro de Arte Reina Sofía, Madrid, Spain.

El Carro de Fenc/The Hay Wain, Centre d'Art Santa Mònica, Barcelona, Spain.

Galeria Alfons Alcolea, Barcelona, Spain.

1992

Memorial, Hirshhorn Museum and Sculpture Garden, Smithsonian Institution, Washington, DC.

Crónica del extravío, Church of San Luís de los Franceses, Seville, Spain.

Galería Elba Benítez, Madrid, Spain.

The Bohen Foundation, New York.

Instituto de Cooperación Iberoamericana, Buenos Aires, Argentina.

1993

Silk Stockings, Kijkhuis, The Hague, Holland.

Too Late for Goya, Memorial Art Gallery, University of Rochester, Rochester, New York.

Too Late for Goya: Works by Francesc Torres, Arizona State University Art Museum, Tempe, Arizona.

Major Video, Film and Multi-media Installations

1975

Almost Like Sleeping, Artists Space, New York.

Personal Intersections, 112 Greene Street Gallery, New York.

1976

Synchronic Attempts, 112 Greene Street Gallery, New York.

The Construction of the Matrix, *Spain - Artistic Avant Garde and Social Reality 1936-1976*, Venice Biennale, Venice, Italy.

La Casa de Tothom (es crema)/Everybody's House (is burning), Galería "G", Barcelona, Spain.

1977

Repetition of the Novelty, PS 1, Long Island City, New York.

Accident, 112 Greene Street Gallery, New York.

Scenography of Labor, in an abandoned factory, Sabadell, Spain.

1978

Residual Regions, Whitney Museum of American Art, New York.

1979

Look, Look, Look At It!, Autonomous University of Barcelona, Spain.

Aquesta és Una Instal.lació Que Té Per Títol.../This Is An Installation That Has As A Title..., Fundació Joan Miró, Barcelona, Spain.

John Doesn't Know What Paul Does, Everson Museum, Syracuse, New York.

1980

Rock-Solid-Thin-Air, The Hudson River Museum, Yonkers, New York.

Seen Elsewhere, Watson Gallery, Wheaton College, Norton, Massachusetts.

The Assyrian Paradigm, Williams College, Williamstown, Massachusetts.

Running Speech, Elise Meyer Gallery, New York.

1981

The Head of the Dragon, Whitney Museum of American Art, New York.

1982

Field of Action, Johnson Museum, Cornell University, Ithaca, New York.

Airstrip, School of Art, University of Hartford, Hartford, Connecticut.

1983

Steel Balls, University of Colorado, Boulder, Colorado.

Tough Limo, Virginia Commonwealth University, Richmond, Virginia.

Jean's Lost Notebook, Fine Arts Museum, Santa Fe, New Mexico.

1984

When Boys Play Rough..., Electronic Billboard at Times Square, New York.

Clausewitz's Classroom, Stedelijk Museum, Amsterdam, Holland.

1985

Paths of Glory, New York State University at Stony Brook, New York.

La Casa del Gladiador (té golfes)/The Gladiator's House (has an attic), Palau Robert, Barcelona, Spain.

1986

The Dictatorship of Swiftness, Museum of Contemporary Art, La Jolla, California.

1987

Warszawa, Polytechnic University, Warsaw, Poland.

1988

Belchite/South Bronx, University of Massachusetts, Amherst, Massachusetts.

Plus Ultra, Kunstforum, Nationalgalerie, West Berlin.

The Assyrian Paradigm/Charlottenburg, The Queens Museum, Long Island City, New York.

1989

Oikonomos, Whitney Museum of American Art, New York.

Dromos Indiana, Indiana State Museum, Indianapolis, Indiana.

The Assyrian Paradigm for Indianapolis, Herron Center for Contemporary Art, University of Indiana at Indianapolis, Indiana.

1990

Destiny, Entropy and Junk, Capp Street Project, San Francisco.

1991

Cincuenta lluvias, Centro de Arte Reina Sofía, Madrid, Spain.

El Carro de Fenc/The Hay Wain, Centre d'Art Santa Mònica, Barcelona, Spain.

Amnèsia/Memòria / Amnesia/Memory, Centre d'Art Santa Mònica, Barcelona, Spain.

1992

Memorial, Hirshhorn Museum and Sculpture Garden, Smithsonian Institution, Smithsonian Institution, Washington, DC.

Crónica del extravío, Church of San Luís de los Franceses, Seville, Spain.

1993

Silk Stockings, Kijkhuis, The Hague, Holland.

Too Late For Goya, Memorial Art Gallery, University of Rochester, Rochester, New York.

Single-channel Videography

1973 Elemental Considerations. Black and white, sound, 60 minutes.

1974 Image's Identity. Black and white, sound, 29:44 minutes.

1974 Imitation of Myself. Black and white, sound, 30:21 minutes.

1974 An Attempt to Decondition Myself. Black and white, sound, 30:21 minutes.

1974-75 Behavioral Works. Black and white, sound, 31 minutes.

1983 Tough Limo. Color, sound, 16 minutes.

1988 Belchite/South Bronx, A Trans-Cultural and Trans-Historical Landscape. Color, sound, 39:14 minutes.

1988 Plus Ultra. Color, sound, 30:14 minutes.

1989 Dromos Indiana. Color, sound, 45 minutes.

1990 Sur del Sur. Color, sound, 15:15 minutes.

Filmography

1972 Interaction of Two Elements (Water-Fire [Sun]) on a Sheet of Paper. Super 8, color, silent, 3 minutes.

1977 Historia laica/Profane History. Super 8, color and B/W, sound, 5 minutes.

Sound Works

1973 Sound of a Volume/One Hour of Breathing =540,000 c. One hour.

1973 Comparisons of Urban Sound (Madrid/NewYork). One hour.

1973 Earth's Rotation. One hour.

1973 Sound of a Distance. One hour.

1974 Samples of Human Voice Obtained by Telephone. One hour.

Group Exhibitions

1968

Biennale de Bordeaux, France.

Festival de Nice, France.

1972

Encuentros de Pamplona, Pamplona, Spain.

Comunicación Actual, Barcelona, Spain.

1973

4 Elementos, Colegio de Arquitectos, Valencia, Spain.

4 Elementos, Galería Juana de Aizpuru, Seville, Spain.

Poesía Visual Catalana, Eina School, Barcelona, Spain.

Evanston Art Festival, Evanston, Illinois.

Nature Into Art, The Renaissance Society, University of Chicago, Chicago, Illinois.

Conceptual Art Festival, University of Kentucky, Lexington, Kentucky.

Información de arte, Tarragona, Spain.

Chicago, NAME Gallery, Chicago.

1974

German Institute of Culture, Barcelona and Madrid, Spain.

Realitat, Barcelona, Spain.

Flash Art Show, Milano, Italy, and Dusseldorf, West Germany.

Video and Performance Show, Vehicle Art Inc., Montreal, Canada.

Aidez l'Espagne, CISE, Paris.

Vehicle Art Inc., International Art Fair, Basel, Switzerland.

Prospective '74, Museu de Arte Contemporanea, São Paulo, Brazil.

Galerie des Locataires, 321 E. 12th Street, New York.

112 Greene Street Gallery, New York.

Impact Video Art, Musèe des Arts Decoratifs, Lausanne, Switzerland.

Noves Tendèncics a l'Art, FAD, Barcelona, Spain.

1975

25 Years to 2000, NAME Gallery, Chicago.

Performance, Museum of Contemporary Art, Chicago.

Rencontre Internationale Ouverte de Video, Espace Pierre Cardin, Paris.

Third International Open Encounter on Video, Galeria Civica d'Arte Moderna, Ferrara, Italy.

Impact Video Art, Palais des Beaux Arts, Brussels, Belgium.

Biennale de Paris, Musèe d'Art Moderne, Paris.

1976

Spanish Avant-Garde 1936/1976, Venice Biennale, Venice, Italy.

Spanish Avant-Garde 1936/1976, Fundació Joan Miró, Barcelona, Spain.

L'Objecte, Fundació Joan Miró, Barcelona, Spain.

Art amb nous procediments, Fundació Joan Miró, Barcelona, Spain.

Cornell/Sekula/Torres, Whitney Museum of American Art, New York.

1977

International Communication Event, Huset, Copenhagen, Denmark.

Ten Minutes, Centre Culturel de la Maison de l'Etudiant, Paris.

Works to be Destroyed, West Side Highway, New York.

Small Self-Portrait, Art Core Gallery, Kyoto, Japan.

1978

Small Self-Portrait, Osaka Prefectural Gallery, Osaka, Japan; West Bes Gallery, Nagoya, Japan

Artwords/Bookworks, LAICA, Los Angeles.

Difficult Decisions/Ethical Dilemmas, University of Minnesota, Duluth, Minnesota.

Artwords and Bookworks, Franklin Furnace, New York; Herron School of Art, Indianapolis, Indiana; New Orleans Contemporary Art Center, New Orleans, Louisiana; Artist's Books, National Art Gallery, Wellington, New Zealand; Govett-Brewster Art Gallery, New Plymouth, New Zealand; Auckland City Art Gallery, Auckland, New Zealand; Institute of Modern Art, Brisbane, Australia; Queen Victoria Museum and Art Gallery, Launceston, Australia; Tasmanian School of Art, Hobart, Australia; Experimental Art Foundation, Adelaide, Australia; Undercroft Gallery, Perth, Australia; Geelong Art Gallery, Victoria, Australia; Sculpture Center, Sydney, Australia.

Artist's Books, The New School for Social Research, New York.

1979

Small is Beautiful, Freedman Gallery, Albright College, Reading, Pennsylvania; Center Gallery, Bucknell University, Lewisburg, Pennsylvania; University of Maryland, Baltimore, Maryland; Edinboro State College, Edinboro, Pennsylvania.

Visual Poetry, School of Fine Arts, University of Barcelona, Barcelona, Spain.

Visual Poetry, Perpignan, France.

Pyramidal Influence, Wright State University, Dayton, Ohio.

1980

Pyramidal Influence, Midwest Museum of American Art, Elkhart, Indiana; Freedman Gallery, Albright College, Reading, Pennsylvania; Wesleyan University, Middletown, Connecticut.

Vigilance, Franklin Furnace, New York.

1981

Messages, Freedman Gallery, Albright College, Reading, Pennsylvania; Anderson Gallery, Virginia Commonwealth University, Richmond, Virginia.

CAPS at the State Museum, State Museum, Albany, New York.

Schemes, Elise Meyer Gallery, New York; Emily Lowe Gallery, Hofstra University, Hempstead, New York; Johnson Museum, Cornell University, Ithaca, New York.

Alternatives in Retrospect, New Museum, New York.

Lisbon International Drawing Biennale (LIS '81), Lisbon, Portugal.

1982

Schemes, Museum of Contemporary Art, Montreal, Canada.

Decision by Arms, Just Above Midtown/Downtown Gallery, New York.

Visual Politics, Alternative Museum, New York.

American Indian Community House, New York.

Arteder, Bilbao, Spain.

Centro Cultural de la Villa de Madrid, Madrid, Spain.

The Atomic Salon, Ronald Feldman Gallery, New York.

Books by Artists, Ministry of Culture, Madrid, Spain.

1983

Borrowed Time, Baskerville and Watson Gallery, New York.

Video as Attitude, Fine Arts Museum, Santa Fe, New Mexico.

Film as Installation, The Clocktower, New York.

Damon Brandt Gallery, New York.

Watching Television, School of Art and Design, University of Illinois at Urbana-Champaign, Illinois.

Hispanic Achievement in the Arts, The Equitable Gallery, New York.

Commentaries, University of Colorado Art Galleries, Boulder, Colorado.

1984

Apocalyptic Visions: The Impact of The Bomb in Recent American Art, Mount Holyoke College Museum of Art, Mount Holyoke, Massachusetts.

Art and Ideology, The New Museum of Contemporary Art, New York.

Automobile and Culture, The Museum of Contemporary Art, Los Angeles.

The Vanguard of the New, Museum of Contemporary Art, Chicago.

Art as Social Conscience, Bard College, Annandale On Hudson, New York.

Galeria Alfons Alcolea, ARCO, Madrid, Spain.

Disarming Images, nationally touring show, 1984-1986.

Montbeliard Video Festival, Montbeliard, France.

Locarno Video Festival, Locarno, Switzerland.

San Sebastián International Film Festival, Video Section, San Sebastian, Spain.

The Luminous Image, Stedelijk Museum, Amsterdam, Holland.

1985

Film and Video on Art, Whitney Museum of American Art, New York.

Disinformation, The Alternative Museum, New York.

The Big Car Show, Herron Gallery, University of Indiana at Indianapolis, Indiana.

Barcelona-Paris-New York, Palau Robert, Barcelona, Spain.

Biennale des Friedens, Kunstverein and Kunsthaus, Hamburg, West Germany.

Images for Survival, Arthur A. Houghton Gallery, Cooper Union, New York; Hiroshima Museum of Art, Hiroshima, Japan.

1986

Psychodrama, Philadelphia Art Institute, Philadelphia, Pennsylvania.

Oppression/Expression, Contemporary Arts Center, New Orleans, Louisiana.

Group Show, PPOW Gallery, New York.

Disarming Images, The Bronx Museum, New York.

II International Video Festival, Fine Arts Circle, Madrid, Spain.

Video: Installed, New Langton Arts, San Francisco.

1987

ETC., Polytechnic University, Warsaw, Poland.

Japan '87 Video and Television Festival, Spiral Hall, Tokyo, Japan.

All the News That's Fit for Prints, PPOW Gallery, New York.

La imagen sublime, Centro de Arte Reina Sofía, Madrid, Spain.

1988

Committed to Print, Museum of Modern Art, New York;Wright Art Galleries, Wright State University, Dayton, Ohio.

All the News That's Fit for Prints, Contemporary Arts Museum, Houston, Texas.

Fukui International Video Biennale, Fukui, Japan.

The Wolf at the Door, Hartwick College, Oneonta, New York.

Art and the Law, Temple University, Philadelphia, Pennsylvania.

Atelier Berlin, DAAD Gallery, West Berlin, West Germany.

Group Show, Damon Brandt Gallery, New York.

American Film Institute Video Festival, Los Angeles.

Montbeliard Video Festival, Montbeliard, France.

The Bonn Videonnale, Bonn, West Germany.

1989

The Whitney Biennial, Whitney Museum of American Art, New York.

The Whitney Biennial Film/Video Exhibition, Instituto de Estudios Norteamericanos, Barcelona, Spain; National Gallery, Ottawa, Ontario, Canada; University of North Carolina, Greensboro, North Carolina; Cornell University, Ithaca, New York; Museum of Art, University of Georgia, Athens, Georgia; Vancouver Art Gallery, Vancouver, Canada.

Art and the Law, Rose Art Museum, Brandeis University, Waltham, Massachusetts.

Internationale Filmfestspiele, VideoFest '89, Medien Operative, West Berlin.

Committed to Print, Wright State University, Dayton, Ohio; The Peace Museum, Chicago, Illinois; Glenbow Museum, Calgary, Alberta, Canada.

Japan '89 Video and Television Festival, Spiral Hall, Tokyo, Japan.

L'Avanguarda de l'Escultura Catalana, Centre d'Art Santa Mònica, Barcelona, Spain.

1990

Committed to Print, New York State Museum, Albany, New York; Spencer Museum of Art, Lawrence, Kansas; Newport Harbor Art Museum, Newport Beach, California.

If Buildings Could Talk, Pacific Film Archive, University Art Museum, University of California at Berkeley.

Nearness and Distance, Walter Phillips Gallery, The Banff Center for the Arts, Banff, Alberta, Canada.

Construction in Process, Lodz, Poland.

Re-Writing History, Kettle's Yard Gallery, University of Cambridge, United Kingdom.

Bienal de la imagen en movimiento, Museo Nacional Centro de Arte Reina Sofía, Madrid, Spain.

On the Road: Selections from the Permanent Collection of the San Diego Museum of Contemporary Art, Duke University Museum of Art, Durham, North Carolina.

1991

El sueño imperativo, Círculo de Bellas Artes, Madrid, Spain.

Re-Writing History, Ikon Gallery, Birmingham, United Kingdom; Cornerhouse, Manchester, United Kingdom.

On the Road: Selections from the Permanent Collection of the San Diego Museum of Contemporary Art, J.B. Speed Art Museum, Louisville, Kentucky; Springfield Museum of Fine Arts, Massachusetts; San Diego Museum of Fine Arts, La Jolla, California; Memorial Art Gallery of the University of Rochester, New York.

Work in Progress, Galeria Alfons Alcolea, ARCO, Barcelona, Spain.

Artists of Conscience, The Alternative Museum, New York.

The Whitney Biennial, Whitney Museum of American Art, New York.

Dénonciation, GNAC, Usine Fromage, Ecole d'Architecture de Normandie, Rouen, France.

1992

On the Road: Selections from the Permanent Collection of the San Diego Museum of Contemporary Art, Utah Museum of Fine Arts, University of Utah, Salt Lake City, Utah; The Philbrook Museum of Art, Tulsa, Oklahoma.

Denontiation, Centre d'Art Santa Mònica, Barcelona, Spain.

Idees i Actituts, Entorn de l'Art Conceptual a Catalunya, 1964-1980..., Centre d'Art Santa Mònica, Barcelona, Spain.

The Power of the City/The City of Power, Whitney Museum of American Art at Federal Reserve Plaza, New York.

Galeria Alfons Alcolea, ARCO, Madrid, Spain.

Art at the Armory: Occupied Territory, Museum of Contemporary Art at the Illinois National Guard Armory, Chicago.

Exposición de Documentación Plus Ultra, Museo de Arte Contemporáneo, Seville, Spain.

America Discovers Spain, The Spanish Institute, New York.

Bienal de la imagen en movimiento, Museo Nacional Centro de Arte Reina Sofía, Madrid, Spain.

Fragments, Palau Episcopal, Girona, Spain.

1993

The Whitney Biennial, Whitney Museum of American Art, New York.

World Wide Video Festival, Kijkhuis, The Hague, Holland.

Montage 93, Rochester, New York.

Desmontaje, Museo Nacional Centro de Arte Reina Sofía, Madrid, Spain; IVAM, Centre Julio Gonzalez, Valencia, Spain.

1993 Whitney Biennial in Seoul, National Museum of Contemporary Art, Seoul, South Korea.

Markets of Resistance, White Columns, New York.

Bibliography

Articles, Essays, Interviews and Reviews

Ancona, Victor. "Francesc Torres: Sociopsychological Video." *Videography* Oct. 1981: 64-73.

Artner, Alan G. "Question: When Is an Art Object not an Art Object." *Chicago Tribune* 6 Jan. 1974, sec. 6: 7.

Atkins, Robert. *Village Voice* 27 June 1989: 95.

Baker, Kenneth. Review. *San Francisco Chronicle* 9 June 1986: 70.

______________. Review. *San Francisco Chronicle* 8 Nov. 1992: 58.

Berkson, Bill. Review. *Artforum* Nov. 1990: 174.

Birringer, Johannes. "Invisible Cities/Transcultural Images." *Performing Arts Journal* 33-34 (1989): 134-38.

______________. "The Damnation of Culture in Modern Video Sculpture." *Tema Celeste* July-Oct. 1990: 30-33.

Bonet, Eugeni. "Polivídeo: El vídeo en plural." *Telos* Mar.-May 1987: 109.

______________. "The State of the (Video) Art." *Lápiz* Feb. 1990: 42-55.

______________. "La soledad de cuatro vídeo-artistas de fondo." *Vídeo Actualidad* Apr. 1983: 18-23.

Borràs, Maria Lluïsa. Review. *La Vanguardia* 1 Oct. 1991, Culture and Arts sec.: 7.

______________. Review. *La Vanguardia* 3 Dec. 1991, Culture and Arts sec.: 2.

Bradley, Kim. "Spanish Vignettes." *Art in America* Oct. 1991: 138-9, 171.

Brenson, Michael. Review. *The New York Times* 18 Oct. 1985: 26C.

Bufill, Juan. "La caída de la historia." *ABC* 8 Nov. 1991: 30.

Calhoon, Sharon L. "Process Revealed: Dromos Indiana at the Indiana State Museum." *Arts Indiana* June 1989: 15-17.

Cameron, Dan. "Four Installations: Francesc Torres, Mierle Ukeles, Louise Lawler/Allan McCollum and Todt." *Arts Magazine* Dec. 1984: 66-68.

Canal, Charo. "A la busca de la verdadera naturaleza humana." *El Sol* 4 Feb. 1991: 27.

______________. "En este fin de siglo, la cueva primigenia es el museo." *El Sol* 17 Oct. 1991: 57.

Carr, Cindy. "The Complex Implications of the Invisible." *Chicago Express* Feb. 1973: 10-11.

Casado, Luis. "El Carro de Fiemo." *El País* 4 Nov. 1991: 38.

Castaño, Adolfo. "Las reflexiones de Francesc Torres." *ABC* 14 Feb. 1991: 127.

Cembalest, Robin. "La Bienal del Whitney/Un escenario para provocar." *El País* 3 June 1989, Art sec.: 1, 5.

______________. "Zeus con un bate de béisbol." *El País* 3 June 1989, Art sec.: 5.

______________. Spain. *ARTnews* Nov. 1990: 127-29.

Chacón, José Antonio. "Memoria reflexiva." *Diario 16* 10 May 1992: 22.

Codina, Rosa. "Polèmica a Nova York per l'Obra d'Art d'un Català." *Diari de Barcelona* 25 June 1989.

Cohrs, Timothy. "A Report Back from the Other-World of Printmaking." *Arts Magazine* Nov. 1986: 43.

Combalia, Victòria. "Francesc Torres: La casa de todos (se quema)." *Batik* Mar. 1977: 30-31.

______________. "Francesc Torres, obra reciente." *Batik* Oct. 1980: 77-79.

______________. Review. *Batik* Jan./Feb. 1981: 41.

______________. "La velocidad detenida/La provocación como arte." *El País* 12 Aug. 1989, Art sec.: 1, 3.

______________. "Exposiciones en Nueva York." *El País* 23 May 1992, Art sec.: 4-5.

Conal, Robbie. Review. *LA Weekly* 6-12 Mar. 1987.

Corredor-Matheos, José. "Francesc Torres: Cuando la casa de todos se quema...." *Destino* 9 Dec. 1976: 69.

Cotter, Holland. "A Bland Biennial." *Art in America* Sept. 1989: 83, 85.

Da Vinci, Mona. Review. *Soho Weekly News* 20 Mar. 1975: 17.

______________. Review. *Soho Weekly News* 29 Jan. 1976: 18.

Decker, Andrew. "Clash of the Titans." *Art & Auction* Sept. 1989.

Duguet, Anne-Marie. "The Luminous Image - Video Installation." *Camera Obscura* 13/14: 31, 42-43.

Durán, Manuel. "Francesc Torres: Las lluvias de la historia o la escenografía de los medios." *El Guía* May-June 1991: 79-81.

Editorial. "Francesc Torres, Colón y un templo." *El Correo de Andalucía* 8 May 1992: 35.

Esche, Charles and Anna Harding. "Re-Writing History." *AND Journal of Art* 23/24 (190-91): 3-9.

España, Ramón de. "El arte no es un refugio." *El País* 28 Oct. 1991: 31.

Espinosa, María José. Interview. *Europ-Art* Sept. 1991: 25-32.

Estevez, Isidre. Review. *Diari de Barcelona* 18 Oct. 1991: 35.

Farrés, Ramon. Interview. *Avui* 29 Dec. 1988, Culture sec.: 38.

Fernández, Ángel. "Un escultor de la memoria social." *El Mundo* 5 Feb. 1991: 34.

Figueres, Abel. "Objectes, Imatges, Idees i Simbols." *Avui* 9 Oct. 1991, Art sec.: 3.

____________. "Una Estrategia Vital, Estética i Social." *Avui* 27 Nov. 1991, Art sec.: 3.

____________. "Francesc Torres' Latest Installations." *Catalonia* Nov. 1991: 37-41.

Findsen, Owen. "Art from the Other Side of the Atlantic." *The Cincinnati Enquirer* 11 June 1989: E3.

____________. "Artist Caught in Spat, by Zeus." *The Cincinnati Enquirer* 28 May 1989: E3.

Fontana, Juan C. Interview. "La instalación: Una forma del arte contemporáneo." *¿Qué Hacemos?* Feb. 1993: 22-23.

Fontova, Rosario. Article. *El Periódico* 17 Oct. 1991: 36.

Fontrodona, Oscar. Review. *ABC* 17 Oct. 1991: 11.

Fudge, Jane. Review. *Muse* Dec./Jan. 1983-84: 10, 15.

García Sevilla, Ferran. "Análisis de los trabajos conceptuales de Francesc Torres 1." *Artes Plásticas* Jan. 1976: 20-22.

García Sevilla, Ferran. "Análisis de los trabajos conceptuales de Francesc Torres 2." *Artes Plásticas* Feb. 1976: 15-18.

____________________. "Análisis de los trabajos conceptuales de Francesc Torres." 3. *Artes Plásticas* Mar. 1976: 13-16.

Gambrell, Jamey. "All the News That's Fit for Prints: A Parallel of Social Concerns of the 1930's and the 1980's." *The Print Collector's Newsletter* May/June 1987: 52-55.

Garmel, Marion. "In Love with Art and Cars, Art Should Say Something About Reality." *The Indianapolis News* 18 May 1989: D1, D4.

Gelavert, M. "Francesc Torres/El arte de la instalación." *RS* Winter 1991: 40-44.

Gibson, Eric. Review. *The Washington Times* 18 Mar. 1992: E6.

Glueck, Grace. "Met Throws Thunderbolts at Zeus." *The New York Times* 18 May 1989: 13, 16.

____________. "Met's Zeus Is Home Free as Whitney Finds Another." *The New York Times* 17 June 1989: 13.

Goldberg, Vicky. "A Brave New World of Electronic Art and Images." *The New York Times* 25 July 1993, Arts & Leisure sec.: 30, 31.

Guardiola Román, Juan. Interview. *El Guía* Mar. 1990: 38-44.

____________________. "La Memoria Rota." *Ars Video* May 1992: 39-45.

Guasch, Anna. Review. *Diari de Barcelona* 24 Oct. 1991: 35.

Guillamon, Julià. Interview. *Cultura* Oct. 1991: 12-19.

______________. "L'Espai Interdit." *Cultura* Oct. 1991: 20-21.

Hall, Jacqueline. Review. *Columbus Dispatch* 25 June 1989.

Hanhardt, John. "Video Installation: Expanded Forms." *American Federation of the Arts Newsletter* Oct. 1982: 2-4.

______________. "Seis instalaciones que cuestionan e interrogan al vídeo y a la televisión." *El País* 14 Jan. 1984, Art sec.: 4-5.

Haydon, Harold. Review. *Chicago Sun-Times* 15 April 1973:16.

Hoge, Helmut and Sabine Vogel. "Konkrete Poesie in Warschau." *Die Tageszeitung* 27 June 1987: 17-18.

Johnson, David Torbet. "Francesc Torres: Belchite/South Bronx." *Dialogue* Sept.-Oct. 1989: 17.

Knight, Christopher. Review. *Los Angeles Times* 30 Sept. 1992: F1, F6.

Krebs, Betty Dietz. Review. *The Dayton Daily News* 13 May 1989: C3.

Kreis, Elfi. "Das Karussell de Geschichte." *Berliner Kunstblatt* Fall 1988: 83-84.

Kuspit, Donald. Review. *Art in America* Mar. 1981: 130-31.

____________. Review. *Artforum* Jan. 1989: 113.

____________. Reprint from the Barcelona-Paris-New York exhibition catalogue. *RS* Winter 1991.

La Cruz, Elena de. "Las instalaciones de Francesc Torres en el Reina Sofía invitan a reflexionar sobre nuestro tiempo." *Diario 16* 5 Feb. 1991: 27

Lautreamont, Isadore Ducasse. "Nearness and Distance." C Winter 1991: 46-47.

Levi Strauss, David. Interview. "Francesc Torres Tough Limo." *Artscribe* Nov./Dec. 1991: 39-51.

Levin, Kim. "Coming Up Empty." *Village Voice* 9 May 1989: 99-100.

Lewis, Jo Ann. "War's Dilemma, Gone Up in Smoke." *The Washington Post* 12 Feb. 1992: C1, C4.

Lieberthal, Mary Louchheim. "On the Spanish Easel." *Saturday Review* 29 Oct. 1977: 24-25

Lippard, Lucy R. "A Small Slice of Whose Pie." *Village Voice* 8 June 1982.

Lipson, Karin. "Get Ready for the Barbs." *New York Newsday* 26 April 1989, Part II: 8-9.

López Anaya, Jorge. "Con Francesc Torres." *Diario La Nación* 30 Jan. 1993, Sec. 3: 6.

Loughery, John. "Whitney Upsets Met." *New Art Examiner* Summer 1989: 11.

Macía, Albert. Interview. *Avui* 17 Jan. 1990, Art sec.: 4.

Mannheimer, Steve. Review. *The Indianapolis Star* 21 May 1989: E10.

Mason, M.S. Review. *Colorado Daily* 14-15 Oct. 1983: 21, 23.

Minton, David. "Artist Uses Junked Car, Basketballs To Make Point." *Lexington Herald Leader* 11 June 1989: H5.

Montagut, Albert. "El Metropolitan modifica una instalación de Francesc Torres para la Bienal del Whitney." *El País* 6 June 1989, Culture sec.: 36.

Moreno, Alberto. "Francesc Torres: Explorador de la memoria." *El Europeo* Feb. 1991: 84-89.

Morse, Margaret. "Staging Scenes of Loss." *Video Networks* Oct./Nov. 1990: 9-12.

Nungesser, Michael. "Collage aus Botschafsresten." *Der Tages Spiegel* 27 Oct. 1988: 4.

Ocón, María. "Francesc Torres: Reflexión sobre unos Escombros." *La Vanguardia* 9 Dec. 1988, Culture sec.: 40.

Olivares, Rosa. "Arte es lo que hago, pero no en lo que pienso." *Lápiz* April 1991: 24-35.

Ortega, Julio. "Belchite/South Bronx." *Diario 16* 9 Sept. 1989, Culturas.

Ortega, Julio. "Francesc Torres: la serie Newsweek." *El Nuevo Día* 21 Feb. 1993: 18, 19.

Palacio, Manuel. "Francesc Torres: El arte crítico en el II Festival Nacional de Video." *Fundesco Magazine* Feb. 1987: 16.

Palacio, Manuel. "Dromos Indiana, una video-instalación de Francesc Torres." *Fundesco Magazine* Mar. 1990: 1, 20.

Paoletti, John. "Francesc Torres." *Arts Magazine* Nov. 1982: 42-43.

Paoletti, John. "Learning from Experience: Francesc Torres." *Arts Magazine* June 1981: 88-91.

Penn, Michelle. "Culture Crash." *Street Wise* Oct. 1992: 19.

Pérez Ornia, J.R. "Los juguetes se rompen...." *El País* 23 Dec. 1986, Culture sec.: 34.

Picazo, Gloria. "Juegos de Guerra." *Lápiz* Nov. 1989: 54-59.

Piett, Nicole. Review. *The New Mexican Pasatiempo* 20 May 1983: 21.

Portell, Susanna. "Francesc Torres: Una Escenografia per a les Idees." *Papers D'Art* Jan.-Feb. 1992: 11.

Price, Max. Review. *Denver Post* 20 Sept. 1983: B1, B3.

Princenthal, Nancy. "Political Prints: An Opinion Poll." *The Print Collector's Newsletter* May/June 988: 47.

Queralt, Rosa. Review. *Artforum* Feb. 1992: 126.

Rapko, John. Review. *Artweek* 13 Sept. 1990: 14-15.

Restany, Pierre. "Barcelona-Parigi-New York." *Domus International* Feb. 1986: 187-88.

Reveaux, Tony. Review. *LA Artweek* 25 Jan. 1990: 16.

Ricart, Maite. "Francesc Torres. El arte sólo es un vehículo."RS Fall 1989: 70-71.

Rice, Shelley. Review. *Artforum* Sept. 1981: 81."

___________. "Francesc Torres: The Tyranny of the Past." *Afterimage* Dec. 1982: 4-7.

___________. "The Luminous Image - Video Installations at the Stedelijk Museum." *Afterimage* Dec. 1984: 14.

Robertson, Jean. "A Spanish-Born Artist's View of the 500 and Interview." *New Times* 6.2 (June 1989): 22.

Samaniego, Fernando. "La práctica de la instalación." *El País* 20 Jan. 1990, Art sec.: 8.

_________________. "Francesc Torres expone sus instalaciones de la memoria en Madrid." *El País* 4 Feb. 1991: 29.

Sargent-Wooster, Ann. "Censorship vs. Appropriation at the Whitney." *High Performance* Fall 1989: 14-15.

Sei, Keiko. "European Media Art (Part II)." *Limbo* 4.

Serra, Catalina. "Carretades de Fenc." *El País* 17 Oct. 1991: 1-3.

Smith, Roberta. Review. *The New York Times* 28 Apr. 1989: C32.

Spiegel, Olga. Interview. *La Vanguardia* 14 July 1991: 51, 54.

Stepken, Angelika. "DAAD-Gäste in Berlin. Francesc Torres." *Berliner Kunstblatt* Jan. 1987: 25-26.

Swartz, Jeffrey. "The Imperative Dream." *Flash Art News* May/June 1991: 173.

Thai, Quynh. "Clash of the Titans: The Met Protests Video Installation at the Whitney." *The Independent* Aug./Sept. 1989: 5-6.

Thomson, Patricia. "Struggling with the R-Complex." *High Performance* 26 (1984): 75, 77.

______________. "Video and Electoral Appeal." *Afterimage* Feb. 1985: 8-9.

Van Den Brink, H.M. "The Foute Wereld Op Zijn Kop." *NRC Handelsblad* Cultureel Supplement 3 Mar. 1991: 2.

Vidal, Jaume. Article. *El Observador* 16 Oct. 1991: 52.

Villaespesa, Mar. "Torres y Tatafiore." *Figura* Fall 1985: 88-93.

______________. "History's Broken Toys." *Artforum* Jan. 1991: 109-115.

Vogel, Sabine. "Die Botschaft Ist das Medium." *Die Tageszeitung* 27 Oct. 1988: 19.

Wiley, Jocelyn. "Nearness and Distance." *Parachute* Jan.-Mar. 1991: 66-67.

Wright, Patricia. Review. *Art New England* May 1988: 24.

Yagüe, Antonio M. Interview. *Fundesco* Feb. 1, 87: 5-6.

Yalkut, Jud. "Videospace/Interface." *Dialogue* Sept./Oct. 1989: 13-17.

Yard, Sally. "The Shadow of the Bomb." *Arts Magazine* Apr. 1984: 79.

Yau, John. "Official Policy. Reflections on a Decade of the Whitney Biennial." *Arts Magazine* Sept. 1989: 53.

Zabalbeascoa, Anatxu. "El Compromís del Artista." *Diari de Barcelona* 20 Oct. 1991: 4-5.

______________. Review. *Art Press* Feb. 1992: 86.

Zaya, Octavio. Hartísimo entrevista a Francesc Torres. *Hartísimo* Fall 1985: 117-28.

______________. "El revisionismo de FrancescTorres." *Diario 16* 27 Apr. 1986, Cultural sec.: 8.

Exhibition Catalogues

Berkowitz, Terry. *La Casa de Tothom (es crema)*. Barcelona: Galeria "G," 1976.

Bonet, Eugeni. "Cinema i Vídeo experimental i d'Artistes a Catalunya (Un Megamix)." *Idees I Actituds. Entorn a L'Art Conceptual a Catalunya, 1964-1980*. Barcelona: Centre d'Art Santa Mònica, Generalitat de Catalunya, 1992.

Combalia, Victòria. "Francesc Torres: Biografía, biología, historia." *La cabeza del dragón*. Madrid: Museo Nacional Centro de Arte Reina Sofía, 1991.

Gordon, Kelly. *Francesc Torres, Memorial*. Washington, DC:Hirshhorn Museum and Sculpture Garden, Smithsonian Institution, 1992.

Grisebach, Lucius. "Die Gegenwart der Vergangenheit in den Dingen." *Francesc Torres, Plus Ultra*. West Berlin: Berliner Künstlerprogramm des DAAD; Nationalgalerie Berlin, 1988.

Hanhardt, John. "Francesc Torres: The Limits of Discourse." *Francesc Torres, Works From the Field, a Selection*. Ithaca: Herbert F. Johnson Museum of Art, Cornell University, 1982.

______________. "Landscapes of History: The Art of Francesc Torres." *Francesc Torres, Plus Ultra*. West Berlin: Berliner Kunstlerprogramm des DAAD; Nationalgalerie Berlin, 1988.

______________. "The Discourse of Landscape Video Art: From Fluxus to Post-Modernism." *American Landscape Video, the Electronic Grove*. Pittsburgh: The Carnegie Museum of Art, 1988.

______________. *1989 Biennial Exhibition*. New York: Whitney Museum of American Art; Norton, 1989.

______________. "La excavación de lo real: El arte multi-media de Francesc Torres." *La cabeza del dragón*. Madrid: Museo Nacional Centro de Arte Reina Sofía, 1991.

______________. "Media Art Worlds: New Film Expressions in Film and Video 1991-93." *1993 Biennial Exhibition*. New York: Whitney Museum of American Art, 1993.

______________. "Silk Stockings." *1993 World Wide Video Festival*. The Hague: Kijkhuis, 1993.

Judson, William. "Francesc Torres." *Francesc Torres: Tough Limo*. Pittsburgh: The Carnegie Museum of Art, 1985.

______________. "Context i Apropiació: Un Lloc en la Història." *El Carro de Fenc*. Barcelona: Centre d'Art Santa Mònica, 1991.

Kuspit, Donald. "Symptoms of Critique: Nancy Spero and Francesc Torres." *Art and Ideology*. New York: New Museum of Contemporary Art, 1984.

______________. "Francesc Torres." *Paths of Glory*. Stony Brook: Fine Arts Center, State University of New York, 1985.

______________. Francesc Torres. *Barcelona-Paris-New York*. Barcelona: The Autonomous Government of Catalonia, 1985.

Levi Strauss, David. Catalogue Essay. *Capp Street Project 1989-1990*. San Francisco: Capp Street Project, 1991.

______________. **"Colón más allá."** *Plus Ultra Intervenciones*. Sevilla: Pabellón de Andalucía, Expo 92, 1992.

London, Barbara. "Four Points of View." *Commentaries*. Boulder: University of Colorado Art Galleries, 1983.

Lubar, Robert. "Centers and Peripheries: Eight Artists from Spain." *America Discovers Spain 1*. New York: The Spanish Institute, 1992.

Macià, Albert. "Conversa mantinguda entre Albert Macià i Francesc Torres," 1 de juliol de 1991. *El Carro de Fenc*. Barcelona: Centre d'Art Santa Mònica, 1991.

Mignot, Dorine. Introduction. *The Luminous Image*. Amsterdam: Stedelijk Museum, 1984.

Nye, Timothy. "Conceptual Art: A Spatial Perspective." *The Power of the City/The City of Power*. New York: Whitney Museum of American Art, 1992. 21-23.

Onorato, Ronald J. "Francesc Torres: The Dictatorship of Swiftness." *Parameters*. La Jolla: La Jolla Museum of Contemporary Art, 1986.

______________. "Collecting in Context." *San Diego Museum of Contemporary Art/Selections from the Permanent Collection*. La Jolla: San Diego Museum of Contemporary Art, 1990.

Palacio, Manuel. "Tough Limo." *La imagen sublime*. Madrid: Museo Nacional Centro de Arte Reina Sofía, 1987.

Parcerisas, Pilar. "Memòria Històrica contra Amnèsia Col.lectiva." *El Carro de Fenc*. Barcelona: Centre d'Art Santa Mònica, 1991.

Picazo, Gloria. "It Is Difficult To Bungle a Good Idea." *Idees i Actituds. Entorn de l'Art Conceptual a Catalunya, 1964-1980*. Barcelona: Centre d'Art Santa Mònica, Generalitat de Catalunya, 1992.

Posner, Helaine. Introduction. *Belchite/South Bronx, A Trans-Cultural and Trans-Historical Landscape*. Amherst: University of Massachusetts, 1988.

Pritikin, Renny. *Video Installed*. San Francisco: New Langton Arts, 1987.

Rose, Barbara. *Memory and Amnesia: Spanish Artists Abroad. America Discovers Spain 1*. New York: The Spanish Institute, 1992.

Simonot, Beatrice. "Francesc Torres." *Dénonciation*, GNAC. Rouen: Ecole d'Architecture de Normandie, 1991.

Villaespesa, Mar. "The Ultimate Reason." *Belchite/South Bronx, A Trans-Cultural and Trans-Historical Landscape*. Amherst: University of Massachusetts, 1988.

Wasserman, Nadine. Catalogue Essay. *Art at the Armory: Occupied Territory*. Chicago: Museum of Contemporary Art, 1992.

Wyle, Deborah. *Committed to Print*. New York: Museum of Modern Art, 1988.

Wright, Beryl J. "Artifact and Art: The Armory as Exhibition Site." *Art At The Armory: Occupied Territory*. Chicago: Museum of Contemporary Art, 1992.

Zeitlin, Marilyn. *Masters of Contemporary Drawing I: Francesc Torres*. Richmond: Anderson Gallery, Virginia Commonwealth University, 1983.

______________. "Honor Roll." *Belchite/South Bronx, A Trans-Cultural and Trans-Historical Landscape*. Amherst: University of Massachusetts, 1988.

By The Artist

Image's Identity, documentation. On Site/On Energy. New York: Site Inc., 1974.

About Behavior: Three Works, book. Edicions Alternes #5. Barcelona: Fundació Anselm Turmeda, 1975.

Everybody's House (is burning), book. New York: Francesc Torres, 1977.

"Site: Empresa Deconstructora," article. *Artes Plásticas* Apr. 1977.

"Escuela Pública 1," article. *Artes Plásticas* May, 1977.

"Notas sobre el arte como comportamiento," essay. *Artes Plásticas*, 1977.

Mira, Mira, book. Barcelona: Autonomous University of Barcelona, 1979.

"The Crimean Trick," catalogue text. **Film as Installation.** New York: The Clocktower, 1983. 7.

"Disinformation - Information Before Television (long ago and far away), catalogue text." *Disinformation, the Manufacture of Consent*. New York: The Alternative Museum, 1985.

"Notas Sueltas," essay. *Hartísimo* Fall 1985: 119.

"Tough Limo," text. *Francesc Torres: Tough Limo*. Pittsburgh: The Carnegie Museum of Art, 1985.

"Clausewitz's Classroom," art text. *Alles und Noch Viel Mehr, das Poetische ABC*. Bern: Benteli Verlag, 1985. 958-61.

"Turmoil in the Barracks," art text. *Art Criticism* 2.3 (1986): 85-88.

"Arte en la Baja Edad Media," article. *Telos* Mar.-May 1987: 128-30.

"Absolute Fire," essay. *Belchite/South Bronx, A Trans-Cultural and Trans-Historical Landscape*. Amherst: University of Massachusetts. 74-104.

"About Plus Ultra," catalogue text. **Francesc Torres, Plus Ultra.** West Berlin: Berliner Kunstlerprogramm des DAAD; Nationalgalerie Berlin, 1988. 23-27.

Text. *Blick Wechsel*. West Berlin: Argon/DAAD, 1988. 340.

"El fuego absoluto," essay. *Balcón* 3 (1989): 42-54.

"Plus Ultra," text. *Arena* April 1989: 94-97.

"Dromos Indiana," essay. *Artforum* May 1989: 113-15.

"Policías y ladrones al mismo tiempo: Arte, financiación estatal y reacción política en USA," article. *Lápiz* Feb 1990: 36-39.

"Una práctica equívoca," essay. *El País* 17 Feb. 1990, Art sec.: 4-5.

"El fuego absoluto," essay. *Historia y Fuente Horal*. No. 3. Barcelona: University of Barcelona, Barcelona, 1990. 5-20.

"Clarity That Hurts," lecture excerpts. *Contemporary Art in Context*. New York: The Museum of Modern Art, 1990. 57-58.

"El museo flexible," article. *El País* 24 Nov. 1990, Culture sec.: 9.

"The Art of the Possible," article. *Illuminating Video/An Essential Guide to Video Art*. New York: Aperture; San Francisco: Bay Area Video Coalition, 1991.

"La gran pantalla," article. *El Europeo* Jan. 1991: 92-93.

"Estado y cultura," article. *El País* 19 June 1991, Opinion sec.: 18.

"Respuesta a la Quinta Columna," article. *Lapíz* Oct. 1991: 28-29.

"El accidente contextualizado," catalogue essay. *La cabeza del dragón*. Madrid: Museo Nacional Centro de Arte Reina Sofía, 1991. 29-36.

"El Carro de Fenc," catalogue essay. *El Carro de Fenc*. Barcelona: Centre d'Art Santa Mònica, 1991. 24-31.

"Amnèsia/Memòria," catalogue essay. *El Carro de Fenc*. Barcelona: Centre d'Art Santa Mònica, 1991. 66-69.

"Objectes Freds," catalogue essay. *El Carro de Fenc*. Barcelona: Centre d'Art Santa Mònica, 1991. 86-114.

"Pot Ser Fer Art amb Contingut Social i que no Acabi Essent Decoració," catalogue essay. *El Carro de Fenc*. Barcelona: Centre d'Art Santa Mònica, 1991. 116-19.

"Destiny, Entropy and Junk," catalogue essay. *Capp Street Project 1989-1990*. San Francisco: Capp Street Project, 1991. 22.

"The Art of the Possible," original version. *ARS Video* 1992: 91-96.

"Paseo por un campo minado," article. *El País* 25 Apr. 1992, Culture sec.: 10.

"Lo que el viento se llevó," article. *Lápiz* May-June 1992: 22-25.

"Crónica del extravío," transcript of a fragment of the soundtrack for the installation by the same title. *Plus Ultra Intervenciones*. Sevilla: Pabellón de Andalucía, Expo 92, 1992: 36.

"The Newsweek Series: An Act of Revenge in the Recoding of This Week's News," exhibition brochure. New York: The Bohen Foundation, 1992.

"Objectified Events: The Gallery as a Beach for Historical Flotsam," exhibition brochure. New York: The Bohen Foundation, 1992.

Article, *Cinevídeo* Dec. 1992: 72.

"La caja de los sueños," text. *Photovisión* 24 1993: 15-16.

"Arte en el arsenal, conversation with Beryl Wright, Associate Curator at the Museum of Contemporary Art, Chicago." *Lápiz* Feb. 1993: 28-35.

Books by the Artist

Ombra: Obscuritat Relativa. Barcelona: Quaderns, 1972.

About Behavior: Three Works. Edicions Alternes #5. Barcelona: Fundació Anselm Turmeda, 1975.

Everybody's House (is burning). New York: Francesc Torres, 1977.

Belchite/South Bronx, A Trans-Cultural and Trans-Historical Landscape. Amherst: University of Massachusetts, 1989.

¿Qué Hacer? Barcelona: Galeria Alfons Alcolea, 1991.

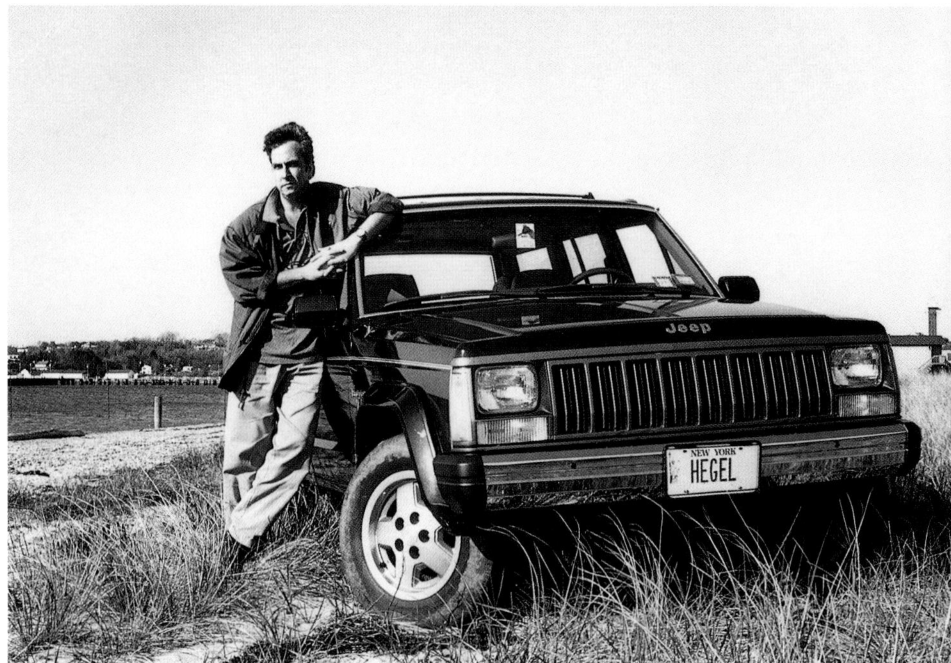

Francesc Torres with Hegel Cum Auto, 1993

Books:

Albertazzi, Liliana and Beatrice Simonot. *Dénonciation*, GNAC. Rouen: Ecole d'Architecture de Normandie, 1991.

Brentano, Robyn, ed. with Mark Savitt. *112 Workshop/112 Greene Street: History, Artists and Artworks*. New York: New York U P, 1981.

Cortés, José Miguel G. *La creación artística como cuestionamiento/Artistic Creation at Stake*. València: Institut Valencià de la Joventud, Generalitat Valenciana, 1990.

Decker, Edith and Wulf Herzogenrath. *Video-Skulptur, Retrospektiv Und Aktuell*. Koln: DuMont Buchverlag, 1989.

Dyckes, Williams. *Contemporary Spanish Art*. New York: Art Digest Inc., 1975.

Kriesche, Richard. *Artists' Statements*. Graz: Richard Kriesche, 1987.

Lippard, Lucy R. *Overlays: Contemporary Art and the Art of Prehistory*. New York: Pantheon, 1983.

Marchan Fiz, Simon. *España: Vanguardia artística y realidad social, 1936-1976*. Barcelona: Editorial Gustavo Gili, 1976.

Silk, Gerald. *Cultural Reconstruction, Explosion and Reflection. Automobile and Culture*. New York: Abrams, 1984.

Administration & Advisory Board
Arizona State University Art Museum

Administration

Lattie F. Coor
President

Milton D. Glick
Provost and Senior Vice President

Brent W. Brown
Vice President, University Relations

Ben R. Forsyth
Vice President, Administrative Services
Provost and Vice President, West Campus

Seymour L. Rosen
Dean, College of Fine Arts

Advisory Board

John Armstrong

Elaine Cohen

Ted Decker

LaReal Eyring

Betsy Fahlman

Dorothy Fratt

Richard Goldsmith

Edward Jacobson, *honorary member*

Richard Levinson

K. David Lindner

Barbara Meyerson

Daniel Moquay

Joanne Rapp

Joseph Segura

Kurt Weiser

Richard Whitney, *honorary member*

Marilyn Zeitlin, *ex officio*

Charles W. Anderson
Security Officer

Manuel Bingochea
Security Officer

Linda Calvin
Secretary/Receptionist

Dianne Cripe
Public Information Coordinator

Rebecca Dalvesco
Security Officer

Joseph DeMasi
Security Officer

Bruce Erno
Security Officer

LaReal Eyring
Museum Store Manager

Stephen Johnson
Chief Preparator

Bernie LaMagna
Security Officer

Heather S. Lineberry
Curator

Linda A. McAllister
Senior Curator

Jean Makin
Print Collection Manager

Juanita R. Rodriguez
Accounts Secretary

Gregory Strange
Assistant Preparator

Deanna DePass-Stulgaitis
Acting Administrative Assistant

Mary Jane Williams
Registrar

Marilyn A. Zeitlin
Director

Credits

Too Late for Goya Installation

Technical Director:	Dan Harnett, New York
Multi-media Systems Integrator:	Wayne Armour, New Jersey
Mechanical Engineering:	Eli Buk, New York
Video Production and Post-Production:	Broadway Video, New York
Laser Disk Elaboration:	Magno Sound and Video, New York
Primate Sculpture:	Taller de Manolo Martín, Valencia, Spain
Historical Footage:	Sherman Greenberg Film Archives, New York

Too Late for Goya Catalogue

Catalogue design and production:	Terry Berkowitz, New York
English to Spanish translations:	Teresa Sàrries, New York
Spanish to English translations:	Alisa Tager, New York
Coordinator of catalogue:	Linda McAllister, Phoenix, Arizona
Photography:	David Allison, New York; Miquel Bargalló, Barcelona, Spain; Terry Berkowitz, New York; Richard Bloes, New York; Geoffrey Clements, New York; Ferran Freixa, Barcelona; Martín García, Barcelona; Stephen Nichols, Amherst, Massachusetts; Lee Stalsworth, Washington, DC; Francesc Torres, New York; Jim Via, Rochester, New York; and Mark Woods, Phoenix
Goya Print:	Courtesy of Memorial Art Gallery, Rochester, New York
Printing:	Land O' Sun Printers, Phoenix
Typography:	Goudy Oldstyle Regular, Bold and Italic Copperplate Gothic 31BC and 32BC
Color separations:	Color Masters, Phoenix
Binding:	Roswell Bookbinding, Phoenix

Three thousand five hundred copies published by Arizona State University Art Museum, 1993.